AUTOMOTIVE ELECTRICAL SYSTEMS

SECOND EDITION

Herbert E. Ellinger

PRENTICE-HALL, INC., Englewood Cliffs, New Jersey 07632

Library of Congress Cataloging in Publication Data

ELLINGER, HERBERT E.
   Automotive electrical systems.

   Includes index.
   1. Automobiles—Electric equipment—Maintenance
and repair.   I. Title.
TL272.E639 1985   629.2'54   84-24853
ISBN 0-13-054271-7

Editorial/production supervision
and interior design: *Theresa A. Soler*
Manufacturing buyer: *Anthony Caruso*

Printed in the United States of America

10 9 8 7 6 5 4 3 2 1

ISBN 0-13-054271-7 01

Prentice-Hall International, Inc., *London*
Prentice-Hall of Australia Pty. Limited, *Sydney*
Editora Prentice-Hall do Brasil, Ltda., *Rio de Janeiro*
Prentice-Hall Canada Inc., *Toronto*
Prentice-Hall Hispanoamericana, S. A., *Mexico*
Prentice-Hall of India Private Limited, *New Delhi*
Prentice-Hall of Japan, Inc., *Tokyo*
Prentice-Hall of Southeast Asia Pte. Ltd., *Singapore*
Whitehall Books Limited, *Wellington, New Zealand*

CONTENTS

Contents

PREFACE

Electricity is one of the most difficult subjects with which an automotive service technician works. Vehicles are now being made with complex electrical and electronic equipment that replaces familiar mechanical, vacuum, and hydraulic parts. It is therefore increasingly important for you to understand electricity so that you will be able to diagnose problems and service electrical systems in these vehicles. This book is designed to help you understand how electrical systems operate, how problems are diagnosed, how the systems are tested, and how they should be serviced.

Electrical test and diagnosis procedures specified by the vehicle manufacturers often differ from those given by the manufacturers of test equipment. Test procedures described by vehicle manufacturers are keyed to the specific type of equipment the dealers have. This often includes specialized test equipment. Equipment manufacturers, on the other hand, have developed test equipment that can be used rapidly on many different makes of vehicles. This type of test equipment is the type generally described in this book.

The most common electrical test procedures are described in this book. Manufacturers may recommend test procedures that are somewhat different from the ones described here. You should always review the procedures given in the service manuals to see if there are any special instructions before you work on vehicles with which you are unfamiliar.

This book is organized to give you experience working with parts that use electricity. It starts with the theory of electricity. This is followed by simple service on lights, flashers, fuses, and batteries. A chapter on testing electrical systems and motors follows to reinforce your understanding of the electrical theory.

By this time you have studied the first seven chapters. You should then have enough knowledge of electricity so that you can start to learn about electronics. Charging systems and ignition systems use electronics. Studying these systems, after you have an introduction to electronics, will reinforce your knowledge of both electricity and electronics.

Microcomputers have been added to vehicles to control ignition timing, fuel metering, and vehicle systems. Sensors keep checking on how the engine and vehicle are operating. Electrical sensor signals are sent to a microcomputer. The microcomputer processes the signals, then sends electrical signals to control actuators that readjust the operating system. The sensors see the adjustment to complete a closed-loop control. These control systems are discussed in this book because they operate with electricity. They are checked using normal electrical system test equipment. In some shops they are checked using specialized test equipment. The discussion in this chapter is limited to the electrical parts of the control systems. There is no discussion in this book of adjustments or of servicing for engine performance.

Each chapter is followed by study questions. The questions are listed in the order in which the material is discussed in each chapter. This should make it easy for you to find the correct answer for each question.

I wish to express my sincere thanks to all who have helped make this book possible. Special thanks are given to the automobile manufacturers and equipment companies for their use of technical literature. For the use of illustrations, I must acknowledge American Motors Corporation, Champion Spark Plug Company, Chrysler Corporation, The Prestolite Company, and the following divisions of General Motors Corporation: AC Spark Plug, Buick Motor, Cadillac Motor Car, Chevrolet Motor, Oldsmobile, and Delco-Remy. Thanks are also given to Western Michigan University for the unrestricted use of the automotive laboratories to take photographs. Help received from the automotive teaching staff and students is appreciated. Finally, thanks to Marilyn Brown for many hours of typing and proofing the manuscript for this book.

Herbert E. Ellinger

1

PRINCIPLES OF ELECTRICITY

Electricity is used by each of us every day. For example, we turn a switch and a light comes on, a radio pleases us with music, or an electric motor starts to run. It is hard for us to think of living without electricity as the founders of the United States did in 1776.

Many of the effects of electricity were recognized a long time ago. Scientists were finally able to learn enough about electricity to use it, even though they did not understand it. Once electricity was used, scientists began to discover more of its characteristics. Characteristics are the way it acts and the way it can be used. By 1800 the basic characteristics of electricity were understood. Each discovery of a new characteristic led to the discovery of another new characteristic of electricity. The dry cell was one of the early useful sources of electricity. The dry cell was followed by batteries and the generator. Dry cells and early batteries had to be replaced when they would no longer produce electricity. The generator produced electricity as long as it was kept running. Early uses of electricity were for heat, light, and power. It was soon discovered that a generator could be used to recharge batteries. Electricity was used for ignition in the first automobiles built in the late 1800s. By 1900 the most common characteristics of electricity had been identified. In 100 years electricity had moved from laboratory experiments to common use in homes and in industry.

Benjamin Franklin thought that electricity acted like flowing fluid. He suggested that electrical current flowed from the charge he called positive toward a negative charge. This Franklin current theory is used in technical literature because it has been accepted and is used by scientists, engineers, authors, and teachers. As the science of electronics developed it was found that electricity is the movement of electrons through a conductor. In an electrical circuit the electrons move from the negative charge toward the positive charge. This is the opposite of the accepted Franklin current theory. Because the Franklin theory is used in textbooks and reference material, many technicians think of electricity going from positive toward negative. Many automotive training and reference sources describe electrical current flow using this well-known current theory (positive to negative). A few use the technically correct electron flow theory (negative to positive). It really makes no difference which electrical theory you use in automotive electricity as long as you correctly connect the vehicle electronic units and test instruments. You must connect positive leads to positive terminals and negative leads to negative terminals.

1-1 NATURE OF ELECTRICITY

Technical words in this section you will need to learn:

Atom	Ion
Charges	Negative
Conductor	Nucleus
Current	Orbit
Direct current	Positive
Electromotive force	Proton
Electron	Voltage
Insulator	

All matter is made of atoms. Each atom is made of very small parts called protons, electrons, and neutrons. The way the atom is made is often compared to that of the solar system. The center of the atom, called the nucleus, is made of neutrons and protons. Neutrons have a neutral electrical charge and protons have a positive electrical charge. The electrons of the atom rapidly spin around the nucleus. Electrons have a negative charge and weigh only 1/1800 as much as a proton or a neutron.

It is difficult to understand that atoms, even in solids, are mostly space. This is like the solar system. It might help you if you think of a fan with two blades. When the fan is spinning it looks like a flat disk, even though you know there is mostly space between the blades. This spinning disk would act more like a solid than like empty space if you tossed a rubber ball at it. The ball would be hit by a blade and would bounce off. If this spinning flat disk could be tumbled fast enough, it would look and behave like a solid ball. The atom acts in much the same way. Electrons rapidly spinning around a nucleus at speeds as high as 4000 miles per second makes the atom act like a solid. The electron orbits of atoms interlock to form molecules of matter.

When the number of electrons in an atom is equal to the number of protons, the atom has a neutral charge. The negative charge of one electron will balance the posi-

Figure 1-1 Particles of an atom.

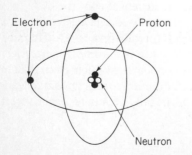

tive charge of one proton. You can see this in Figure 1-1. Electrons spinning about the nucleus rotate at different distances away from the nucleus. As they rotate, they form orbits at different energy levels, as illustrated in Figure 1-2. The electrons rotate around the nucleus like a satellite rotates around the earth. Some satellite orbits are so close to the earth that they go around the earth each hour. Others are so far into space that it takes 24 hours to go around the earth. Electrons close to the nucleus are bound tightly to the nucleus, while electrons in the outer orbits of many materials are loosely bound. In some materials the electrons can be removed from or added to the loosely bound outer orbit.

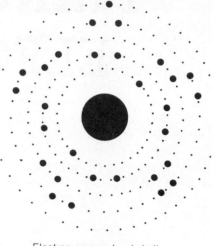

Electron energy level shells

Figure 1-2 Electrons orbit around the nucleus at different energy levels.

An atom is a very small particle. Usable matter is made up of large groups of atoms or combinations of atoms. For instance, water is made from hydrogen and oxygen atoms, petroleum is made from hydrogen and carbon atoms, and steel is made from iron, carbon, manganese, phosphorus, and sulfur atoms.

The electrons from the outer orbit of the atoms in conducting material can be knocked from their orbit. These electrons will enter the orbit of other atoms or they may become free electrons. Electrons normally move or drift through materials. That is, every electron that leaves the orbit of an atom is replaced by an electron from another atom as shown in Figure 1-3. Metallic materials have many free-drifting electrons. These materials are called **conductors.** Conducting materials have three or less electrons in the outer orbits of their atoms. Materials with five or more electrons in the outer orbit have a tighter bond to the nucleus with few drifting electrons. These materials are called **insulators.**

Atoms that pick up an extra electron in their outer orbits have more electrons than protons and therefore the atom is said to have a negative charge. If an atom were

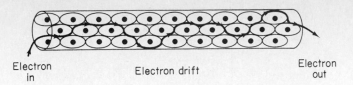

Electron in   Electron drift   Electron out

Figure 1–3 Electrons leaving an atom are replaced with other electrons.

to give up one of its electrons to a neighboring atom, it would have one more proton then electron. It would then have a positive charge. Atoms with either extra or missing electrons are called **ions.** If they have extra electrons, they are negative ions. When they are missing some electrons, they are positive ions.

Copper is a good conductor because it has many free electrons drifting within it. If you look at Figure 3–9 you can see how copper conducts compared with some other conducting materials. Most conductors in automobile electrical systems are therefore made from copper. When the conductor has one end connected to a source of extra electrons and the other end connected to an object that lacks electrons, the general drift of electrons in the conductor will be away from the source of electrons and toward the part that has less electrons. The electrons will drift away from the source of electrons because like charges repel each other. They move toward the part that has less electrons because unlike charges attract each other. You can see this in Figure 1–4. The forced drift from the collision of the electrons will make an energy wave that moves through the conductor at a speed approaching the speed of light. This wave moves like a series of rear-end collisions on a crowded highway. The collision rate of one car hitting the one in front moves ahead much faster than the movement of any of the cars in the collision.

The drift of electrons through a conductor in one direction is **electricity.** The amount of electrons drifting in one direction is called **current** expressed in **amperes** (A). Current that flows in one direction is called **direct current** (dc). The electrical force that causes electrons to drift in one direction is called **electromotive force** (EMF). In automobiles, electromotive force is formed by a battery or charging system. The electromotive force (amount of

electrical pressure) is expresed as **voltage** (V). The higher the voltage, the greater the electrical force to move electrons through the conductor.

Often, as an automotive service technician, you will be asked to install electrical equipment on automobiles. It is important for you to know how much current this equipment will need so that you will use the correct-size wires. You need to know the total effective resistance of the circuit, then using Ohm's law, you can find the current the system will use. The following sections show you how you can determine the resistance of an electrical circuit.

1–2 SERIES ELECTRICAL CIRCUITS

Technical words in this section you will need to learn:

Amperes	Ohm's law
Circuit	Polarity
Electrical load	Resistance
Ground	Series
Ohms	Volts

Symbols you will need to learn:

+ Positive   —o◄—o Switch closed

– Negative

—o◄ o— Switch open   ⏚ Ground connection

If a battery is connected to an open conductor (Figure 1–5), free electrons will fill the conductor. They can not drift in one direction. You must have a complete electrical circuit (Figure 1–6) for electrons to drift in one direction. A **complete electrical circuit** means that you can follow all the way around the circuit without running into openings. In addition, the electrons need an electromotive force (voltage) to make them drift in one

Figure 1–4 Electrons are forced to drift in one direction when added electrons repel electrons already in a conductor.

EMF forcing electron into conductor

Repelling force moves electrons along conductor

Figure 1–5 There is no electron movement when a battery is connected to an open circuit.

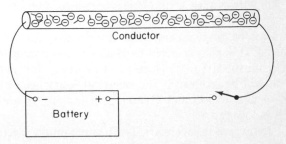

Conductor

Battery

3

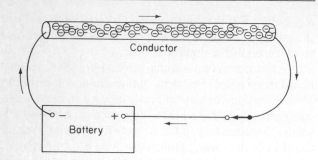

Figure 1-6 Electrons move when a battery is connected to conductors, forming a complete circuit.

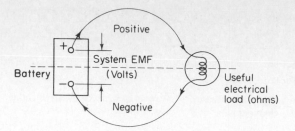

Figure 1-7 A complete electrical circuit can be thought of as a circle. Electricity can leave one terminal of the battery, flow through the circuit, and return to the other terminal of the battery.

direction. Remember, the forced drift of electrons is called an electric current. An electric current cannot flow unless there is a different voltage at each end of the closed or complete electrical circuit.

As electrical current flows in a conductor, the forced drift of the free electrons is slowed as they bump into atoms in the conductor. This bumping heats the conductor, which, in turn, increases free-electron activity. The movement of electrons knocks free electrons from the outer shell around atoms. As they do this some of the energy of the free electron is used up. This use of energy is resistance to the electron drift or electrical current flow. Resistance to electron movement is expressed in units called ohms.

There is a fixed relationship between the electrical pressure, **volts**; the electrical current, **amperes**; and the electrical resistance, **ohms.** This relationship is shown by an algebraic expression, called Ohm's law:

$$\text{ohms} = \frac{\text{volts}}{\text{amperes}}$$

If two of the values are known, the third can be calculated. If the resistance of a circuit (in ohms) is constant, the ampere flow in a conductor is directly proportional to the circuit voltage.

A complete electrical circuit is illustrated in Figure 1-7 by a circle. A battery is at one point in the circle, and a part that uses electricity, called an **electrical load,** is at another point in the circle. The circuit is positive on one side of the circle and negative on the other side. Electricity will flow as long as the circle is complete. The amount of current flowing in the circle results from the different electromotive force on each side of the battery (measured in volts). It is also effected by the load and conductors that cause the circuit resistance. The current flow in the circuit will be reduced if the electrical resistance of the load or circuit becomes greater or if the electromotive force is lowered.

In automobile electricity the maximum electro-

motive force is battery voltage when the engine is not running. When the charging system is operating, the maximum electromotive force is the regulated voltage (except in special circuits within some electronic accessories).

In the following description of a series electrical circuit we will use battery voltage. The battery supplies electrical current through action of the chemicals in the battery. As electrical current is drawn from the battery, chemical reactions form additional free electrons to replace the electrons going through the electrical circuit. Battery voltage is the same as long as the chemical reactions within the battery can supply the required current. If the electrical load is greater, like a starting motor, it will allow more current to flow than the battery can quickly supply. This will lower the battery terminal voltage. The lower voltage will force less current to flow through the circuit so that at some point the current flow (amperes) becomes constant. The circuit volts times current flow in amperes equals electrical power in watts:

$$\text{watts} = \text{amperes} \times \text{volts}$$

For instance, if a starter were cranking at 10 volts (V) drawing 160 amperes (A) the starter would be using 1600 watts (W) of power. One horsepower (hp) equals 746 W, so this starter is producing 2.28 hp (1600/746 = 2.28).

A battery in a circuit has a given amount of electrical power. This power is limited by the battery size and the chemical action in the battery. Current flow in an electrical circuit will increase as resistance in the circuit is reduced when electrical loads are added. Increased current flow will lower the system voltage. When the electrical load is reduced the system voltage will rise and current flow will decrease. The electrical system has maximum voltage when the system resistance is infinite. This occurs when the circuit is opened with a switch and no current is flowing.

The total resistance of a conductor increases as:

1. The length of the conductor increases
2. Its cross section decreases
3. Its temperature increases

Wires normally used in automobiles have as small a cross section as possible without causing too much resistance.

The following examples should help you understand the relationship between volts, amperes, and resistance by comparing an electrical system to the shop compressed-air system. If you have worked in an auto shop you have used compressed air. You know that the pressure in the air compressor tank is measured with a gauge. If you put a pressure gauge on the shop air pressure outlet before you connected the air hose coupling (Figure 1-8) it would show the same pressure as the compressed-air tank. This is like an open switch in the electrical circuit shown in Figure 1-9.

When the hose coupling is connected and air is being used by an air gun, as pictured in Figure 1-10, the pressure at the hose coupling will be less than the pres-

sure in the compressed-air tank. A pressure gauge at the air gun will show a lower pressure than the pressure at the coupling. The pressure becomes zero just after the air leaves the air gun. Comparing Figure 1-11 with Figure 1-10 will help you to see how the voltage drops in an electrical system as electricity is being used.

The amount of air you can get from an air gun depends on three things: (1) the amount of pressure in the compressed-air tank, (2) the length of the air lines and air hoses, and (3) the size of the lines and hoses.

More pressure will push more air through the lines, hoses, and air gun. This works the same way with electri-

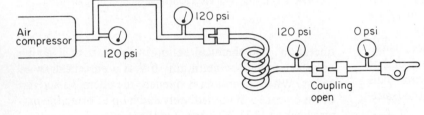

Figure 1-8 Pressure in a shop air supply when the coupling to an air gun is open.

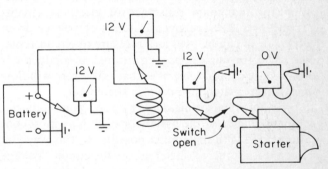

Figure 1-9 Voltage in an electrical system when the switch to the electrical load is open.

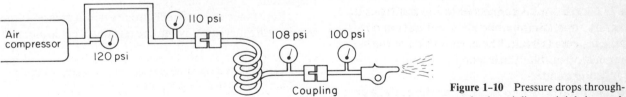

Figure 1-10 Pressure drops throughout the shop air line as air is being used.

Figure 1-11 Voltage drops in an electrical circuit as electricity is being used.

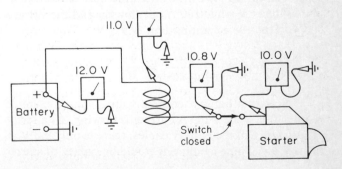
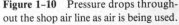

city. A higher voltage will push more current through the electrical wiring and electrical load.

If you connect several lengths of air hose together to reach the job you are doing, you will have less working pressure at the air gun. The loss in working pressure is caused by resistance to airflow through the long air hose. Added resistance of a long electrical wire will also reduce the amount of voltage available to operate the electrical load.

If you need a long length of hose to reach your work, you can get more working pressure at the air gun by using a larger air hose. The larger air hose will have less resistance as you use the air. Larger wires in an electrical system have less resistance so more current can flow to operate the electrical load with a higher voltage. This would be most noticeable if the battery and starter are at opposite ends of a vehicle.

You can find the resistance of a conductor, usually a wire, by measuring the voltage between each end of the conductor and the amperes that it is carrying. This is called **voltage drop.** You can then calculate the resistance by using Ohm's law. In automotive service, specification for maximum resistance of electrical circuits carrying over 3 A are given in terms of voltage drop. Voltage drop can be used as a measure of circuit resistance when the current passing through a conductor is known. You should remember that no current will flow unless there is a voltage drop in the circuit.

Circuit voltage is measured by placing one voltmeter lead on each side of the battery or load. You must connect the lead with the correct polarity. In this way you are connecting the voltmeter across the circuit. Voltage drop is measured along a conductor with both voltmeter leads on the same side of the circuit while current is flowing. The insulated wire is connected to the positive side of the battery, in all automobile electrical circuits. This is called the **insulated circuit.** The negative side of the battery is connected to the vehicle body and engine metal. This is called **ground.**

Voltage drop is used to measure resistance of a circuit by applying Ohm's law. This is illustrated in Figure 1-12. The resistance of the operating unit in this example is 0.0613 Ω while 160 A are flowing and the voltage drop across the operating unit is 9.8 V.

$$\text{ohms} = \frac{\text{volts}}{\text{amperes}} = \frac{9.8}{160} = 0.0613$$

Note that battery-terminal voltage in this example is only 10 V while a 160 A current is flowing. As a result of resistance in the battery cables, there is only 9.8 V at the battery. These conditions would be typical of starter

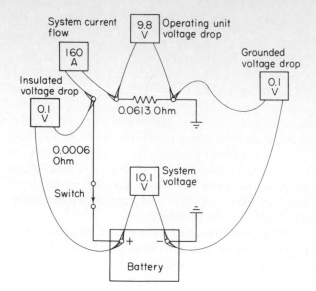

Figure 1-12 Typical voltage drop in an operating electrical circuit.

operation. The chemical action in the battery is acting only fast enough to maintain 10 V at a current draw of 160 A. When the switch is opened, the chemical activity of the battery will immediately catch up to bring the battery back to 12 V. Resistance in the insulated and ground sides of the circuit limit the voltage at the operating unit.

Too much resistance in the charging system will reduce the amount of electrical current the system can carry. Normally, the charging system operates at about 14 V. This voltage is above the open-circuit battery voltage. As a result, the battery will be charged while the charging system is working.

Figure 1-13 shows a discharged battery being charged. In this illustration 14.2 V is forcing 20 A through the charging circuit to recharge the battery. The insulated circuit of the charging system has 0.01 Ω resistance, so the battery is being charged by 14.0 V.

Resistance in electrical circuits will increase as the temperature increases, when the terminals get loose, and

Figure 1-13 Voltage drop in an operating charging system. Amperage is being checked with an inductive ammeter.

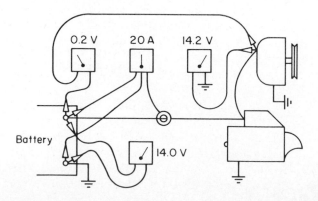

when electrical units are added. If the electrical units with resistance are added, one after the other, so that the only electrical path is through each unit in turn, the resistors are said to be connected in **series**. You can determine the total resistance of electrical units in a series circuit by adding the resistance of each unit and the connecting wire. Each resistance is called R.

$$R = R_1 + R_2 + R_3$$

The cranking circuit is used to illustrate series resistances. The starter has a large current draw. As a result, it is easy to measure the voltage drop of each unit in the circuit.

Each cable, each junction, and each switch in the cranking circuit has some resistance. The starter motor itself has the most circuit resistance while the starter is cranking. The *SAE Handbook* specifies that the maximum allowable voltage drop is 0.2 V per 100 A for cables between the battery and starter. Resistance in most starter circuits is well below this. Voltage drop in the cranking circuit results from the size of the battery cable and the number of wire strands in the cable.

The cranking circuit voltage drop is measured by placing the positive voltmeter lead of an expanded-scale voltmeter (1 to 4 V full scale) at the positive battery terminal. The negative voltmeter lead is connected on the insulated starter terminal. The voltage reading is taken while the starter is cranking. This is illustrated in Figure 1-14. Any voltage reading on the voltmeter indicates resistance. The greater the voltage reading, the greater the resistance, assuming constant current flow to the starter.

Each cable, switch, and connector causes some resistance to current flow. When these current-carrying units are connected, one after the other, as they are in the cranking circuit, they form a series electrical circuit. Resistances in series add directly in ohm units. The voltage drops across the conductor, switches, and operating units in a circuit while current is flowing will add up to equal the measured battery voltage. Remember that voltage drop is a measure of resistance. There is no voltage drop when no current is flowing. Full battery voltage will be measured across an open switch. You should notice that the voltmeter is used without disconnecting any circuit connections. This is also true with new-style inductive ammeters, illustrated in Figure 1-13. The circuit had to be separated at a junction to connect the old-style ammeters into the circuit (Figure 1-12).

Some automotive series circuits have a variable resistance. A good example of this is the fuel gauge. A float in the fuel tank is connected to the variable resistance. When the fuel tank is full the float is up. The variable resistor has almost no resistance. This allows the maximum current to flow. The float lowers to add resistance to the fuel gauge circuit as the fuel level lowers. This restricts the current flow. The float is at the bottom and

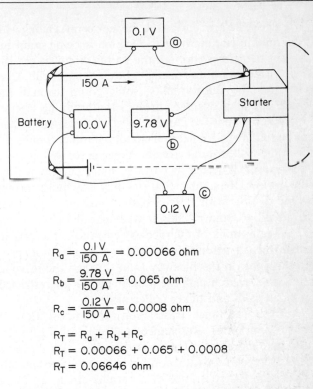

$$R_a = \frac{0.1\ V}{150\ A} = 0.00066\ ohm$$

$$R_b = \frac{9.78\ V}{150\ A} = 0.065\ ohm$$

$$R_c = \frac{0.12\ V}{150\ A} = 0.0008\ ohm$$

$$R_T = R_a + R_b + R_c$$
$$R_T = 0.00066 + 0.065 + 0.0008$$
$$R_T = 0.06646\ ohm$$

Figure 1-14 Measuring voltage drop in the series circuit of a cranking system.

there is maximum resistance in the fuel gauge circuit when the fuel tank is empty. This allows the least current to flow. The fuel gauge is actually measuring current flowing in the circuit.

Series resistance is similar to a line of traffic going into a raceway. The restrictions are the drive-in gate, the ticket sales and the ticket collector. Each car that goes through the gate also goes through each of these restrictions in series, one after the other.

The grounded side of the cranking circuit is just as important as the insulated side. All the current that flows through the insulated and switch side of a series circuit also flows through the grounded side. The grounded side of the circuit is often overlooked when automotive electrical circuits are being tested. The grounded side is tested in the same way you test the insulated side of the circuit. You can see that the voltage drop across the ground circuit in Figure 1-14 is 0.12 V.

1-3 PARALLEL ELECTRICAL CIRCUITS

Technical words in this section you will need to learn:

Parallel   Wheatstone bridge
Shunt

The switch circuit for the starter operates along with the cranking circuit while the engine is being cranked. Current that flows through the switch circuit is not the same current that flows through the cranking circuit. Current from the battery splits, some going through the switch circuit and some through the cranking circuit. Systems that split the current to go through more than one circuit are called **parallel circuits**. Parallel circuits are sometimes called **shunt circuits**. You can see that as more circuits are connected in parallel, more current will be able to flow. Remember that the only way more current is able to flow with a fixed battery voltage is to lower the circuit resistance. This is what parallel circuits do.

Again, think of the raceway entrance. If a walk-in gate is opened in addition to the drive-in gate, more people can get into the raceway than through the drive-in gate alone, even though the walk-in people are restricted by ticket sales and ticket collectors.

Each resistance (restriction) to current flow is measured in ohms. Resistances added parallel to a circuit make more paths for current to flow. This reduces the resistance of the total combined circuit. You can calculate the total resistance of a parallel circuit by using the following form:

$$R = \frac{1}{1/R_1 + 1/R_2 + 1/R_3}$$

Figure 1–15 Voltage drop and resistance of parallel crank and switch circuits.

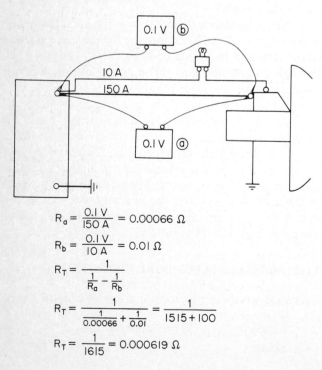

$$R_a = \frac{0.1\,V}{150\,A} = 0.00066\ \Omega$$

$$R_b = \frac{0.1\,V}{10\,A} = 0.01\ \Omega$$

$$R_T = \frac{1}{\frac{1}{R_a} - \frac{1}{R_b}}$$

$$R_T = \frac{1}{\frac{1}{0.00066} + \frac{1}{0.01}} = \frac{1}{1515 + 100}$$

$$R_T = \frac{1}{1615} = 0.000619\ \Omega$$

If the cranking circuit resistance is 0.00066 Ω in Figure 1–15 and the starter switch circuit resistance is 0.01 Ω, the total resistance of the parallel circuits would be

$$R = \frac{1}{1/0.00066 + 1/0.01} = \frac{1}{1515 + 100}$$

$$= \frac{1}{1615} = 0.000619\ \Omega$$

Another example of a typical parallel electrical use in automobiles is the lighting circuit shown in Figure 1–16. Each lamp is connected between the insulated electrical circuit and ground. In this example each headlamp has a resistance of 2 Ω and each parking and tail lamp has 16 Ω resistance. Putting these resistance values in the equation for calculating parallel resistances, you have

$$\text{ohms} = \frac{1}{\underbrace{1/2 + 1/2}_{\substack{\text{head-}\\\text{lamps}}} + \underbrace{1/16 + 1/16}_{\substack{\text{parking}\\\text{lamps}}} + \underbrace{1/16 + 1/16}_{\substack{\text{tail}\\\text{lamps}}}}$$

$$= \frac{1}{0.5 + 0.5 + 0.0625 + 0.0625 + 0.0625 + 0.0625}$$

$$= \frac{1}{1.25} = 0.8$$

If there were no resistance in the wires or ground, this lighting circuit would carry 17.5 A while the charging

Figure 1–16 Resistances in a parallel light circuit.

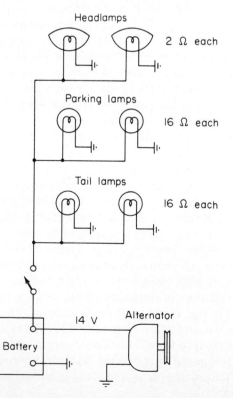

system is operating at 14 V. This was determined by Ohm's law. Using algebra, Ohm's law is converted from

$$\text{ohms} = \frac{\text{volts}}{\text{amps}} \qquad \text{to} \qquad \text{amps} = \frac{\text{volts}}{\text{ohms}}$$

Substituting the operating voltage (14 V) and the circuit resistance (0.8 Ω), you have

$$\text{amperes} = \frac{14\ V}{0.8\ \Omega} = 17.5$$

As more circuits with some resistance are added, the total circuit resistance will decrease. **Resistances used in parallel form an electrical load.**

The Wheatstone bridge can be used to illustrate the principle that no current will flow when the voltage is the same on both ends of a conductor.

The Wheatstone bridge in Figure 1–17 is connected across a battery. The circuit is complete and current will flow through the circuit. The voltage drop across R_1 is the same as the voltage drop across R_2, when the resistance of R_1 equals R_2, and R_3 equals R_4. The voltage at V_1 is the same as the voltage at V_2. No current flow will be shown on ammeter A_2 because the voltage is the same at both of its terminals. You will remember that there must be a voltage drop from one end of a conductor to the other end to have any current flow. As a result there is no current flow when the voltage is the same at each terminal of the ammeter. The current on ammeter A_1 is the same as the current on ammeter A_3. Remember the total current flowing in one series part of the circuit is the same as the total current flowing in any other series part of the circuit.

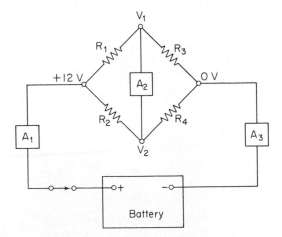

Figure 1–17 Wheatstone bridge circuit.

1–4 SERIES–PARALLEL CIRCUITS

Few electrical circuits in automobiles have a combination of series and parallel circuits. Series–parallel circuit resistance can be determined if you know the resistance of

each part of the system. First you need to determine the **effective resistance** of the parallel part of the circuit. This is done in the same way that you would determine the total resistance of any parallel resistances. Finally, you would add the effective resistance of the parallel resistance with the series resistances in the circuit. This will give you the total resistance of the circuit.

In most automotive electrical circuits it would be much quicker and easier to determine the resistance of any part of a circuit, or even the whole circuit, by using the voltage drop test. In this test you would connect an ammeter in the circuit you are going to measure. When current is flowing, measure the voltage drop from one end of the circuit to the other end. The resistance in this part of the circuit can be quickly calculated by dividing the voltage reading by the amperage reading. You are using Ohm's law when you do this.

1–5 MAGNETISM

Technical words in this section you will need to learn:

Magnetic field   Magnetic pole

Magnetic keeper   Permanent magnet

Magnetic lines   Reluctance
of force

Electricity and magnetism affect each other. This effect is used in all electric motors, relays, solenoids, generators, alternators, and electrical test equipment. You need to understand this effect to know how many electrical parts work. A brief review of magnetism will help you to understand this effect.

Magnetism was first noticed in stones called lodestones. When these stones were tied on the end of a string one part of the stone would always point toward the north pole. As a result, the first practical use of lodestones was their use as a compass in ships to aid in navigation. Modern compasses use human-made permanent magnets that act in the same way. The end of the magnet that points north is called the *north pole* of the magnet. The other end is called the *south pole*.

You may have used toys that have magnets in them. When one part of the toy is moved the other part also moves, even when the parts are not connected. As you played with these toys you found that like magnetic poles try to push away from each other (repel), while unlike poles pull toward each other (attract). Both poles of a magnet attract iron and steel. In the auto shop you often use a magnet to pick up a small iron or steel part that accidentally dropped into a small space.

You can also see the effect of the magnetic lines of force if you put a sheet of plastic over two magnets. Sprinkle iron chips from a brake lathe on the plastic. The iron chips will collect in lines as pictured in Figure 1–18. Notice that the chips bridge across the space from one magnet to the other when the poles are different. They push away from each other when the poles are the same. The chips will line up along magnetic **lines of force.** All the magnetic lines of force taken together are called the **magnetic field.**

Figure 1–19   Iron chips on a plastic sheet that covers a horseshoe magnet taken from an instrument.

(a)

(b)

Figure 1–18   Effects of polarity shown by iron chips from a brake lathe on a plastic sheet over two magnets: (a) unlike poles attract; (b) like poles repel.

on the ends of the horseshoe. Lines of force concentrate between the poles as shown in Figure 1–19.

Magnetic fields cause other interesting effects. If soft iron is placed in the magnetic field the lines of force move into the iron rather than moving through air. An iron bar is often placed across the open end of a horseshoe magnet to act as a **keeper.** The iron bar forms an easy path for the magnetic lines to move through rather than move through air. The keeper helps the magnet keep its magnetic strength. This characteristic of iron to attract lines of force is due to the low **reluctance** of iron compared to that of air. Magnetic lines of force move through other materials, such as copper, aluminum, and plastic, in nearly the same way as they move through air.

If a magnet is cut, it will form two magnets, end to end, each having a north and a south pole. This shows

Figure 1–20   Magnetic field as shown by iron chips on a plastic sheet over thin sections of a bar magnet.

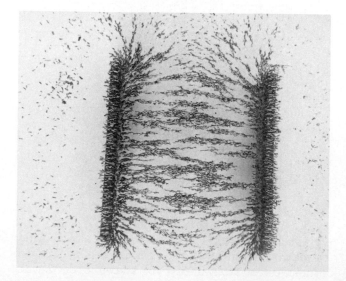

The lines form also when the bar magnet is rotated on its axis. This shows you that the lines of force are actually a section view of magnetic shells that form the magnetic field. The magnetic shells **never cross each other.** The shells all come together at the poles at both ends of the magnet. The magnetic force goes from the **north to south pole** of the magnet along the outside of the magnet. The magnetic shells, called lines of force, complete a closed loop as they go through the magnet. If the bar magnet is bent in the form of a horseshoe, the poles stay

that the magnetic field completes a closed loop through the magnet. Each cut will make smaller but complete magnets. Two small sections of magnets are shown in Figure 1-20. If this example were carried to the extreme, one atom would be left and it would still be a magnet.

1-6 ELECTROMAGNETISM

Each atom acts like a very small magnet, having north and south magnetic poles. Current flowing through a conductor will align the electrons of the atoms around the conductor so that the magnetic poles of the atoms are generally in the same direction. This action makes a magnetic field around all current-carrying conductors. As in permanent magnets, the magnetic field around a conductor is directed from the north pole toward the south pole. If you place your right thumb on the wire pointing toward negative, as in Figure 1-21, your fingers will be pointing in the direction that the magnetic field goes around the conductor.

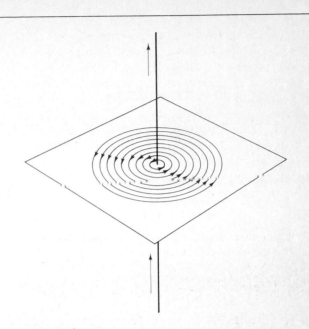

Figure 1-22 A flat surface perpendicular to a current-carrying conductor is used to show the magnetic field around the conductor.

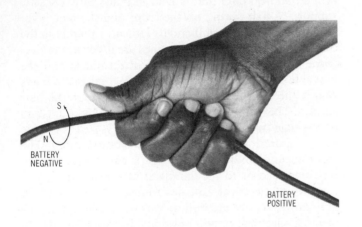

Figure 1-21 Right hand being used to show the direction of the magnetic field. The thumb points toward the negative battery terminal and the fingers point in the direction that the magnetic force goes around the conductor.

shown in Figure 1-23. Magnetic fields around the two conductors run in the same direction between the conductors. Because the fields are in the same direction between the conductors their lines of force are pushed away from each other. The eccentric-shaped magnetic fields tend to force the conductors apart. The conductor is forced toward the center of the fields. This always happens when current flows in opposite directions in each of the side-by-side conductors.

When the magnetic lines of force around current-carrying conductors would normally go in opposite

Figure 1-23 Magnetic lines of force around two conductors repel each other to force the conductors apart when the direction of their fields go in the same direction between the conductors.

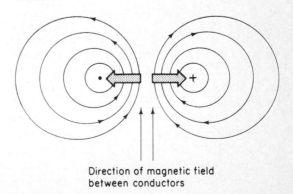

Direction of magnetic field between conductors

The strength of the magnetic field around a current-carrying conductor becomes stronger as more current flows in the conductor (Figure 1-22). The magnetic force can be seen as lines if iron chips are sprinkled on a flat surface around a current-carrying conductor. Lines of force actually stretch along the conductor in the third dimension to form magnetic shells along the conductor.

You will remember that magnetic lines of force will not cross each other. When they are going in the same direction, the magnetic lines of force repel each other. As the magnetism becomes stronger, the lines separate farther from each other. Two side-by-side conductors are

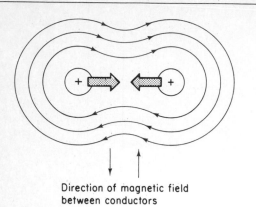

Direction of magnetic field
between conductors

Figure 1-24 Magnetic lines of force around two conductors join up and pull the conductors together when the direction of their fields would normally go in opposite directions between the conductors.

directions between the conductors, the lines join up. This is shown in Figure 1-24. The combined lines of force will form a large displaced field that tries to pull the conductors together. This force always happens when the current flow in the two conductors is flowing in the same direction. All magnetic fields try to become as small as possible and move the conductor to the center of the magnetic field.

All moving electrical parts of an automobile use electromagnetism. Some type of electromagnet is used in these parts.

Electromagnets are formed by wrapping a current-carrying coil around an iron core. The magnetic field around each wire turn of the coil combines (using the principle shown in Figure 1-24) to form a single large magnetic field. The iron core has low reluctance, so it

concentrates the magnetic lines to increase the effective strength of the magnet. The principle of an electromagnet is illustrated in Figure 1-25.

1-7 ELECTROMAGNETIC INSTRUMENTS

Electrical instrument operation is another important use of electromagnetism. High-quality electromagnetic instruments are based on a D'Arsonval movement. This instrument movement uses a moving coil suspended in the magnetic field of a horseshoe magnet. An electromagnetic field is formed around the coil when current flows through the coil wires. The effect between the permanent magnetic field and electromagnetic field makes the moving coil rotate to a new position. This movement is shown by a pointer that is connected to the moving coil (Figure 1-26).

The moving coil is a winding of many turns of very fine wire wound on a nonmagnetic frame. The frame has a short shaft on each end. It is supported by and pivots in jeweled bearings. This allows the coil to rotate freely around an iron core that is held in place with a plastic support. A hair spring on the front and the rear pivot shaft holds the meter coil and its indicator pointer in the "at rest" position. The hair springs are used for the electrical leads between the instrument terminals and the movable coil. Reaction between the two magnetic fields causes the coil to rotate against the force of the hair springs. The meter is calibrated by adjusting the anchors of the hair springs. The back anchor is used for basic meter calibration when the meter is manufactured. The front anchor can be adjusted with a small screw on the instrument cover to set the meter at zero.

Most electrical test instrument meters used in automotive service are built in this way. The test instrument has electrical circuits, switches, resistors, and shunts

Figure 1-25 Magnetic field around a typical electromagnet.

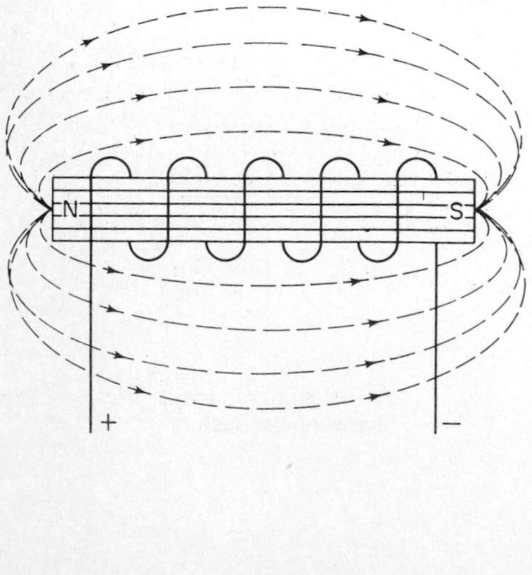

Figure 1-26 Instrument pointer connected to a current-carrying coil suspended in the magnetic field of a horseshoe magnet.

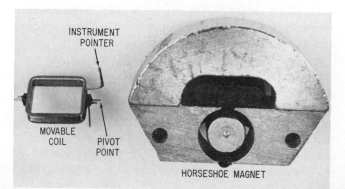

that sense electricity at the instrument test leads. A part of the electricity from the circuit being tested reaches the meter coil. Current flowing through the moving coil of the meter is directly proportional to the voltage at the coil terminals because the moving coil has a fixed resistance.

This type of meter is used as a voltmeter. With the correct-size resistors connected in series through switch positions, the meter can be used for different voltage ranges (see Figure 5–27). The same meter is also used as an ammeter to measure current. This type of ammeter is connected in series in the circuit. All the current of the circuit goes through a fixed-resistance shunt inside the ammeter. The meter in the ammeter measures voltage drop across the shunt. This voltage drop is proportional to the current flowing through the shunt. Different-sized shunts are used for different ampere ranges (see Figure 5–28).

The basic electromagnetic instrument can be connected to other circuits when the test signal is modified by electronic parts within the test instrument. Instruments of this type measure engine rpm, dwell, ohms, microfarads, ignition output, hydrocarbons, carbon monoxide, and so on.

It is necessary to separate a circuit to install the standard-type ammeter. The ammeter is connected in series between the wire removed and the junction from which it was removed. Inductive ammeters have been developed because it is difficult to separate many junctions and there is a chance of making a poor connection at the junction. The inductive ammeter test lead is clamped around the conductor (see Figure 1–13). As a result there is no need to disconnect wires and there is no chance of making a poor connection. The inductive ammeter measures the strength of the magnet field around the conductor as current flows through the conductor. You will remember that the strength of this magnetic field is proportional to the current flowing in the conductor. The ammeter has an electronic circuit to convert the effect of the magnetism to a voltage strong enough to operate the meter. The electronic circuit in the ammeter needs a source of electricity to operate. The meter will be either a D'Arsonval type or a digital type, like the reading on the calculator you use.

1–8 ELECTROMAGNETIC SWITCH

In automobiles, electromagnetism is used in an electrical switch called a **relay**. A common use of the relay is in circuits that carry high current, such as the starter, horn, and electrically heated window defroster. Relays are also used where one circuit cannot operate unless a second circuit is working. Examples of this are the neutral safety

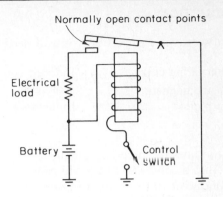

Figure 1–27 Schematic drawing of a typical relay with normally open contact points.

switch and trunk lid release that only allows the starter to crank or the trunk lid to be opened while the transmission is in neutral or park. The relay is placed between the battery and the operating unit (electrical load) so the wires will be as short as possible. This keeps resistance low so there is less voltage drop. Relays are operated with a control switch that is placed within easy reach of the driver.

A relay with normally open (NO) contact points is illustrated in Figure 1–27. When the control switch is closed, a small current flows through the coil to form an electromagnet. Magnetism pulls on the arm to close the contact points. The contact points carry the main current flowing through the electrical load.

A relay can also have the contact points normally closed (NC), as shown in Figure 1–28. When the control switch is closed, magnetism pulls the arm to open the contact points. The electrical load is turned off when the control switch is closed.

Figure 1–28 Schematic drawing of a typical relay with normally closed contact points.

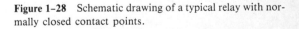

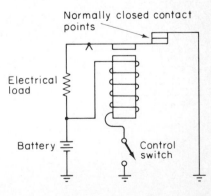

1-9 INDUCTION

Technical words in this section you will need to learn:

Alternating current

Electromagnetic
 induction

Induced counter
 voltage

Inductance

Henry

If the lines of force in a magnetic field are made to cut across a conductor, they will cause the electrons in the conductor to try to drift in one direction. More magnetic lines of force cutting across the conductor will cause a stronger force on the electrons in the conductor. The electromagnetic force in the conductor, caused by the magnetic lines of force cutting across the conductor, is measured in volts. These are the same volt units you used to measure the electrical pressure of batteries. **An electromotive force made by relative motion between a conductor and a magnetic field is called electromagnetic induction.** The strength of the induced electromotive force depends on the number of magnetic lines of force cutting across the conductor each second.

The alternator is one of the common automotive parts that uses electromagnetic induction. The rotating part of the alternator (the rotor) is an electromagnet. As the rotor is forced to rotate by a drive belt, the magnetic lines of force around the rotor cut across the wire coils of a stationary conductor (the stator) located in the alternator frame, as illustrated in Figure 1-29. This action forms a voltage in the stator coils. The voltage in the stator coils forces a current to flow through the automotive electrical system. In this case electromagetic induction is caused when moving magnetic lines of force cut across a stationary conductor.

Current in an alternator rapidly reverses its direction of flow a number of times each rotor revolution. This action is called **alternating current** (ac). The amount of current flowing increases and decreases as it alternates. As the current flow alternates in the stator, it forms a second expanding and contracting magnetic field around the stator windings. This newly formed moving magnetic field cuts across the side-by-side wires within the stator coil winding. This is illustrated in Figure 1-30. The moving field forms a counter voltage in the side-by-side wires. The counter voltage opposes the voltage induced by the rotor magnetic field. The principle of inducing a counter voltage in a coil wire that is carrying an increasing or a decreasing current is called **inductance**. Maximum alternator current output is limited by the induced counter voltage. The amperage output of the alternator is held at a maximum safe value when the counter voltage becomes nearly as strong as the alternator voltage.

A coil has inductance only when there is an increasing or decreasing current flowing in side-by-side conductors. When the current changes at the rate of 1 A per second inducing 1 V, the system has an inductance unit of 1 **henry.** Henry units are not used in automotive servicing. They are used in electrical equipment design and they can be used as an aid to understanding the operation of some electrical equipment.

An ignition coil has a similar type of electromagnetic induction. When the ignition contact points close, current will flow through the heavy primary windings of the coil. This makes the coil into an electromagnet. A magnetic field builds up around the coil (Figure 1-31). When the ignition points open, the primary ignition current stops and the magnetic field collapses. The magnetic lines of force in the collapsing field rapidly cut through

Figure 1-29 Electromagnetic induction in an alternator.

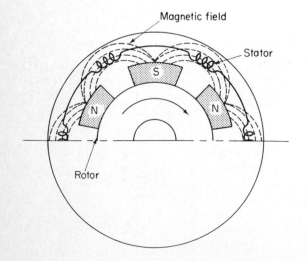

Figure 1-30 Voltage induced in a conductor that is next to a conductor carrying an alternating current.

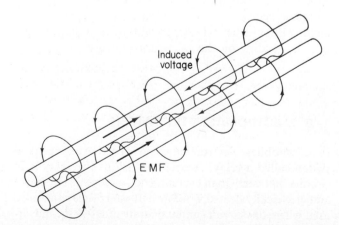

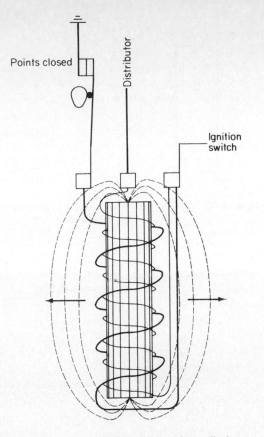

Figure 1-31 A magnetic field builds up in a coil when current begins to flow.

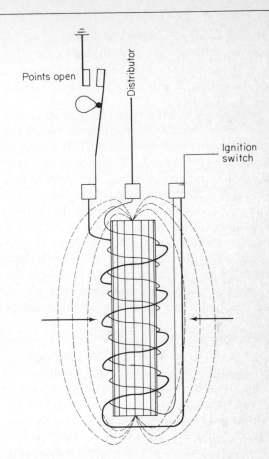

Figure 1-32 When the current flow through a coil stops, the magnetic field collapses through the coil wires. This induces a voltage in the coil wires.

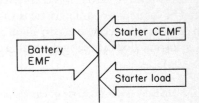

Figure 1-33 The counter electromotive force developed in the starter, added to the mechanical load on the starter, opposes the electromotive force of the battery to limit the maximum starter rotating speed.

the coil secondary windings (Figure 1–32). These rapidly moving magnetic lines of force induce a high voltage in the secondary windings of the coil. This high voltage is used to make the arc or spark at the spark plug. Here again the lines of force cut across a conductor to make a voltage. The faster they cross the conductor, the more voltage is made.

Electromagnetic induction is also used in motors. As the motor armature turns, it cuts through the magnetism of the motor field. This produces an electromotive force in a direction that is opposite to the battery voltage. It is, therefore, called a **counter electromotive force (CEMF)**. The strength of the counter electromotive force is proportional to armature speed. As motor speed increases, its counter electromotive force increases. When the mechanical load plus the counter electromotive force equals the electrical energy of the battery, the motor will not rotate faster. This is illustrated in Figure 1–33. In a motor the rotating armature is the conductor. It rotates in a stationary magnetic field to produce the counter voltage. A weaker magnetic field in the motor produces less counter electromotive force at the same armature speed. As a result the armature will keep rotating faster until it produces enough counter electromotive force to balance system voltage and starter load.

There will be electromagnetic induction any time there is relative motion between the lines of force of a magnetic field and a conductor. This can happen in three ways:

1. The lines of force can be made to cut across the conductor.

2. Expanding or contracting magnetic lines of force can move across a conductor.

3. The conductor can be moved through a stationary magnetic field.

Let us look at what happens as a result of inductance in a circuit with a coil. Closing the switch puts full voltage across the ends of the coil. This causes current to start to flow very rapidly. A magnetic field builds up rapidly around each coil winding. The building magnetic field induces a counter voltage in the side-by-side coil windings. The counter voltage opposes the current flowing into the coil. This induced counter voltage slows the rate that the current goes into the coil. The action graphed in Figure 1–34 shows that induction controls the time it takes to build up full current flow in a coil. After the magnetic field has reached its maximum strength, current through the coil is limited only by the resistance of the coil wire.

When the switch is turned off the voltage across the ends of the coil drops to zero. Then the magnetic field around the coil collapses through the windings. The collapse causes a voltage in the coil that tries to keep current flowing in the same direction it had been flowing with the switch on. This continues until the magnetic field has completely collapsed. The graph in Figure 1–35 shows how inductance affects the voltage in a coil right after the switch is turned off.

You will notice that the current will build up to full strength **after** the voltage has reached full strength during inductance. It will also cause some current flow after the voltage has dropped to zero if it is connected in a complete circuit. The inductive characteristic is shown on the photograph of an oscilloscope trace in Figure 1–36. The upper trace is current flowing through an alternator field.

Figure 1–34 Induction slows the rate of current going into a coil to control the time it takes to build up a full current flow in the coil.

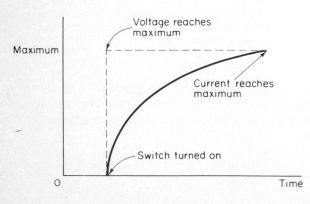

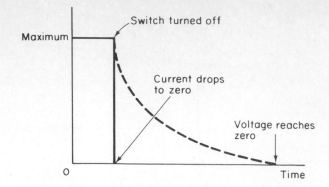

Figure 1–35 Inductance from the collapse of the magnetic field in a coil produces a voltage that tries to keep the current flowing.

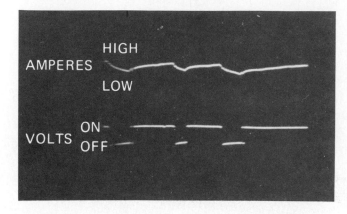

Figure 1–36 Oscilloscope trace of current and voltage flowing through an alternator field as the regulator turns off and on.

Voltage is shown in the lower trace as the regulator turns off and on. This characteristic is part of the reason for the phase shift that causes **voltage to lead current** in alternating-current (ac) electrical equipment.

1–10 CAPACITANCE

Technical words in this section you will need to learn:

Charging a capacitor	Farad
Discharging a capacitor	Microfarad

Capacitance is another electrical characteristic that affects the electrical system. When two conductor materials are close together but insulated from each other, the negative electrical charge in one conductor will attract the positive electrical charge in the other conductor. These electrical charges will remain as long as the conductors are insulated from each other.

Typical capacitors (also called condensers) used in automobiles are made from two long strips of electrically conductive foil called **plates.** The plates are separated by insulating paper. The typical capacitor is illustrated in Figure 1–37. The amount of electrical charge held on a plate is limited by the plate size and the distance from the other plate. The larger and closer together the plates are, the more electrical charge they can store. The electrical charge is made up of a very large number of electrons. **The ability to store electrons is called capacitance.** The electrical measurement of capacitance is a farad. It is a very large unit, so the smaller unit, **microfarad** (mF = 1/1,000,000 farad), is used to describe the electrical capacity of automotive capacitors.

Let us take a look at how a capacitor works. The electrical circuit of a radio in Figure 1–38 has a capacitor The switch and capacitor shown in this drawing are built inside the radio. They are shown outside to illustrate their action. When the switch is turned on, electricity goes to both the radio and the capacitor. Keep in mind that the action in the following discussion happens very quickly.

When the switch is turned on, the capacitor must fill with electrons before the voltage can build up. This is called charging the capacitor. Note that there is current in the circuit **before** voltage builds up. Once the cir-

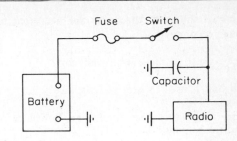

Figure 1–38 Circuit with a capacitor to keep a sudden voltage surge from damaging electronic parts.

cuit has full voltage and the capacitor is fully charged, the capacitor does not enter into the operation of the circuit. Connected in this way the capacitor controls how fast the voltage will build up. This keeps a sudden voltage surge from damaging the electronic parts of the radio.

Have you ever wondered why the sound from radios gradually fades out after you have turned off the switch? This is caused by current going through the radio as the capacitor discharges.

The capacitance characteristic of electrical circuits causes the current to flow before the voltage builds up in some alternating-current (ac) electrical circuits. In this way the **current leads the voltage** in the ac circuits.

In addition to capacitors, a number of other parts of the automobile electrical systems have capacitance. Any two current-carrying conductors that are close together but insulated from each other have capacitance. A good example of this is a wire coil, like an electromagnet or ignition coil. In addition to carrying the required current, these coils have capacitance as well as inductance, which affects the way they work.

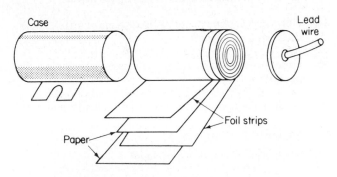

Figure 1–37 Parts of a typical ignition capacitor.

STUDY QUESTIONS

Section 1–1

1. How does the electron theory differ from the current theory?

2. From which orbit of an atom can electrons be removed from or added to?

3. How many electrons are in the outer orbit of atoms in conductor materials?

4. How many electrons are in the outer orbit of atoms in insulator materials?

5. Why is copper used for wires in automotive electrical systems?

6. How do electrical charges affect each other?

7. What should you call the one-way drift of electrons through a conductor?

8. What should you call the amount of electrons drifting in one direction?

9. What unit is used to express electrical current?

10. What unit is used to express electromotive force?

Section 1–2

11. What should you call a circuit that you can follow all the way around without running into an opening?

---

12. What two things are necessary for a current to flow through a conductor?

13. What causes resistance in a conductor?

14. What unit is used to express resistance?

15. If circuit resistance does not change, how is current affected by doubling the voltage?

16. If circuit voltage does not change, how is current affected by doubling the resistance?

17. How can you determine electrical power?

18. When is the electrical system voltage the greatest?

19. List three things that increase the resistance of a conductor.

20. What must you know to use voltage drop as a measure of resistance?

21. How is circuit voltage measured?

22. How is voltage drop measured?

23. How can you determine the total resistance of a circuit with several resistances connected in series?

24. What voltage will you have when you add all the voltage drops in a series electrical circuit?

25. What part of the electrical system is often overlooked when making electrical tests?

Section 1–3

26. What is a parallel circuit?

27. What is another name used for a parallel circuit?

28. How do parallel circuits affect current flow?

29. How do parallel circuits affect the total resistance?

30. What makes an electrical load?

Section 1–4

31. What do you call the effect of parallel resistances?

32. What is the quickest way to determine the resistance of a part of an electrical circuit?

Section 1–5

33. How do magnetic poles affect each other?

34. Why is it stated that lines of force are actually a section view?

35. What happens to a magnetic field when an iron bar is placed in the field?

36. What happens to a magnet when it is cut in two?

Section 1–6

37. What makes the magnetic field around all current-carrying conductors?

38. What happens to the magnetic field around a current-carrying conductor when the current increases?

39. What force is put on two side-by-side conductors when the magnetic fields between the conductors go in the same direction?

40. What force is put on two side-by-side conductors when the magnetic fields between the conductors go in opposite directions?

41. What is an electromagnet?

Section 1–7

42. What holds the instrument needle in the zero or center at rest position?

43. What causes the instrument needle to move?

44. How can the same meter be used to make different electrical measurements?

45. How does an inductive ammeter measure current in a conductor?

46. What is the main advantage of an inductive ammeter?

Section 1–8

47. What type of circuit uses relays?

48. What is meant by normally open and normally closed relay contact points?

Section 1–9

49. What happens in a conductor when magnetic lines of force are made to cut across the conductor?

50. On what does the strength of the induced electromotive force depend?

51. List three ways voltage can be induced in a conductor.

52. What controls the length of time it takes to build up full current flow in a coil?

Section 1–10

53. What controls the amount of charge a capacitor can hold?

54. How can an electrical circuit have current before voltage?

55. Make a graph to show how the voltage builds up after current starts to flow.

ROUTINE SERVICE OPERATIONS

Automobiles will last longer when faults are corrected and preventive maintenance is done. Except for a change in appearance or performance, these are the only reasons a customer will have an automobile serviced by automotive service technicians.

When you work on a vehicle you should work in a safe manner so that you do not get hurt or damage the vehicle on which you are working. To start with, you should wear the right clothing. Loose clothing may catch on a moving part and pull you into it. Long sleeves will help protect your arms from hot engine parts. You should remove rings and wristwatches so that they do not catch on parts and injure your hands. Metal in rings and watches will get hot and burn you if they contact between an electrical junction and ground. Proper safety glasses are recommended any time you work on vehicles to minimize the chance of damage to your eyes.

Fender covers and seat covers should be used. They will protect the vehicle from scratches and soil caused by tools and dirty vehicle parts. It is much easier to use covers than it is to clean the vehicle after it has become dirty or to repair scratches made by careless work.

Routine service work done by an automobile service technician includes lubrication, oil changes, filter changes, seasonal service, and tune-ups. As a service technician you will be expected to repair faulty parts rapidly

and correctly. Faulty small electrical parts are usually replaced. Major electrical units, such as starters and alternators, are disassembled and repaired when they do not operate normally. Damaged connecting wires are usually repaired. The biggest problem you will face in electrical service is to find the specific part that is causing the failure. Checking a system to identify a faulty part is called **diagnosis**.

Service manuals have very good troubleshooting charts. They give specific test procedures that you should follow to find the cause of the problem. New car dealerships also have service bulletins. The service technician often overlooks this valuable information. Instead, parts are often changed until the faulty system operates. Even though each car type and model is different, many electrical systems have a number of things in common. An understanding of the common things will be a great aid in helping you solve problems as you follow the servicing procedures provided by the manufacturer.

Service technicians usually find it difficult to service electrically operated accessories. The technician will usually work with mechanical parts where movement can be seen or touched. On the other hand, electrical parts seem to operate in a mysterious way with no moving force that you can see. When you learn to understand electrical force or power, often in terms of fluid or air movement, you should have less difficulty in diagnosing electrical accessory problems or in locating and correcting the faulty part.

To service electrical accessories properly, you must understand the principles upon which the electrical units operate. You also need to develop a systematic testing procedure to pinpoint the cause of the problem. When you have done this, you will be able to rapidly diagnose, repair, and adjust electrical parts.

2-1 LIGHTING

Technical words in this section you will need to learn:

Adjuster frame	Candlepower
Beam	Filament
Bulb socket	Lamp
Candela	Lamp base
	Lens

The most common cause of lighting system failure is lamp bulb failure. Bulb life depends on several things. These include the way the bulb is made, electrical system voltage, number of hours the bulb has been in use, and the amount of vibration. Many of the bulbs will last as long as the automobile is in use. Other bulbs must be replaced several times during the lifetime of the vehicle.

Lighting is a safety item. The lamps on the outside of the vehicle (exterior) help the driver light the roadway and warn other drivers that a vehicle is there. They also indicate that the driver plans to slow or to change direction. The lamps inside the vehicle (interior) give the passengers light for entry into and exit from the automobile. Instrument lamps help the driver to keep track of the vehicle operating conditions to prevent dangerous or destructive malfunctions. Any time a lamp does not work, vehicle safety is affected.

In most cases, lamp failure results from a burned-out filament in the bulb. This is easily corrected by replacing the bulb. Lamp failure can also be caused by the wiring, terminals, or a faulty bulb socket. When a whole set of lamps fail, it is usually caused by a blown fuse.

The lamp bulb must be of the correct type. It must have a base to match the bulb socket and it must have the correct filament. Bulbs have identifying marks on the glass or base. The brightness of the bulb is controlled by the filament size and design. The bulb must be bright enough to give the necessary light, but not so bright that it uses too much current.

Bulb Identification. Lamp bulbs are given a commercial number that is used by both the bulb manufacturer and automobile manufacturer. Bulbs are designed with different base sizes (some are baseless), locking pin arrangements, single or double contacts, and voltage and amperage requirements. A number of typical automotive bulbs are shown in Figure 2-1. The bulb must have the correct base size, locking pins, contact arrangement, and voltage range. The bulb number for each lamp is shown

Figure 2–1 Typical automotive lamp bulbs.

in the owner's handbook that is usually kept in the glove box of the automobile. It is also listed in the service manual and in bulb manufacturers' catalogs. If you do not have any of these, replace the bulb with the same number as the bulb you removed. This should always be the *last* way to select a bulb, because the bulb you are replacing may have been the wrong bulb, which caused it to burn out.

Bulb Replacement. Exterior lamps are sealed from dust and moisture. The body of the exterior lamp is mounted in a body panel. It is covered with a lens. A gasket forms a seal between the lens and lamp body. The bulb is usually replaced by removing Phillips head lens-mounting screws, and then lifting the lens off. The bulb is removed by pushing it inward and turning it counterclockwise to release the pins; then the bulb can be lifted from its socket. This is illustrated in Figure 2–2. The bulb may corrode and seize in the socket if the lens seal is damaged or if moisture follows the wire into the socket. Special bulb-removing tools are made to remove these bulbs. When you do not have these special tools you can remove the bulb by covering it with a shop towel, then breaking the glass of the bulb. Remove the bulb base with pliers. Sometimes the base is corroded so badly that the entire socket will have to be replaced. Figure 2–3 shows the parts of a typical bulb socket assembly. Be sure to seal the new socket from moisture so that it will not seize again.

The new bulb base is pressed into the socket and turned clockwise to lock it in place. Turn the switch on to make sure the new bulb will light. If it does, install the gasket and lens.

Figure 2–3   Parts of a typical bulb socket assembly.

Some tail lamp bulbs can easily be changed from inside the trunk. An example is shown in Figure 2–4. Spring clips on the bulb socket hold it in the lamp body. From inside the trunk the socket is pulled from the lamp body. The bulb is replaced in the socket; then the socket is replaced in the lamp body. Be careful to line up the tab that correctly positions the socket.

Instrument panel lamps have removable sockets. The socket is made of molded plastic with fingers to contact the conducting surfaces of the printed circuit board. The sockets are difficult, if not impossible, to see under the dash panel so that you will have to learn to feel for the socket. The voltage under the dash is so low that it will not give you a shock if your hand touches electrical connections. Remember, you should not wear rings and wristwatches while doing this, to avoid burns. Metal on

Figure 2–2   Replacing a lamp bulb after removing the lens.

Figure 2–4   Replacing a tail lamp bulb from inside the trunk.

your hand or arm can short across a circuit. The current flow through the metal will make it hot and burn your skin.

The instrument bulb socket is turned counterclockwise to remove the socket from the printed panel circuit. The baseless bulb is put in the socket, as shown in Figure 2–5. The socket is then reinstalled in the panel. Check the lights to see that the new bulb is operating correctly.

The lens must be removed to replace other interior light bulbs. Interior lamps are not sealed. On some lamps the lens is fastened with screws around a frame. In other lamps the lens is made of flexible plastic that can be bent slightly to release tangs from the lamp body. The burned-out bulb is removed and a new bulb is installed. Be sure to test the operation of the new bulb before you replace the lens.

Headlamps. The most critical lights on the automobile are the headlamps. They must be bright enough for the driver to see the road ahead but not so bright that they will blind the oncoming driver. Many state laws limited the headlamp brightness to a maximum of 75,000 candle-power. **Candlepower** is a standard unit used to measure the brightness of light. In 1978 the Department of Transportation raised the legal light output of headlamps to 150,000 candela. **Candela** is the metric unit of light brightness. This change in regulations has made it possible to use halogen headlamps in the United States.

Headlamps are made to direct the light onto the road and still not blind the oncoming driver. This is done by the shape of the reflector and the inside surface of

the lens on the front of the headlamp. The shape of the lens widens the beam and reduces glare. Careful location of the bulb filament helps to aim the light beam onto the road.

Automobiles have high-beam and low-beam headlamps. Most of the driving in cities and on busy highways is done using low beams. High beam is used only when there is no traffic in front of the vehicle.

Two types of sealed-beam headlamp units are used to meet driving needs. Type 1 sealed-beam units have one filament aimed to put maximum light on the road. They are used as the inboard lamps in the four-headlight system. Type 2 sealed-beam units have two filaments. The main filament is the low-beam filament. It is placed in the unit where it will give maximum light. The second filament in type 2 units is used for high-beam light. It is placed to put light down the road as far as possible. It does not give as much high-beam light as the type 1 unit because the low-beam filament is placed where it will give the most light. Type 2 units are used for the outboard lamps in the four-headlight system and for all two-headlamp systems. The four-headlamp system uses 5 3/4 in. (146 mm) round or 4 × 6 1/2 in. (100 × 165 mm) rectangular units. Sealed-beam units used in the two-headlamp system are 7 in. (178 mm) in diameter or 142 × 200 mm (5.6 × 7.9 in.) rectangular. The type number is at the top of the lens face for easy identification. The location of the type number is shown in Figure 2–6. In addition, the mounting lugs are offset at different angles so that they will only fit in the correct position. Type 1 units have two electrical terminals, while type 2 units have three.

In July 1978 the National Highway Traffic Safety Administration (NHTSA) amended the Federal Motor Vehicle Safety Standard 108 to allow the use of head-

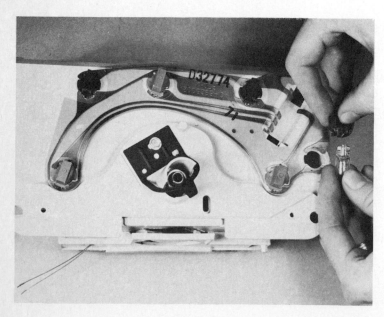

Figure 2–5 Lamp bulb being replaced on an instrument panel that has a printed circuit. The instrument assembly has been removed from the vehicle to make this illustration.

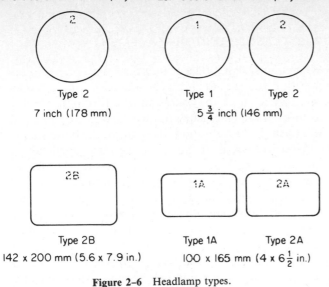

Type 2

7 inch (178 mm)

Type 1   Type 2

5 3/4 inch (146 mm)

Type 2B

142 x 200 mm (5.6 x 7.9 in.)

Type 1A   Type 2A

100 x 165 mm (4 x 6 1/2 in.)

Figure 2–6 Headlamp types.

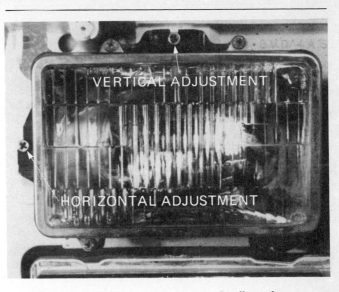

VERTICAL ADJUSTMENT

HORIZONTAL ADJUSTMENT

Figure 2–7 Adjuster screws on a headlamp frame.

lamps with a fixed lens and reflector. This type of head-lamp uses a small replacement bulb. The amended standard also allows the use of only two small 4 × 6 1/2 in. (100 × 165 mm) type 2A rectangular sealed-beam units. The change in the standard gives the vehicle manu-facturer more flexibility to design vehicles with less aerodynamic drag, and this results in better fuel economy.

Headlamp Aiming. Headlamps can be designed and manufactured correctly, but they will only light the road correctly when they have been properly aimed. Poor headlamp aiming is the largest single fault in vehicle safe-ty inspections. Headlamps can easily be aimed with mini-mum equipment.

The headlamp sealed-beam unit is fastened in an **adjuster frame**. The adjuster frame has one screw that controls side-to-side (horizontal) movement and another that controls up-and-down (vertical) movement. The ad-juster screws are shown on a headlamp in Figure 2–7. The frame is adjusted to place the hot spot of the headlamp to give the driver maximum road lighting.

Before the headlamps are aimed, the automobile should be on a level floor, have a full tank of fuel, the spare tire should be in place, all tires should be inflated correctly, and all other equipment regularly carried should be loaded. Headlamp aiming is based on a distance of 25 ft (7.6 m) between the front of the headlamp lens and a viewing screen, which may be a wall. Use masking tape to place vertical lines on the viewing screen directly in front of the headlamps. Also place a horizontal line on the screen at the same height as the center of the head-lamps. The lines and headlamp hot-spot high-intensity zone should be located as shown in Figure 2–8. Use the adjusting screws to position the hot-spot correctly. Type

Figure 2–8 Location of the hot-spot high-intensity zone on a screen 25 feet in front of the headlamp when the headlamps are adjusted correctly.

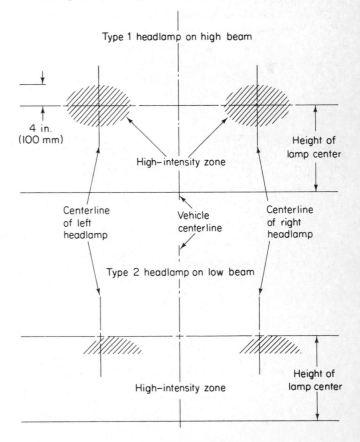

Type 1 headlamp on high beam

4 in.
(100 mm)

High–intensity zone

Height of lamp center

Centerline of left headlamp

Vehicle centerline

Centerline of right headlamp

Type 2 headlamp on low beam

High–intensity zone

Height of lamp center

1 units are aimed with the high beam turned on, and type 2 units are aimed with the low beam turned on.

Whenever possible, headlamps should be aimed with mechanical aimers. They can aim the headlamps more quickly than the light-beam method. Mechanical aimers are seated against locating lugs on the front outer edge of the sealed-beam unit. Specific operating details differ between mechanical aimers. In general, they use spirit levels, strings, and reflecting mirrors with split images to align headlamp pairs. Some aimers used in daylight use the headlamp beam with optics so that the pattern in the aimer appears the same as it would be on the viewing screen. A typical mechanical headlamp aimer is shown in Figure 2-9.

No matter what method is used, headlamps should be correctly aimed. Any light less than the maxi-

mum gives the driver less time to react in case there is an unexpected change in the road conditions ahead.

2-2 FLASHER UNIT REPLACEMENT

When a turn signal flasher unit does not operate in one direction you should check for a burned-out bulb. One easy way to check the condition of a turn signal bulb is to turn on the emergency hazard flasher. A good bulb will flash. If the bulb still fails to flash, the bulb, socket, or electrical circuit is faulty. If the turn signal fails to operate in both directions it is very likely that the flasher unit has failed. The flasher unit is mounted under the dash. It is a small metal or plastic can with wires connected on one end, or it is plugged into a junction on the fuse block. Sometimes it is clipped into a bracket and at other times it hangs freely. You will have to reach under the dash and feel for the flasher. When it is not on the fuse block the flasher unit can be pulled low enough so that the socket can be removed (Figure 2-10). Plug a new

Figure 2-9 Typical headlamp aimer. (Courtesy Cadillac Motor Car Division, General Motors Corporation.)

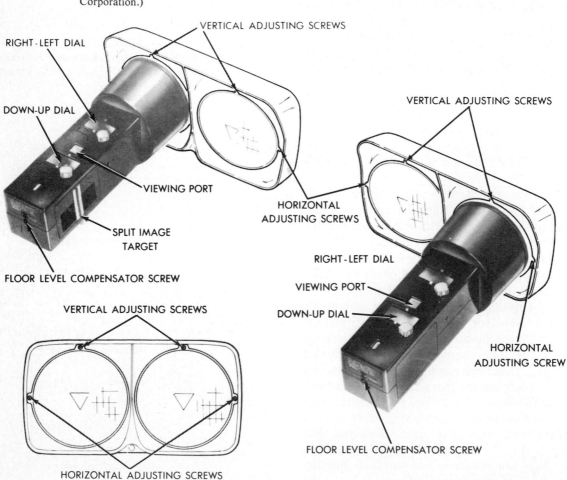

Figure 2–10 Turn signal flasher unit lowered below the instrument panel for replacement.

insulation from damage. Safety devices used in automobiles take three forms: fuses, circuit breakers, and fusible links.

Fuse. A fuse is a small metal strip in a glass tube (cartridge type) or plastic body (blade type). The metal strip burns out to break the circuit when high current flows. Fuses are usually grouped together in a fuse block under the dash. Figure 2–11 pictures a typical fuse block that uses blade-type fuses. Sometimes, a fuse is mounted separately in a circuit. This is usually done when electrical accessories are added to the vehicle. A fuse will carry a 10% amperage overload. It will burn out immediately with a 35% amperage overload. The circuit opens when the fuse burns out. This protects the wiring and the operating units. Fuses are used in low-amperage light and accessory circuits. Circuits that draw high current usually have circuit breakers.

Circuits that use a lot of electricity, such as windshield wipers, radio, hazard warning flasher, heater, and air conditioner, have an individual fuse. Circuits that are not used all the time, such as courtesy lights, trunk lights, and glove-box lights, are grouped together, on one fuse. If the entire circuit fails to operate, a blown fuse is most likely the cause of the failure. Fuses are easy to replace. Most fuse blocks can be found under the dash panel where you can see them. In some cases the fuse block is hinged so that it can be lowered. This makes it easy

Figure 2–11 Typical automotive fuse block.

flasher in the socket. Automobiles use two flasher units, one for the turn signals and one for the hazard warning lights. Be sure to check both systems *before* you start to work on the flasher unit. Check them again when the flasher unit has been removed to be sure that you are changing the correct flasher unit. Make sure that the flasher system operates correctly with the new unit installed before you put the flasher unit in its retaining clip.

2–3 SAFETY DEVICES

Technical words in this section you will need to learn:

Bimetal arm	Fuse block
Circuit breaker	Fusible link
Fuse	

Electrical circuits are protected with safety devices. **A safety device in an electrical circuit opens the circuit when too much current flows.** This keeps the wiring and

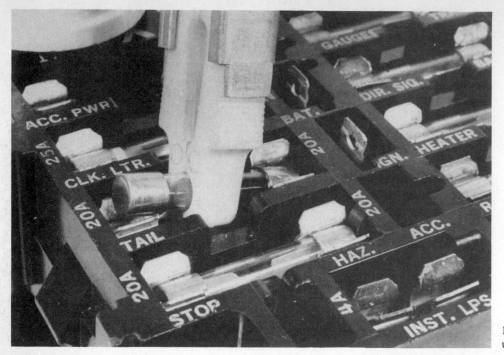

Figure 2-12 Special puller being used to remove a cartridge-type fuse.

for you to find a blown fuse. The circuit that the fuse protects and the fuse type are often marked on the fuse block. The burned fuse is pulled from the clip and replaced with a new fuse of the correct amperage. Cartridge-type fuses must usually be pried out. Special plastic pullers, like the one in Figure 2-12, make it easy to replace cartridge-type fuses. The amperage rating of the cartridge-type fuse is marked around one of the metal ends. Blade-type fuses are color-coded (Figure 2-13) to show their amperage size.

You should always find the cause of a blown fuse. The only way a fuse can blow is to have too much electrical current flow in the circuit. This is caused by a faulty operating unit, a short or grounded wire, or an accidental grounding while you are working on the circuit. The cause

Figure 2-13 Color codes used on blade-type fuses.

Blade – type fuse Identification	
Amperes	Identification
3	Violet
5	Tan
10	Red
15	Light blue
20	Yellow
25	White
30	Green
Over 30	Circuit breaker

should be corrected before a new fuse is installed or the new fuse will blow out (see Section 5-3).

If a fuse is replaced with a larger-amperage fuse, it could allow too much current to flow. This could ruin a partly malfunctioning unit. It could also burn insulation from the wires. This, of course, would increase the repair cost to the customer.

Circuit Breaker. Circuit breakers are used as safety devices in circuits that carry more than 30 A. A circuit breaker has a set of normally closed contact points mounted on a bimetal arm as illustrated in Figure 2-14. It has a metal or plastic cover. When too much current flows, the bimetal arm heats. Heat causes the two metals to expand at different rates. This makes the arm bend, opening the point contact to stop current flow in the circuit. When the arm cools, the arm returns to close the contact. This completes the electrical circuit so that current can flow again. Circuit breakers are used in the headlamp circuit for safety. In case of a short in the circuit, the headlamps flash on and off to give the driver a chance to stop the automobile safely. Circuit breakers are also used on high-current-drawing units, such as power windows and power seats. The circuit breaker is placed under the dash or beside the operating unit.

Some circuit breakers do not reset automatically, so the circuit remains open until repairs are made. These breakers are reset manually after being tripped.

A remote reset breaker is another type of circuit breaker. It has a resistance wire coiled around the bimetal spring. The ends of the coil are connected across the normally closed points. When the points are closed, no

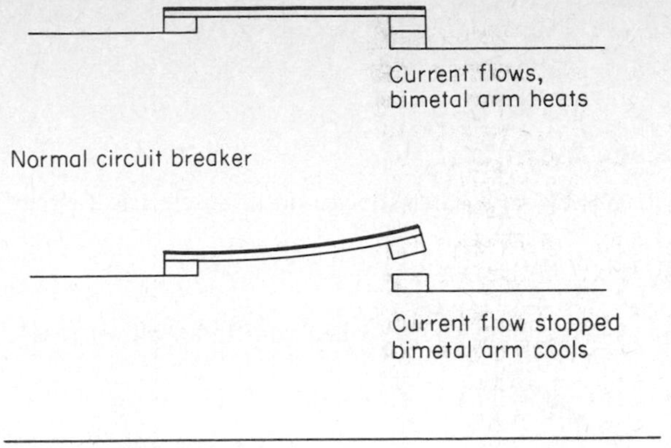

Current flows,
bimetal arm heats

Normal circuit breaker

Current flow stopped
bimetal arm cools

Figure 2-14 Operation of a typical circuit breaker.

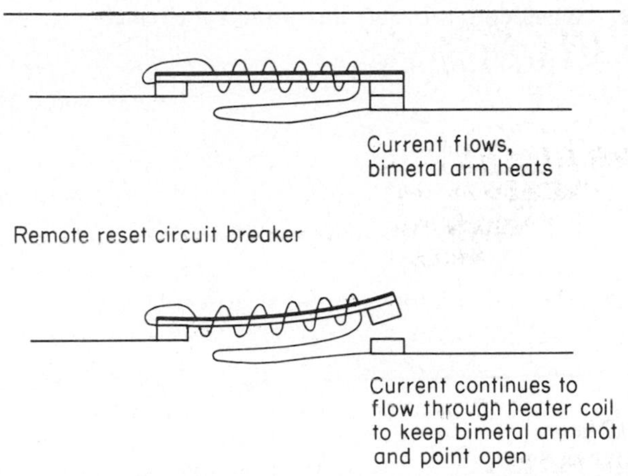

Current flows,
bimetal arm heats

Remote reset circuit breaker

Current continues to
flow through heater coil
to keep bimetal arm hot
and point open

Figure 2-15 Operation of a remote reset circuit breaker.

current will flow through the heating coil. Too much current in the operating circuit causes the bimetal spring to get hot and open the points. With the points open current will flow through the resistance coil and the coil gets hot. Coil heat keeps the bimetal arm hot so that the points stay open (Figure 2-15). The circuit breaker will automatically close when the switch for the circuit is turned off or when the battery is disconnected.

Fusible Link. Many circuits are protected with a fusible link. Fusible links are used in circuits that do not have a fuse or a circuit breaker. They are also used in some circuits that have fuses and circuit breakers. Fusible links protect the circuit if one of the other safety devices accidentally shorts out. **A fusible link is a short piece of wire four AWG sizes smaller than the circuit wire it protects.** AWG wire sizes are described in Section 5-5. For example, the AWG 10 wire in the charging circuit is protected by an AWG 14 fusible link. An AWG 16 light wire is protected by an AWG 20 fusible link. The fusible link is covered with thick Hypalon plastic insulation that will melt but will not burn. The size of the insulation looks like a large wire. When the link fails, the grounded point that caused the failure must be repaired before a new link is installed. Some fusible links are connected with terminals. Others are soldered in the circuit.

When a safety device breaks the circuit, faults in the electrical system must be found and repaired properly. This is discussed in Sections 5-3, 5-4, and 5-5. A new fuse or fusible link is installed after the circuit is repaired.

STUDY QUESTIONS

Introduction

1. Why do customers have their automobiles serviced?

2. Why should wristwatches be removed when working on the electrical system?

3. What is usually done to repair small faulty electrical parts?

4. What is the biggest problem faced by automotive service technicians?

5. Why do service technicians find it difficult to locate the cause of electrical problems?

Section 2-1

6. What is the most common cause of lighting system failure?

7. What two ways do lights help vehicle safety?

8. What is the most common cause of lamp bulb failure?

9. What is the most common reason for the failure of a whole set of lamps?

10. Why should you use the bulb number taken from specifications rather than the number from the old bulb?

11. Describe the way you should remove a bulb from a corroded socket.

12. Why is it difficult to replace instrument lamp bulbs?

13. How does an exterior lamp lens differ from an interior lamp lens?

14. What are the most critical lights on a vehicle?

15. What is the metric unit of light brightness?

16. How do type 2 headlamp bulbs differ from type 1 bulbs?

17. How can you tell a type 2 headlamp bulb from a type 1 bulb?

18. What is the largest single fault in vehicle safety inspections?

19. How are headlamps aimed?

Section 2-2

20. How can you be sure you are removing the faulty flasher unit?

Section 2-3

21. What does a safety device do in an electrical circuit?

22. How much overload will a fuse carry?

23. What should you do when you find a blown fuse?

24. How do you know what size of fuse to use?

25. What circuits use a circuit breaker rather than a fuse?

26. Why are circuit breakers used in headlamp circuits?

27. What is done to reset a remote reset circuit breaker?

28. When does a fusible link protect a circuit?

3

THE AUTOMOTIVE BATTERY

The lead-acid type of battery is the primary source of electricity for starting engines. It also serves as a reserve source of electricity for the electrical running load of the vehicle. Its size depends on how it will be used. Vehicles with large engines require a greater cranking power and therefore they need a large battery. Large batteries are also used in vehicles with many electrically operated accessories. Small batteries are found in vehicles with small engines and light electrical loads.

A properly maintained lead-acid battery (the type used in automobiles) will give from three to four years of trouble-free service. Proper maintenance is keeping the battery clean, charged, full of water, and correctly held in the battery carrier. When a battery fails to crank the engine, you must be able to check the battery and the rest of the electrical system to find the cause of the cranking failure. Only then can you repair the problem. The battery may have failed or other electrical system parts may have failed. The types of failure are discussed in Chapter 4.

It is important for you to know what is in a battery and how it works when you are diagnosing battery problems. It is also important for you to know about different battery materials and construction. This knowledge will let you help your customer make intelligent choices in the selection of a replacement battery.

3-1 BATTERY OPERATION

Technical words in this section you will need to learn:

Ampere-hour	Electromotive force
Cell	Element
Counter electromotive force	Ion
	Lead peroxide
Discharge	Plate
Electricity	Separator
Electrochemical	Specific gravity
Electrolyte	State of charge

Electron movement in one direction is an electrical reaction that we call electricity. Chemical reactions between different materials cause electrons in the materials to move from some atoms to other atoms. The movement of electrons is described in Chapter 1. When electron movement results from a chemical reaction, it is called an **electrochemical** process.

A lead-acid automotive battery is an electrochemical device. It has a voltage (electrical pressure) and it can produce a current (movement of electrons) as the result of chemical reactions that use up battery materials. A current forced backward through the battery will cause chemical reactions that restore battery materials. Chapter 1 describes voltage and current in more detail.

Battery Cell.   A simple storage battery **element** has two different active materials. Each is formed on grids to make **plates**. The two materials in the element are kept apart with a **separator**. The element is put in a liquid sulfuric acid electrolyte solution to make a battery **cell**. Battery parts are shown in Figure 3–1. **Electrolyte** is a material whose atoms become ionized in solution. **An ion is an atom that is either missing electrons (positive ion) or has extra electrons (negative ion)**. These ionized atoms move in the electrolyte. The acid in the electrolyte loosens electrons from the plate materials so that the electrons can drift through the plates. This causes positive and negative ions to be formed in the plate material.

The active material on one of the plates is lead dioxide, usually called **lead peroxide** (PbO_2). It is a brown, small-grain crystalline material. The crystalline type of structure is very porous, like a sponge, so the electrolyte

Figure 3–1   Parts of a typical lead-acid automotive battery. Notice how the connector goes through the wall between the cells. (Courtesy Chevrolet Motor Division, General Motors Corporation.)

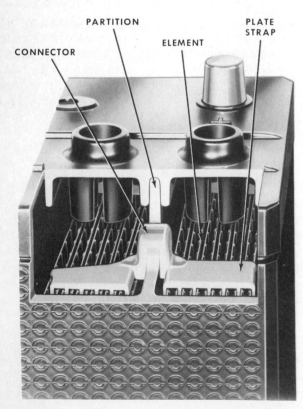

CONNECTOR

PARTITION

ELEMENT

PLATE STRAP

can soak through the plate. Electrons leave the lead peroxide plate and enter the electrolyte, leaving positive ions behind in the lead peroxide plate. This is the **positive plate**.

The active material on the second plate is porous or **sponge lead**. Electrolyte with many electrons from the positive plate soaks through this second plate. Electrons leave the electrolyte and go into the lead of the second plate, as shown in Figure 3–2. This gives the sponge-lead plate extra electrons that form negative ions in the plate. This second plate is the **negative plate**.

The electromotive force (volts) between the lead peroxide positive plate and sponge-lead negative plate is 2.13 V. **The cell voltage of a battery is caused by the type of materials used in the plates**. The voltage is not affected by the plate size, plate shape, or number of plates in a cell.

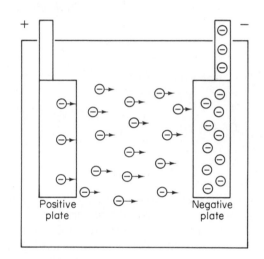

Positive plate

Negative plate

Figure 3–2   Electron movement within a cell that has no external connection.

If a wire connects the plates through a light bulb outside the cell (Figure 3–3), electrons can leave the terminals of the negative plate and flow through the wires and bulb to the terminals of the positive plate. Electrons will continue to flow as long as chemical action inside the cell can transfer electrons from the positive plate to the negative plate. This process is called **discharging** the cell.

Cell Chemical Action.   Look at Figure 3–4 as you read the following description. During discharge, electrons leave the sponge-lead negative plate through the wire. This leaves postive lead ions (Pb^{2+}) on the plate. Negative sulfate ions (SO_4^{2-}) from the electrolyte are attracted to the positive lead ions. They combine to form neutral lead sulfate ($PbSO_4$) on the negative plate. During this time, the lead peroxide (PbO_2) of the positive plate combines with hydrogen (H^+) from the electrolyte.

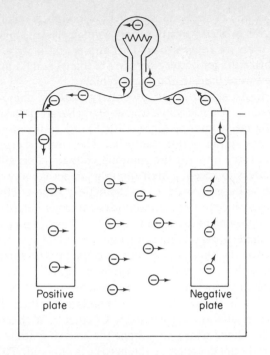

Figure 3-3 Electron movement through a cell when an external circuit is complete.

Figure 3-4 Ion movement in a cell during discharge.

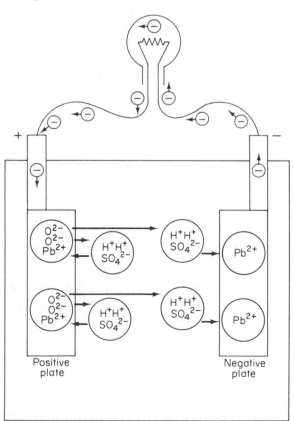

This releases electrons as positive lead ions (Pb^{2+}) and water (H_2O) are formed. The positive lead ions from this reaction combine with negative sulfate ions (SO_4^{2-}) of the electrolyte. This reaction also forms neutral lead sulfate ($PbSO_4$) on the positive plate. You should note that in a perfect battery both of the plates in the cell become neutral lead sulfate when the battery is completely discharged. The electrolyte becomes water.

Battery Performance. During discharge, electricity will be produced by the battery as long as it has active material. You can see in Figure 3-5 that the terminal voltage drops as more current (discharge amperage) is taken from the battery. This voltage drop is used to rate batteries as discussed in Section 4-4. The electrolyte of a fully charged battery has a specific gravity of 1.27; that is, it is 1.27 times as heavy as pure water. The specific gravity of water is 1.00. **The specific gravity of the electrolyte indicates the amount of chemical activity remaining in the cell to supply electricity.** A measurement of the specific gravity in a battery cell is called the cell **state of charge.**

You will remember that the electrochemical process in a lead-acid battery is reversible. If the terminals of a battery are connected to a voltage higher than the battery voltage, electrons will flow backward. This reverse electrical current causes a reverse chemical action in the battery. The plates again become lead and lead peroxide. The cell can only be discharged or recharged as fast as the electrons can move through the battery. Forcing the electron movement with too much voltage results in the formation of excess hydrogen gas (from the negative plate) and oxygen gas (from the positive plate). These gases leave the cell through a vent in the top of the bat-

Figure 3-5 Battery discharge characteristics.

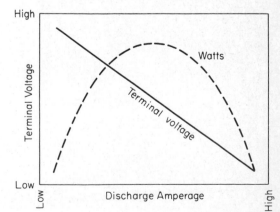

tery. Together, these gases are very explosive. **Keep all sparks and flames away from batteries to minimize the chance of an explosion.**

In operation, battery cells are continually being slightly charged and discharged. They are usually kept near full charge and are seldom fully discharged.

Batteries gradually wear out as they are used. This results from warping of internal parts, loosening of active plate material, hardening of plate material (Figure 3-6), and corrosive action on the separators and plate supporting grids. As the battery begins to wear out, it is not able to produce as much electrical power as it did when it was new. Remember that electrical power is measured in watts (watts = volts × amperes). The electrical power available from an automobile battery has been expressed in **ampere-hours.** This means the number of amperes the battery can supply for 20 hours before the voltage drops to 10.5 V. The electrical power of the battery must be great enough to meet the electrical power needs of the vehicle. As the battery wears out, it will no longer meet

Figure 3-6 Photograph taken of a plate in a battery that would no longer work in an automobile. Notice that some active material has fallen from the grid on the right. The white spots on the plate are sulfated inactive sections of the plate.

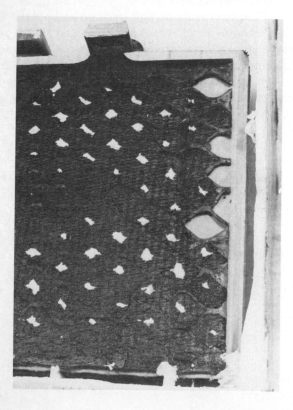

these needs. If a new battery is large enough, it will have reserve power. It will still supply enough electrical power after it begins to wear out. This means that a large battery has a longer battery service life than a small battery if they were used in the same vehicle.

Look at the graph of battery state of charge in Figure 3-7. A battery in a low state of charge has a small counter electromotive force (CEMF) as a result of weak chemical action within the cells. The counter electromotive force opposes the charging voltage . This allows the battery to accept a high charging amperage (current) at a low charging voltage. As the battery state of charge increases, its counter electromotive force also increases, so the charging amperage lowers when the charging voltage is held constant. Charging voltage will have to be increased if the charging amperage is to stay the same or increase. In a normal automotive charging system the voltage stops increasing when it reaches regulated voltage. This is shown by the flat regulated voltage line. Voltage regulation is discussed in Chapter 9. With a constant regulated charging voltage the charging amperage will gradually decrease as the battery is charged. This is caused by the increase in the counter electromotive force of the battery. This action gives a high charging rate on a discharged battery and a low charging rate on a fully charged battery.

Temperature affects the rate at which the chemicals will react within the battery. Low temperature slows the chemical reaction and high temperature speeds the reaction. This is important when starting a cold engine. The cold battery cannot produce as much starting current as a warm battery can. If a battery has a low capacity, it may fail to start a cold engine. In addition, a cold engine needs more power to crank it, so the engine needs above-normal cranking amperage. Thus cold-cranking problems are compounded when an undercapacity or worn-out battery is being used to crank a cold engine.

Figure 3-7 Battery-charging characteristics.

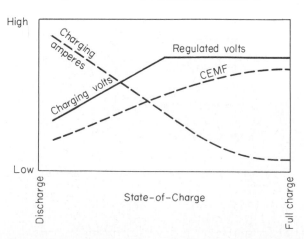

Technical words in this section you will need to learn:

Alloy	Grid
Case	Group
Deep discharge	Microporous
Element	Vent

You will remember that the different material on the plates makes the battery voltage. A number of positive plates are connected together to form a positive group. Negative plates are connected together to form a negative group. The positive and negative **groups** are leafed together, alternating one positive and one negative plate. A separator is put between each positive and negative plate. This assembly (one positive group, one negative group, and separators) is called an **element**. When the element is placed in the battery case and electrolyte is added, it becomes a **cell**.

Only the parts of the plates covered by electrolyte are active. The cell will only be completely active when all the plates are covered with electrolyte. Automotive batteries have a reserve supply of electrolyte in each cell that covers the plates. The electrical capacity of the cell is lowered when so much electrolyte is lost that the top of the plates are above the electrolyte.

Automotive batteries have six cells. Each cell produces slightly over 2 V. A fully charged cell produces 2.13 V. The cells are connected end to end, as shown in Figure 3-8. The positive terminal of one cell is connected to the negative terminal of the next cell. Connections are made through the battery-case partition between the cells. This type of cell connection is called a **series connection**. In series, the voltage of each cell is added to the voltage of the next cell. In this way, six 2 V cells make a 12 V battery (6 cells × 2 V = 12 V battery).

Figure 3-8 Cells connected through the cell partitions.

Plates. The active material on the positive plate is lead peroxide. During manufacture it is mixed to form a paste. The paste is spread on a **grid** to form the positive plate. The negative plate is made in the same way using sponge lead. The grid holds the active material paste. It also forms a path to carry the electricity from the active material to the plate terminal.

The material and design of the grid has a great deal to do with the performance of a battery. The grids are primarily made of lead. This is a good material to use in a battery because lead is not affected by the acid electrolyte. Lead is not a very good electrical conducting material. As a result, the lead connections in the battery have to be quite large. You can see in Figure 3-9 that a wire made from lead can conduct only 0.8% as much electricity as the same-size wire made of silver.

Conductivity of conductor metal	
Material	Percent of silver conduction
Silver	100
Copper	95
Gold	68
Aluminum	60
Lead	8

Figure 3-9 Ability of some metals to conduct electricity when compared to silver.

The electrical capacity of a battery is greater as larger plates or more plates are used. The rate at which electricity can be taken from a battery is based on the surface area of the plates. More thin plates will supply electricity faster than a few thick plates made with the same amount of active material. The length of time this rate can be taken from the battery is based on the total amount of active material in the battery. Thicker plates can supply electricity longer than thin plates of the same size and number.

Have you wondered how golf-cart batteries differ from automotive batteries? The golf-cart battery uses heavy antimony alloy grids with a thick coating of active material. With this type of construction the battery can be recharged after a deep discharge (almost fully discharged). Let's look at an example of the two types of batteries. We will use both batteries until they have only one-fourth of the charge left in them, then we will recharge them (discharge–recharge cycle). About 50 discharge–recharge cycles will ruin a modern automotive-type battery. The golf-cart type of battery can be put through this cycle as many as 400 times before it is ruined.

Pure lead is too soft for the grid metal, so other materials are added to the lead to make it harder. This added material is called an **alloy.** For many years antimony, with a small amount of arsenic, was used as an alloy for the grid metal. In the 1950s the grids had about 11% antimony alloy. Most of the world's supply of antimony comes from China. As a result of the political conditions at that time, an effort was made to reduce the antimony used for grids. Two substitute alloys were used: calcium and strontium. These substitute alloys gave the battery several advantages over the antimony alloy. First, they formed less hydrogen and oxygen gases. Remember, these gases separate from the electrolyte as the battery is used. Less gassing reduces the amount of electrolyte needed by the battery. If the battery can operate without forming gases, there will be less electrolyte lost from the battery. Second, the battery has resistance to overcharging when these substitute alloys are used in the grids. The counter electromotive force while charging goes high enough to minimize overcharging problems. Third, batteries with substitute grid alloys do not self-discharge while standing as batteries with antimony alloys do. This is a big advantage to the automobile manufacturer. New automobiles may stand in sales lots for months before they are sold. Both the dealer and customer expect the engine of the new automobile to start immediately. Batteries with substitute alloys in the grids remain charged. As a result, it is no longer necessary to keep recharging the battery in each car on the sales lot.

As you know, there is usually a disadvantage with every product. Grids with substitute alloys grow in size as they get old. This is just like rust that increases the size of an iron part to pop the paint from the part. The larger size of the grid loosens the active material so that it will no longer produce electricity. Another problem happens when the battery with substitute alloy grids is given a deep discharge. Nonconducting corrosion forms over the surface of the grid under the active material. This insulates the active material from the grid. If there are no cracks in this corrosion, there is no way to recharge the battery. The battery is deep discharged when a light is left on until the battery is discharged.

Low antimony alloy (2.5%) grids were developed as a compromise between high antimony and substitute alloys. There is very little gassing and the battery can be recharged after a deep discharge when these grid materials are used. Batteries have been improved still more by us-ing low antimony alloys in the positive grid and substitute alloys in the negative grid.

Improvements on the grid have had more effect on better battery performance than do changes in any other part of the battery. The design of the grid was changed so that its cross section became thicker close to the terminal. The terminal was placed as near the center of the grid as possible to minimize the distance the electricity had to travel from the active material to the terminal. You can see this in the cells of a battery in Figure 3–8. Most battery grids are made by casting. Modern casting equipment makes the grids close to the exact size needed. Grids are also made by rolling grid metal into a long ribbon. Small cuts are made in the ribbon and it is then pulled to make it longer. This expands the metal into a crosshatch pattern. The plate in Figure 3–6 has this type of grid. Another change was to make a grid support frame from polypropylene plastic. The plastic support frame is covered with pure lead to form an electrical conducting path. This design reduced the weight of the grid by half by using less lead. At the same time, it increased the efficiency of the battery and it eliminated the problems caused by grid alloys.

Separators. If the plates in a cell touched together, electricity would flow between them. This would discharge the cell. An insulating separator keeps the plates from touching. At the same time, the separator must let the electrolyte get into the plates. The positive side of the insulator has ribs that form a path through which electrolyte can flow. This helps the efficiency of the battery. The negative side of the separator fits flat against the negative plate.

In time and with use the active material tends to loosen from the grid. You saw this in Figure 3–6. The loose material will fall to the bottom of the cell. To keep this material from touching the plates, the groups of plates are supported with bridges in the bottom of the case: two bridges for each group. You can see that in this cell design some of the electrolyte reserve is used to fill the space below the plates.

The ideal separator material should not affect the chemical activity of the battery. It must have very small openings (microporous openings) that let the electrolyte get through while holding the active material. Early separators were made of wood or wood fibers called cellulose. Modern batteries have separators made from microporous rubber, poly-vinyl, polyethylene, and fiberglass mats.

A popular separator is designed as an envelope, with ribs on the outside. One of these envelopes is placed over each negative plate before the groups are leaved together. If any active material falls from the positive plate, it will remain outside the envelope. In this way the material cannot short between the positive and negative groups of plates. As a result of this design, the groups can rest on the flat bottom of the case. All the reserve electrolyte is above the plates. This design allows the battery to be used for a longer period of time before electrolyte no longer covers the plates.

Case. Case and cover of modern batteries are made from polypropylene or polyvinyl chloride plastic. These materials are acid and shock resistant. They are light weight and thin. There is room for more active material in the same space when a plastic case is used.

Each cell has a vent even when the battery has no fill caps. Vents are necessary to let the hydrogen and oxygen gases out of the battery. If you look carefully at the cover of a battery, you can see the vents. The vent has a filter to minimize the chance of a spark or a flame igniting the gases inside the battery.

Twelve-volt batteries have six compartments, one for each cell. Ribs on the side and bottom in each compartment support the cell element. This minimizes battery failure from vibration. The ribs are trimmed to the size of the cell element that is to be put into the compartment. Batteries that have the same external size can have a different number of plates and the plates can be different sizes. As a result, the size of the battery case does not indicate the electrical capacity of the battery.

When a battery is built, the cell elements are put in the compartments of the case. The elements are connected by welding the plate connectors through holes in the partitions. You can see this connector in Figure 3–1. This is the shortest electrical path and it uses the least lead. As a result it has the least possible electrical resistance and it lowers the weight of the battery. The cover is heat-sealed to the case to make a permanent joint. Each cell of the assembled battery is filled with weak electrolyte and the battery is given a long charge. This first charge will finish forming the active material on the plates. After charging, the weak acid is replaced with the normal-strength electrolyte. Finally, labels and paint are put on the battery and it is ready for use.

STUDY QUESTIONS

Introduction

1. What is proper battery maintenance?

Section 3–1

2. What is electricity?

3. What parts make up a cell in a lead-acid automotive battery?

4. What makes the voltage of a cell?

5. How long can a cell supply electricity?

6. What happens to the plates and electrolyte in the cell when the battery is discharged completely?

7. What will cause current to flow backward through a battery?

8. What gases are formed at the negative and positive plates?

9. As a result of gas formation in a cell, what precautions should be observed?

10. What units are used to express the electrical power of an automotive battery?

11. How does the battery state of charge affect the charging rate?

12. How does temperature affect the operation of a battery?

Section 3–2

13. What happens to the cell when electrolyte is below the top of the plates?

14. How many cells does a 12 V battery have?

15. What two things does a grid do in a battery?

16. What controls the rate that electricity can be taken from the battery?

17. What controls the length of time electricity can be taken from a battery?

18. List three advantages of using substitute alloys in place of antimony in grids.

19. What are two disadvantages of using substitute alloys in place of antimony?

20. What design feature allows the plates to rest on the bottom of the cell case?

4

BATTERY SERVICE

Like tires, spark plugs, and exhaust systems, batteries will wear out as the automobile is used. The American Automobile Association reports that 45% of all emergency road service calls are for starting troubles. Most of these involve the battery. It may be caused by a faulty battery or the battery may be discharged because the lights were left on or the engine was cranked until the battery discharged. The customer often overlooks the first signs of a weak battery. When the battery fails, the customer usually becomes angry and forgets the excellent service the battery has given. It is your job, as an automotive service technician, to advise the customer honestly about the condition of the battery. To do this, you will need to learn how to service and test batteries correctly. It will help you to diagnose the condition of batteries when you know how batteries are made and how they are rated. This will also help you to advise your customer intelligently on a replacement battery.

For starting the engine, the battery supplies the electrical power to crank the engine, operate the ignition, and on some engines, operate the fuel injection system. After the engine is running, the charging system supplies all the electrical power the vehicle needs for the normal electrical running load. The running load includes the ignition system, lights, wipers, radio, and so on. All of these can be run full time. The charging system also recharges the

battery. The battery acts as a ballast so that the voltage will not be too high or too low. The battery supplies extra electricity for heavy electrical loads that are greater than the charging system output. These loads are used once in a while. They include the horn, power seats, power windows, power door locks, and so on.

Normal battery service is usually done at each oil change. When servicing the battery you will make sure that the battery, cables, and battery carrier are clean and tight. You will seldom be asked to test the battery when there is no sign of a battery problem.

4-1 BATTERY CARE

To operate efficiently, the battery must be big enough and it must be charged. Electrolyte must cover the plates in each cell. Cable connectors need to be clean and tight so that they do not cause electrical resistance. The battery must be held in the battery carrier to keep it from bouncing as the vehicle goes over rough roads. Bouncing could break the case or loosen the plates in the cell.

You should check the battery at every oil change even if there is no sign of battery trouble. Look for moisture on the battery cover. Acid in the moisture will make an electrical leak between the battery terminals. This leak

36

will drain electrical energy from the battery, even when all the switches are turned off. You can check for electrical leakage by touching voltmeter leads on the battery cover. This is being done in Figure 4-1. The battery has electrical leakage if the voltmeter shows voltage. The battery will have to be washed and dried to stop the electrical drain across the cover.

Many batteries are advertised as being maintenance free. This is only a marketing term. What the term means is: When the battery is being used correctly, it will not need to have water added during its normal useful life. All other battery maintenance is needed. These batteries should be called low-maintenance batteries. You know from Chapter 3 how batteries are made and that all batteries will wear out in time. Low-maintenance batteries are designed with little or no antimony alloy in the plate grids to minimize gassing. The negative plates are in envelope separators and the plate groups rest on the bottom of the case so that the electrolyte reserve is above the plates. These battery construction features minimize the need for water to be added to the electrolyte. Remember that as a battery operates, oxygen and hydrogen gases will separate from the electrolyte. Water is a combination of oxygen and hydrogen. Added water replaces the water lost from the loss of these gases.

Figure 4-2 Water should be added to the underfilled cell until it looks like the properly filled cell.

You can check the electrolyte level on batteries that have removable cell caps, like the battery shown in Figure 4-4. If the electrolyte level is low, water should be added to bring it to the correct level, as shown in Figure 4-2. Only distilled water is recommended for use in battery service. Sometimes drinking water is used, but it is not recommended by battery manufacturers.

Cable Connectors. The battery cable connectors must be clean and tight. Deposits build up on the cable connectors and battery terminals, usually on the positive terminal. It must be stressed again that the combination of oxygen and hydrogen gas coming from a battery are very explosive. Blowing the gases from the battery vents will reduce the chance of an explosion. You should always keep flames and sparks away from batteries. Be sure to have all electrical switches turned off when you are connecting or disconnecting battery cables, jumpers, and battery chargers. You will have to remove cable connectors from the battery to clean them. The negative terminal is removed first and connected last. If your wrench should happen to slip while removing the negative cable connector, it could touch metal. This will not cause a spark because the negative terminal connector is already connected to the vehicle metal. After the negative cable has been removed from the battery terminal there will be no chance of a spark while removing the positive terminal connector.

Battery cable connectors are removed from side terminal batteries by loosening the connector bolt with a 5/16 in. wrench (Figure 4-3). The surface of the battery terminal and the cable connector are cleaned with a wire brush. The clean cable connectors are reinstalled and tightened with the 5/16 in. wrench. Do not overtighten the fastener. If the connector bolt needs to be replaced,

Figure 4-1 Touching voltmeter leads on a moist battery cover shows electrical leakage that will drain electricity from the battery.

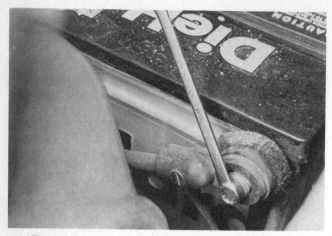

Figure 4–3 Removing a cable connector from a side terminal of a battery.

use only special battery bolts to avoid damaging the terminal or adding electrical resistance. Tightening a long bolt would put a hole through the terminal into the cell.

The nut for the clamp bolt is loosened on the type of cable connector clamped around a top terminal battery post. The connector is usually so tight that it will have to be pulled from the post with a puller (Figure 4–4). The cable and the battery post are cleaned with a special wire brush (Figure 4–5). The clamp should be opened slightly so that it will seat fully on the post. A special tool makes this job easy (Figure 4–6). The clean cable clamps are seated on the posts and tightened securely.

Figure 4–4 Typical puller used to remove a battery cable clamp from a battery post.

(a)

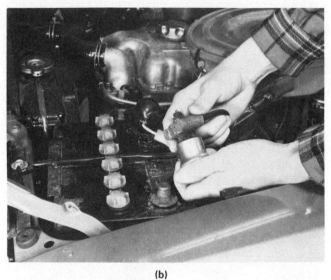

(b)

Figure 4–5 Special battery cable wire brush to clean the post (a) and the cable clamp (b). Notice the hold-down rod across the top of the battery.

Figure 4–6 Using a special tool to expand a battery cable clamp.

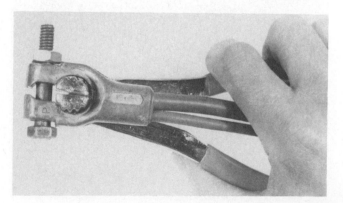

Battery Cleaning. The battery can best be cleaned by removing it from the vehicle. The battery cables are removed as described, then the hold-down clamp is removed to release the battery. The hold-down clamp may go across the top of the battery like the one in Figure 4–5. Others hold at the bottom of the case (Figure 4–7). The battery is lifted from the vehicle by hand or with a battery carrier. Be careful to keep the battery away from your clothing. Battery electrolyte is acid. If it gets on you it will make holes in cloth and it will burn your skin. If you should happen to get acid on your skin or clothing, neutralize the acid by putting baking soda or ammonia on the acid, then flush it with a lot of water. This will minimize the damage caused by the acid.

Acid on the outside of the battery can also be neutralized with baking soda or ammonia. You must be careful to keep the soda or ammonia out of the battery cells. If they get into the battery they will neutralize the acid electrolyte and ruin the battery. Washing the outside of the battery with hot water while brushing it with a soft brush will usually loosen acid, oil film, and dirt from the battery (Figure 4–8). The hot water quickly evaporates, leaving the battery clean and dry.

Give the battery a good visual inspection before you install the original or replacement battery. There should be no signs of cracks in the battery case or cover. The battery cover and sides should be smooth and flat. Internal cell damage will usually cause the sides of the battery case to bulge. The battery terminals should be in good condition. The battery date code should be checked to determine the battery age. Batteries seldom cause trouble if they are less than two years old. Batteries seldom operate longer than four years. The date code is either stamped on the case, punched on a special date tag, or

Figure 4–8 Washing the outside of a battery with water and a brush.

marked on a warranty card. Date coding uses a number to show the year the battery was put into service, for example, 4 for 1984 and 6 for 1986. A letter is also used to show the month, with A for January, B for February, and so on.

The battery carrier and hold downs in the vehicle should be cleaned in the same way you cleaned the battery. Coating the clean battery carrier and hold down with acid-proof paint will help keep them in good condition.

The battery is installed in the carrier and the hold down is clamped securely, not tightly, then the cables are connected. Coating battery cable clamps after they are installed will minimize corrosion that leads to resistance. Some technicians cover them with grease to keep moisture from the clamp and battery post. Others use special materials that are available in spray cans. Side terminal connectors have a plastic cover designed to keep air and moisture from the connection. Finally, you should check the alternator belt condition and tension. Make sure that the belt is not slipping. If the belt slips, the charging system cannot keep the battery charged.

Figure 4–7 Battery hold down at the bottom of the battery case.

SIDE
TERMINAL

HOLD DOWN

It should be noted here that the self-diagnostic memory will be wiped out of the engine control computer when the battery is disconnected. Be sure to check the fault codes **before** you disconnect the battery.

4–2 BATTERY TESTING

Technical words in this section you will need to learn:

Battery capacity	Load test
Hydrometer	Open-circuit voltage

Let us use an analogy to help our understanding of battery testing. We will compare a battery to a tank of compressed air. To be useful, compressed air must have pressure (a battery must have voltage). If it is going to last, it must have a lot of air (battery capacity). All automotive batteries are 12 V, regardless of their size. We could compare this to different size compressed air tanks, each having the same pressure. To do the most work before the tank needs to be refilled with compressed air, we would have to use the largest tank. The same is true of batteries. A large battery can do more work before it must be recharged than a small battery can do.

The pressure in the tank goes down as air is used. The same thing happens in a battery. The battery voltage goes down as the starter cranks the engine. The battery voltage will be lower when the starter uses more electrical power. A normal battery will have enough electrical power to keep the electrical pressure (voltage) high enough to operate the starter, ignition, and electrically controlled fuel systems at the same time. Battery testing measures the battery's ability to do this.

Let's consider the things that cause the voltage to drop too low while trying to start the engine.

1. The battery is too small. It cannot supply all the electricity the starter needs.
2. The battery does not have enough voltage because the battery is discharged.
3. The starter is using the electricity too fast.

The first on the list is the battery size. You will have to think of this when a battery is to be replaced. Effective battery size is important on used batteries. Remember, only the active material on the plates can supply electricity in the battery. The **effective** battery size is smaller when active material loosens from the plate or becomes sulfated (see Figure 3–6). You see that the effective size of the battery becomes smaller and smaller the

longer the battery is used. In time, the battery will not have enough active material to supply the electricity needed to start the engine.

Even a battery with lots of active material cannot start an engine if the battery is discharged. The battery voltage drops too low when you try to take a lot of current from a discharged battery. When we check a battery to see if it is charged we are checking the state of charge of the battery.

State of Charge. The chemical reaction in the battery reduces the acid strength of the electrolyte as electricity is used from the battery. The acid strength is measured by taking a sample of the electrolyte from the cell with the hydrometer. If the acid strength is low, the electrolyte is thin and the hydrometer will float low in the fluid. When the cell is charged, the acid strength is high and the hydrometer floats high. The acid strength of the elec-

Figure 4–9 Hydrometer being used to measure the state of charge of a battery cell. The hydrometer shows a reading of 1225.

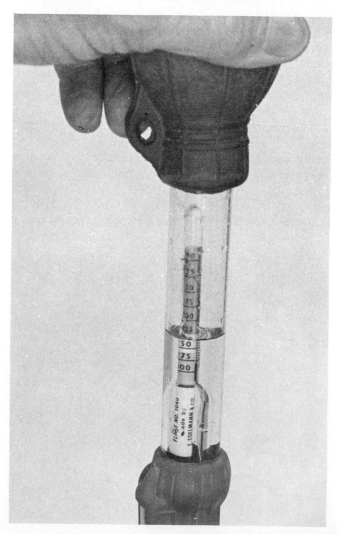

trolyte in each cell, as measured by the hydrometer, is an indication of the battery state of charge (Figure 4-9).

Batteries with sealed covers often have an indicator in a small window in one cell. The indicator will show green (ball is up) when the battery is charged. It will show black (ball is down) when it is discharged. If the window is either white or yellow the electrolyte level is below the indicator. This type of hydrometer is illustrated in Figure 4-10.

A fully charged battery will have a hydrometer reading of 1270 (indicating a specific gravity of 1.27 times that of water). A completely discharged battery will have a hydrometer reading of 1070 (indicating a specific gravity of 1.07 times that of water). You should consider two things when you use a hydrometer. Added water will stay on top of the thicker electrolyte. Checking a cell with a hydrometer right after water is added will show a reading that is lower than the actual battery state of charge. Second, the hydrometer reading is affected by the battery temperature. If the battery is hot, the electrolyte will be thin and the hydrometer will give a false low reading. If the battery is cold, the electrolyte will be thick and give the hydrometer a false high reading. Four points are added to the hydrometer reading for each 10°F (5.5°C) that the electrolyte temperature is above 80°F (27°C). Four points are subtracted for each 10°F (5.5°C), the electrolyte temperature is below 80°F (27°C). Good-quality battery hydrometers have thermometers with the correction scale. The scale on one of these hydrometers is pictured in Figure 4-11. For normal service, a battery should be replaced when the hydrometer reading of the cells differ by more than 50. In the automative service trade this is called 50 points.

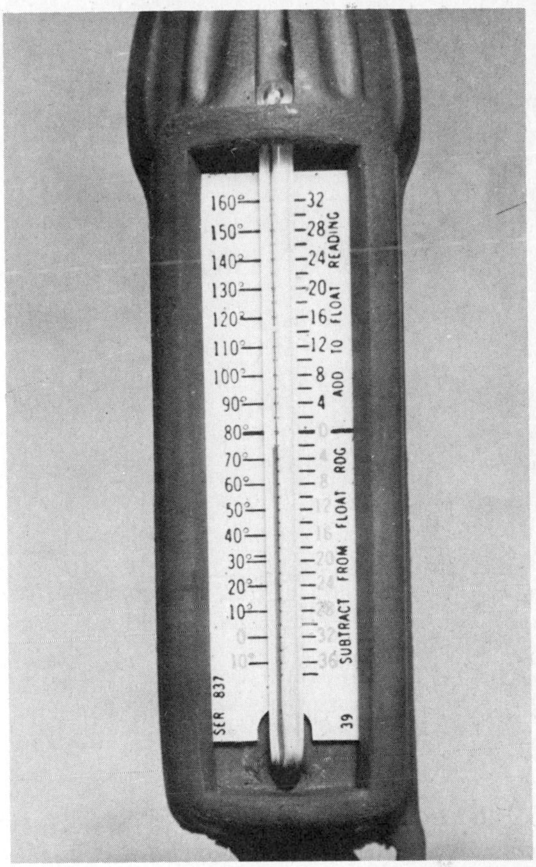

Figure 4-11 Reading corrections are shown by a thermometer on a hydrometer.

Figure 4-10 Type of hydrometer built into one cell of a battery. The ball on the left shows a charged battery. The ball on the right shows a discharged battery.

The open-circuit voltage across the terminals relates to the state of charge of the battery. This is true only if the battery has not been charged or discharged (open circuit) for 12 hours or more. The battery is considered to be discharged when the open-circuit voltage is below 11.9 V (hydrometer reading of 1130). It is fully charged when the open-circuit voltage is above 12.65 V (hydrometer reading of 1270). You can see the relationship of different voltages to the state of charge on Figure 4-12. The open-circuit voltage is the only way that you can measure the state of charge of a sealed-cover battery that does not have a built-in hydrometer.

The open-circuit voltage of a battery will measure only the voltage on the surface of the battery plates. It does not measure the state of charge of the battery. If the battery has been supplying a lot of electricity, the open-circuit voltage will be lower than the actual state of charge of the battery. When the battery has just had a charge, the open-circuit voltage will be higher than the

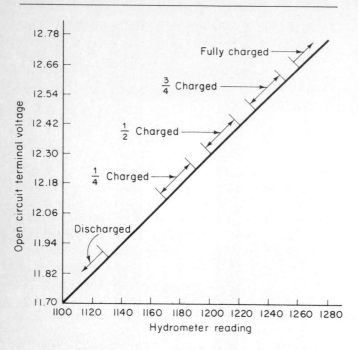

Figure 4–12 Comparison of the hydrometer reading to the terminal voltage after standing with an open circuit for 12 hours or more.

state of charge of the battery. You can see how this works if you connect a voltmeter to the battery in a vehicle. Read the open-circuit voltage, then crank the engine several times, but do not let the engine run. When you stop cranking the engine, notice the voltage. It will be lower than your first voltage measurement. You have taken the surface charge off the plates by cranking the engine. Watch the voltmeter for a few minutes. You will see the voltage gradually climb back to the first voltage reading. Now start the engine and hold the speed at fast idle. Watch the voltmeter as the charging system increases the voltage. Hold the engine at fast idle for a minute after the voltage reaches its highest reading. Notice that the charging voltage is higher than the first voltage reading you took. The charging system has put a high surface charge on the plates. Turn the engine off and watch the voltmeter. The voltage will gradually go back down close to the first voltage reading. Cranking and charging has changed the surface condition of the plates. When the battery is open circuited for a while, the plates gradually reach their normal condition.

Capacity. The capacity test or load test of a battery measures the ability of the battery to change chemical energy to electrical energy. This ability is tested by drawing a heavy current from the battery while watching the

battery terminal voltage. When current is drawn from the battery faster than the chemical action can take place within the battery, the battery terminal voltage is lowered. In the battery capacity test, an open adjustable carbon pile is connected in series with the battery and a high-reading ammeter. A voltmeter is also connected across the battery terminals. The ammeter, voltmeter, and carbon pile are built into battery-starter test units. The electrical circuit in a battery-starter tester is illustrated in Figure 4–13.

The battery capacity test is used only to test batteries with a state of charge over 1225, 12.5 open-circuit voltage (12-hour or more rest period), or on batteries showing a green charge indicator. These indications show that the battery is at least three-fourths charged. Voltage is noted 15 seconds after the carbon pile is adjusted to the test current. The test current is marked either on the battery or given in specification books. If you cannot find the specification, use a test current that is half the cold-cranking rating of the battery. For a healthy, full-charged battery at 80°F (27°C) or above, the battery terminal voltage should not drop below 9.6 V at the end of 15 seconds while the test current is flowing. When the

Figure 4–13 Battery capacity test connections using a battery-starter tester.

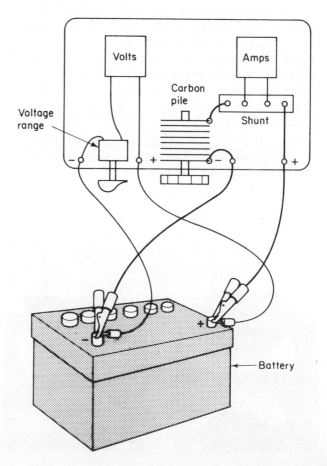

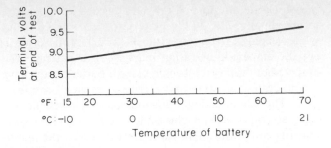

Figure 4-14 Minimum voltage at the end of the battery capacity test at different battery temperatures.

battery is at 30°F (−1°C), the minimum battery voltage needed for this test is only 9.1 V. Minimum voltage readings at other test temperatures are shown in Figure 4–14.

If this test were to be performed on a battery with a low state of charge, the terminal voltage at the end of the capacity test would be very low. This low voltage reading serves no useful purpose in determining the battery condition. The capacity test is valid only when performed on a battery that is three-fourths charged or higher. A battery with a low state of charge should be recharged before making a capacity test.

4-3 BATTERY CHARGING

A battery will charge when a voltage, higher than the battery-terminal voltage, is connected to the battery. The higher voltage forces electricity backward through the battery. This reverses the chemical action within the battery and charges the battery. Charging stores energy in the battery. The battery will charge faster when there is a higher terminal voltage while charging. If the voltage is too high, the chemical action in the battery will occur so fast that the battery will gas excessively, the plates will buckle, active material will break off the plates, and the battery will be destroyed. To minimize damage, battery temperature during charging should never be allowed to go above 110°F (49°C). At higher temperatures the battery has less resistance to an external voltage from the charger. This would allow the charging rate to be too high at a normal charging voltage. The high charging rate will cause the battery to heat rapidly and it will be ruined.

Charging Procedure. A battery charger should be turned off when it is being connected to or removed from a battery. If the charger is turned on, a spark will occur when the charging cable clips are being connected to or removed from the battery terminals. This spark can ignite the gases coming from the battery cell and cause an explosion. The explosion will blow the battery apart and throw acid all around. You can see the value of wearing safety glasses when servicing batteries.

Before charging the battery, make sure that the electrolyte is at the proper level. Connect the red charger cable clips to the positive battery post. The positive terminal is always the larger of the two battery posts and it is usually marked with a plus (+) sign or with red paint. The black charger cable is connected to the negative terminal. The charger is always turned to the lowest charging rate when it is first turned on. The charging rate is then increased to the rate you need to charge the battery. This way of setting the charger prevents a high-voltage surge that could damage the battery.

A normal battery can be fully charged by using a charger that will force from 3 to 5 A through the battery. Chargers have an ammeter that shows the charging rate. A battery will be fully charged when three hydrometer readings taken at 1-hour intervals show no increase in the hydrometer reading. In practice, batteries are usually charged just enough to get the engine running. This is done with a fast charger or with a jump start.

Fast Charger. A battery that is less than three-fourths charged will accept a higher charging rate than a battery that is near full charge. A fast charger can be used for as long as 30 minutes at rates as high as 50 A on a nearly discharged 12 V battery. A fast charger should be used only long enough to get the battery charged enough to start the engine. A normally operating vehicle charging system will finish charging the battery after the engine is running. If the vehicle charging system does not recharge the battery, the charging system will have to be repaired for normal operation of the electrical system.

Most service calls are for battery failure. This means that the battery will not crank the engine. It does not mean that the battery is not good or that it must be replaced. When the automobile battery does not crank the engine, jumper wires are connected from the battery of the service car to the battery of the stalled car. The stalled engine can then be cranked by using electricity from the service car battery.

Jumper wires must be installed correctly to avoid damage to the battery and electronic controls of the vehicle. First the red jumper wire is connected between the positive post of the battery in the stalled vehicle and the positive post of the service car battery. The black jumper wire is then connected between good clean metal of both engines to avoid sparks at the battery. This is illustrated in Figure 4–15. The service car engine is then brought up to a fast idle. This will increase its alternator output to the maximum charging rate. After a minute of charging, the stalled car can be cranked. The charging system of the stalled car will charge the battery after the engine

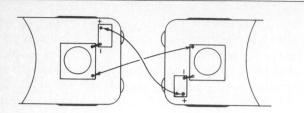

Figure 4-15 Jumper connections for starting an engine with a dead battery.

starts if the battery was discharged by leaving a light or electrical item turned on. If some other problem caused the battery to fail, the automobile should be taken directly to a service garage where the specific problem that caused failure can be identified and corrected.

4-4 BATTERY REPLACEMENT

A battery that failed the battery tests should be replaced. The battery salesperson must first determine the battery requirement of the vehicle. The original equipment battery has the lowest rating that will give satisfactory service when all electrical parts are in excellent condition. A battery with a higher rating will give a longer useful service life in the vehicle. The battery selected must have its terminals in the correct position on the cover or case to match the vehicle cables and it must have dimensions that will fit in the battery carrier.

Battery Ratings.   Battery ratings indicate their capacity. Batteries with the same outside measurements may have different ratings. The rating is marked on the battery or it has numbers or letters that you can use to find the ratings in the sales catalogs.

Most service technicians are familiar with the ampere-hour rating of batteries. The rating comes from the 20-hour battery test. This obsolete test was used to show how well a battery could supply electricity for small electrical loads if the charging system failed. The test measures the amount of amperes needed to lower the terminal voltage of a 12 V battery to 10.5 V in 20 hours while keeping the battery at 80°F (27°C). You may still see the ampere-hour rating marked on a battery. The ampere-hour rating has been replaced. Batteries now have a cold-cranking rating and a reserve capacity rating.

The cold-cranking rating measures how well the battery can crank a cold engine under the most severe engine starting conditions. This rating test is run by the manufacturer on automotive batteries at 0°F (−18°C). The fully charged battery is kept in a cold room until it cools to the test temperature. Then an electrical load is put on the battery. The load is large enough to bring the terminal voltage down to 7.5 V in 30 seconds. The cold-cranking rating of a battery is reported in amperes. The battery can supply more current than the rated amperes when it is warm because the chemical action in a battery is affected by the battery temperature.

The reserve capacity test is a measure of the battery's ability to supply a constant light load for a long time. It measures how long a battery could operate the ignition and lights if the alternator failed. In this test a 25 A load is kept on the battery until the battery terminal voltage reaches 7.5 V. The reserve capacity of the battery is reported in minutes.

Battery manufacturers make a number of other tests when they are developing batteries. These tests include charge rate acceptance, life test, overcharge life test, and vibration test. The results of these tests are not available to the battery user. Therefore, they cannot be used in selecting a replacement battery.

Batteries with the highest cold-cranking rate and the longest reserve capacity with the highest ampere-hour rating will give the longest service before they need to be replaced. Some battery design features (described in Chapter 3) improve the service life of a battery. In general, better batteries are guaranteed for more months. They also cost more. You can help your customer decide on a replacement battery by dividing the cost of the different battery options by the months of the guarantee of each battery. This will indicate the maximum cost per month of each battery. In any case, the replacement battery must have at least the minimum cold-cranking rating and reserve capacity specified for the automobile with its electrical equipment.

STUDY QUESTIONS

Section 4-1

1. Why should the surface of a battery be kept clean?

2. What is being replaced when water is added to the electrolyte?

3. What should be done before connecting or disconnecting battery cables?

4. Why is the negative battery cable removed first and connected last?

5. How are battery terminals and cable ends cleaned?

6. Why should you keep the battery away from your clothing while removing or installing it?

7. What should you do if you get moisture from a battery on your clothes?

8. How is the outside of the battery cleaned?

9. What is the normal life of a battery?

10. Why is a coating put on battery cable clamps after they are connected?

11. Why are fault codes checked before a battery is disconnected?

Section 4–2

12. List three things that cause voltage to drop too low while cranking.

13. What is used to measure the state of charge of a battery?

14. What two things cause faulty hydrometer readings?

15. What is the maximum difference in the hydrometer readings between the cells of a normal battery?

16. How does the state of charge affect the battery terminal voltage?

17. How is the state of charge measured on a battery that has sealed covers?

18. What causes the battery terminal voltage to lower as current is drawn from the battery?

19. What state of charge should the battery have before a capacity test is run?

Section 4–3

20. What reverses the chemical action in a battery?

21. What limits the voltage you can use to charge a normal battery?

22. How can you prevent a high-voltage surge when you start to charge a battery?

23. How long should a fast charger be used on a battery?

24. How should jumper cables be connected?

Section 4–4

25. List three things that a replacement battery must have.

26. What batteries will give the longest service before they need to be replaced?

ELECTRICAL SYSTEM TESTING

Many automotive service technicians find it difficult to service electrical parts. You cannot see a moving electrical force. You know about it when electricity moves a mechanical part or lights a bulb. When you understand electrical force, often in terms of fluid or air analogies, you will have little trouble in diagnosing electrical system problems. Once you locate a part causing the problem, you will have no trouble repairing it. Finding the faulty electrical part is the most difficult part of correcting problems in the electrical system.

The battery and the charging system are the source of automotive electricity. Electricity is carried from the source to the operating unit through a conductor, usually insulated wires. Another conductor returns the electricity back to the source to complete the circuit. The return conductor is usually the metal of the body and frame. You must always remember that an electrical circuit must be complete to operate electrical units. Any opening in the circuit will stop its operation. The circuit must not have leaks that drain away some of the electricity or resistance that will slow the flow of electricity.

5-1 ELECTRICAL CIRCUITS

Electrical wiring diagrams of an automobile are very confusing when you first look at them. You can see this when

you look at the **simplified** drawing of a wiring diagram in Figure 5-1. Wiring diagrams are different for each manufacturer, vehicle model, and body style. They become quite complex when electrical accessories are added to wiring diagrams. It is not surprising that many service technicians try to diagnose electrical system problems by trial and error without using wiring diagrams.

Wiring Diagram. Wiring diagrams are not difficult to follow when you understand the basic requirements of the automobile electrical circuit and the symbols used in the diagrams to identify parts.

Electrical circuits required for engine operation are covered in the next few chapters. The rest of the electrical systems in the vehicle connect to the battery and charging system in the electrical system of the engine.

Electrical parts must have a complete circuit to operate. Wiring diagrams use lines to show how the insulated wires make the circuit connections. In general terms, electrical power flows through the positive battery post, the insulated circuit wires, and to the operating units. Most circuits are connected to battery positive through a fuse block that is part of a junction block. The circuit is completed through the body sheet metal and the battery ground.

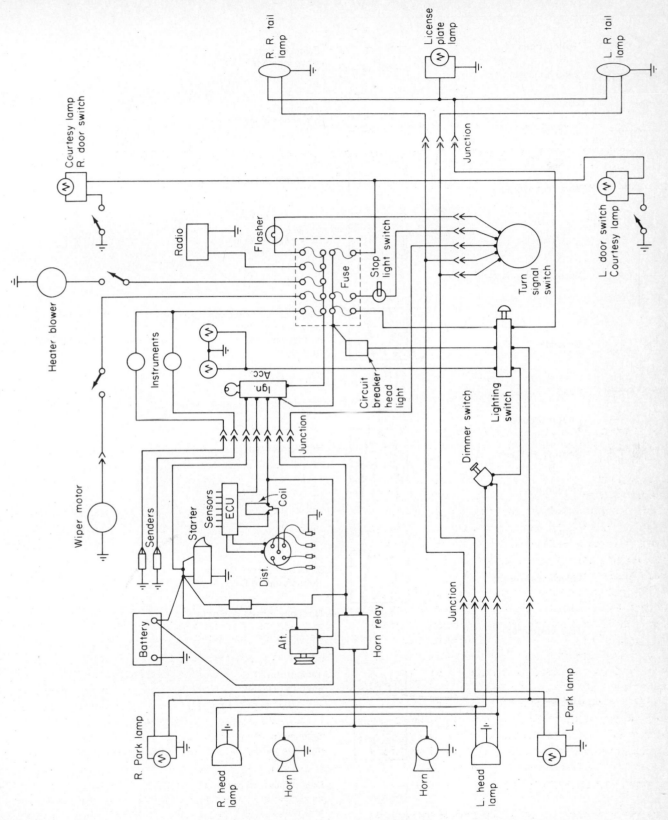

Figure 5-1 Simplified wiring diagram of automotive electrical circuits.

47

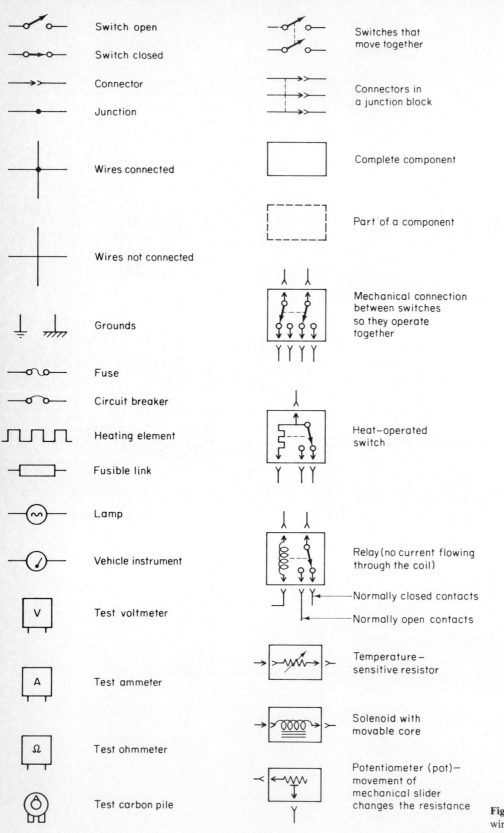

Switch open

Switch closed

Connector

Junction

Wires connected

Wires not connected

Grounds

Fuse

Circuit breaker

Heating element

Fusible link

Lamp

Vehicle instrument

Test voltmeter

Test ammeter

Test ohmmeter

Test carbon pile

Switches that
move together

Connectors in
a junction block

Complete component

Part of a component

Mechanical connection
between switches
so they operate
together

Heat–operated
switch

Relay (no current flowing
through the coil)

Normally closed contacts

Normally open contacts

Temperature–
sensitive resistor

Solenoid with
movable core

Potentiometer (pot)—
movement of
mechanical slider
changes the resistance

Figure 5-2 Electrical symbols used in wiring diagrams.

Each operating unit on the wiring diagram is represented by a symbol, either a simple line drawing picture or an electrical schematic drawing. Examples of typical electrical circuit symbols and drawings are shown in Figure 5-2. The wiring diagram is like a road map between two or more electrical units. It includes a way to identify each wire, each junction, each switch, and each safety device. A simple way to follow one circuit from a complex wiring diagram is to lay a sheet of thin paper over the wiring diagram, then trace the circuit on the thin paper. Most service manuals have separate circuit drawings for each accessory circuit. This makes it less confusing to follow the circuit.

All lines on the wiring diagram that represent wires are given a color code. In general, the same color follows from the fuse to the operating unit (Figure 5-3). Once in a while there are different-colored wires on each side of a junction. You will need to check the color codes carefully in the wiring diagram. The color codes used in the diagram are the same colors as the insulation on the wires in the vehicle. Follow the circuit in the wiring diagram and then find the same color wire in the circuit of the vehicle.

Figure 5-4 One type of fuse block that acts as a bulkhead junction block.

Figure 5-3 Typical symbols used to show circuits and color codes in a wiring diagram.

Vehicle wiring is made of a number of wiring harnesses. One end of each harness is connected to a junction block or connector. The main junction block is often located at the bulkhead between the engine and passenger compartment. An example of this is shown on the drawing in Figure 6-26. In many vehicles the bulkhead junction is also the fuse block. One type is shown in Figure 5-4. The other half of the bulkhead junction is connected to the switch and operating units. The end of most wires have a terminal that snaps into a mating connector. The terminals make an electrical contact when the two halves of the connector are pushed together. One half of the modern connector must be partly compressed or tabs lifted to disconnect it from the other half. Several types of connectors are pictured in Figure 5-5. Many types of connectors are used, so you should look in the service manual to see what you must do to remove the terminal from the connector.

The front-end horn and lighting wire harness runs along the bulkhead and front fenders. The body wiring harness usually runs from behind the dash along the left lower sill to the rear of the car. You can see this in Figure 5-6. Branches run to interior lights. A number of smaller

Figure 5-5 Several types of electrical connectors used in automotive circuits.

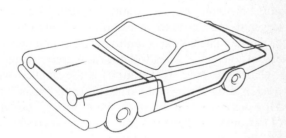

Figure 5-6 Location of typical major wiring harnesses in an automobile.

harness assemblies for electrical accessories connect to the main wiring harness. The harness for the accessories are usually shown as separate wiring diagrams in the service manual.

Wiring Requirements. Automobile wiring is made for safe and efficient operation at a minimum cost. It is installed in the automobile so that it can be easily assembled and serviced. In most cases, the junction connectors are made so that they cannot be connected in the wrong way. This is especially true of connectors for solid-state electronic parts. These parts will burn out if they are connected with reverse polarity.

The best electrical conducting metal is silver. This was shown in Figure 3-9. Copper is also a good conductor. It is the most common metal used for automobile wires. Copper can carry 95% of the electricity carried by silver. Aluminum is also used for wires on some automobiles. It can carry only 60% of the electricity carried by silver in the same-size wire. Aluminum wires can carry 62% of the electricity carried by the same-size copper wires. As a result, aluminum wires must be larger than copper wires to carry the same amount of electricity. Even with the larger wire size, aluminum wires have only 51% of the weight of copper wires when they have the size to carry the same amount of electricity. You can see that aluminum wires are used where minimum weight is very important.

You will remember that lead is used as a conductor in batteries. It is interesting to note that lead can carry only 8% as much electricity as copper, when using the same-size conductor. The lead conductor will weigh 12.6 times as much as copper when the conductor is made large enough to carry the same current. Lead is used in batteries because it is not affected by the acid electrolyte.

Wires must be large enough to carry the required current with minimum resistance to the current. If resistance is high, the wire will get hot and the operating part will not get enough electricity. Wire and connector temperature must not increase more than 225°F (108°C) above the air temperature around the wire. If the wires are larger than they need to be, they will increase the weight of the vehicle, take additional space, and increase vehicle cost. Oversize wires will not cause electrical problems. Generally, No. 16 (1.0 mm²) is the smallest wire size used in body wiring and No. 10 (5.0 mm²) is the largest. Most wire sizes fall between these two. A comparison of customary American Wire Gauge (AWG) size and metric wire size is shown in Figure 5-7.

Wire used for automobile lights, instruments, and accessories is called **primary wiring**. Different colors are used for wire insulation to identify the electrical circuit. Many types of plastic compounds are used for the insulation. They differ in their insulating properties and melting temperature. The one that will meet the operational requirements at least cost is the one used.

Wire Size Conversion Table	
Metric Size (mm²)	AWG Size
0.22	20
0.5	20
0.8	18
1.0	16
2.0	14
3.0	12
5.0	10
8.0	8
13.0	6
19.0	4
32.0	2
52.0	0

Figure 5-7 Table comparing American Wire Gauge (AWG) sizes with metric wire sizes.

Terminals on the ends of wires connect to an operating unit or junction. Many of the original equipment terminals are connected to the wire, then covered with molded insulation (Figure 5-8). Other terminals are connected to the wire by crimping, swaging, welding, or soldering (Figure 5-9). All of these make a good electrical connection that is mechanically strong. A number of wires are held together with a fabric braid, plastic shield, or tape to form a wiring harness. Some electrical harnesses use soldered joints inside a harness cover.

Instrument panels use printed circuits. They have conductor ribbons on an insulator similar to the one in Figure 5-10. If the printed circuit is damaged, the entire printed circuit board will have to be replaced.

Some automobiles have the electrical wires grouped together in a flat plastic ribbon. This keeps the wires properly separated in a harness that takes little room in the vehicle.

There has been a great amount of work done to improve the wiring in automobiles. One development is electronic multiplexing. This is illustrated in Figure 5-11. In

Figure 5-8 Typical terminal-wire joint covered with molded insulation.

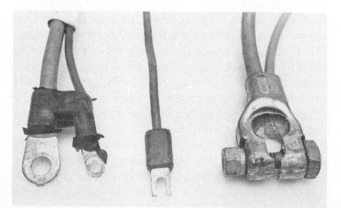

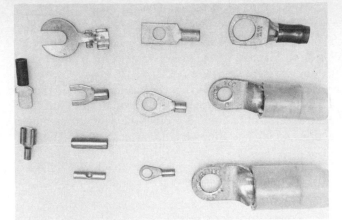

Figure 5-9 Typical terminals that connect to wires by crimping, swaging, welding, and soldering.

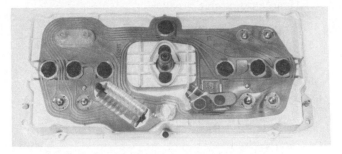

Figure 5-10 Printed circuit used to make connections on the back of an instrument cluster.

Figure 5-11 Drawing illustrating the principle of multiplexing.

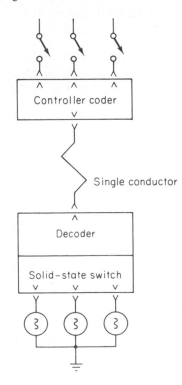

multiplexing, all the switches connect to an electronic black-box controller. The controller converts the switch positions to electronic codes. All the electronic codes are sent through a single conductor to a second black-box decoder. Solid-state switches in the decoder control the accessories. The single conductor carries the signals between the black boxes as electricity in a wire or as light in a fiber-optic conductor. You will learn more about the fundamentals of electronics when you study Chapter 8.

5-2 ELECTRICAL CIRCUIT PROBLEMS

Typical electrical problems include faulty operation of the lights, instruments, electrical motors, solenoids, switches, and electronic equipment. The vehicle operator is usually the first one to notice a problem. To correct the problem the first thing you must do is to **verify the problem.** You do this by setting up the condition that caused the problem. This will show you exactly how the problem acts. It will not be too hard for you to find the cause of a complete failure. The cause of intermittent problems are hard to find. **Intermittent problems** are problems that happen only once in a while. You have heard of a vehicle with a problem that always operated normally when it was taken to the service technician for repair. It is very difficult to correct a problem if the vehicle is operating normally when it is being tested to find the problem. When it is not causing a problem you will have to depend on the customer's description of the problem. Then you will check the parts that might be causing the problem. Wiggling junctions as you test them often helps you spot the cause of an intermittent problem.

To diagnose electrical system problems you need to know how electricity must go from the battery and charging system to the fuses, circuit breakers, switches, and on to the operating units in the malfunctioning circuit. You also need to know when and how each of the electrical units in that circuit should operate so you can set up the conditions that will make them operate.

You know that in time and with use, some parts will fail. Light bulbs burn out in time. Switches and motors wear out with use. These will have to be replaced when they fail. Replacement is a routine service operation after you have found the faulty part. In modern vehicles **the most common cause of electrical problems** is a poor electrical contact between wire connectors or a poor electrical ground connection at the operating unit. You will have to check the circuit to find the poor electrical connection. When you find it, the connection is separated, cleaned, assembled, and tightened to correct the failure. Often connectors are filled with grease to keep air and moisture from corroding the connection. Special silicone grease is used in critical connectors. **Do not clean the grease from the connectors.**

Power Supply.   Electrical power is supplied by the battery when the engine is not running. It is supplied by the charging system when the engine is running. The positive terminal of the battery and the BAT terminal of the alternator are connected together with a wire (see Figure 1–13). In this way each can supply electrical power to the vehicle.

In a typical vehicle a heavy electrical cable connects the positive terminal of the battery to the BAT terminal of the starter relay or solenoid. Smaller primary wires from the positive battery cable clamp or from the starter terminal carry electrical power to the rest of the vehicle. This can be called the **insulated source terminal.** The negative terminal of the battery is connected to the engine with another large cable. A smaller wire or braided metal connects the engine to the body metal. This smaller wire can be called the **ground source terminal.** A diagram of these wires is shown in Figure 5–12. Most of the vehicle electrical systems will not work if these wires are worn out or have faulty connections.

Any terminal that is connected to the battery post by wires without going through a switch or relay is said to be **hot.** A hot wire or hot terminal has battery and charging system voltage.

Electrical power is supplied through fusible links (see Section 2–3) to relays, circuit breakers, and fuses. From here the power goes through switches to the operating units. Figure 5–13 illustrates how electrical power goes through typical vehicle circuits.

A number of wires in a vehicle are hot at all times. They do not feed electrical power through fuses but they depend on fusible links to protect the wires from shorts and grounds. The following are typical of hot circuits:

Horn relay
Electric defroster relay
Power seat relay
Power door lock relay
Sunroof relay
Theft-deterrent relay
Headlamp circuit breaker
Ignition switch
Part of the fuse block

Some hot circuits are fused. The hot wire from the battery goes into the fuse block. It feeds the following circuits through the fuses (Figure 5–14):

Stop light
Interior lights
Clock
Cigar lighter
Glove-box light
Engine electronic controls

These circuits will operate regardless of the position of the ignition switch or light switch.

Figure 5–12 Typical insulated and ground source connections in the engine compartment of a vehicle.

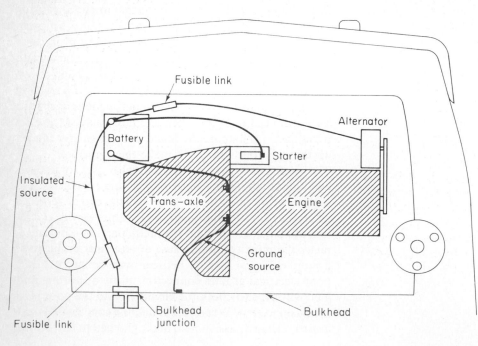

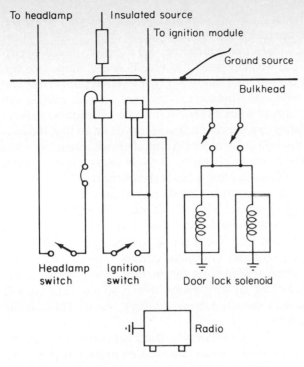

Figure 5-13 Typical electrical circuits in a vehicle.

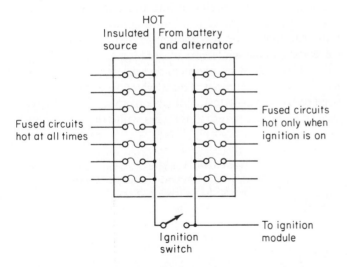

Figure 5-14 Typical fused circuits.

There are a number of circuits that operate only when the ignition switch is turned to the run or accessory positions. Some of the circuits are only needed when the engine is running. Others operate only when the ignition key is turned on so that the circuit will not accidentally be left operating when the operator leaves the vehicle. The following are typical circuits that have electrical power only when the ignition switch is turned on:

Gauges and indicator lights
Electrical engine controls

Windshield wiper and washer
Turn signals
Diesel glow plug
Electrical leveling
Backup lights
Air conditioner and heater
Radio and power antenna
Sunroof control
Power window control
Trunk lid release
Theft-deterrent control deactivation

Several circuits may use the same fuse, especially if the circuits are rarely used at the same time. A group of circuits on the same fuse may include:

Automatic door lock
Cigar lighter
Courtesy lights
Electronic level control
Illuminated entry
Power door lock switch
Power remote mirror
Theft-deterrent deactivator
Trunk light
Vanity mirror light

You can see that a service manual for the vehicle will be very helpful in finding the cause of an electrical problem in one of these circuits. Here is a good place to make an important point. If all the circuits being fed from a fuse fail to operate, the fuse is burned out. If the problem affects only one circuit, the problem is in that circuit.

Ground.   Electrical units use the body metal to complete the ground circuit back to the negative terminal of the battery. The metal frame of the unit may be bolted to a body panel to form the ground circuit. Units mounted in plastic use a wire lead from the unit to body metal. Other insulated units operate through grounding switches to complete the ground circuit. Often, several operating units have ground wires connected to the same ground terminal. Remember, a good electrical ground is just as important to the operation of the electrical unit as good insulated wiring.

Electrical System Failure.   Let's review typical automotive circuits. When operating normally, electrical current

a switch in the off position. The units in the circuit will not operate.

When two conductors make an unwanted electrical contact they cause a short. This is a copper-to-copper connection (Figure 5–16). The electrical current can go from one conductor to the next, so both circuits will get current when either circuit is hot. The short reduces resistance in the circuit that is turned on so that the conductor will carry more current. This will cause the wires in the circuit to get warm. It could cause a fuse to open.

Grounds are a special type of short. The insulation around the conductor breaks so that the conductor makes electrical contact with vehicle metal. A ground is a copper-to-iron connection (Figure 5–17). In vehicles, the frame and structure metal is connected to the negative battery terminal. Grounded current follows the conductor to the ground point, bypassing the rest of the circuit. This failure has very low resistance, so more current will flow and the conductors get very warm. This usually opens the fuse.

If you can follow the electrical circuit wires in the vehicle and have some basic test equipment it is not too hard to find the cause of opens, shorts, and grounds. It becomes more difficult to find the cause of the electrical problem when the problem is intermittent. For example, just connecting a tester to a loose conductor will often move the connection just enough so that it makes a good electrical contact while you are making the test. The circuit test will show no problem as long as the conductor has the electrical contact. This is why you will sometimes need to use a wiggle test. This means that you will have to wiggle the wires and connectors while the test instru-

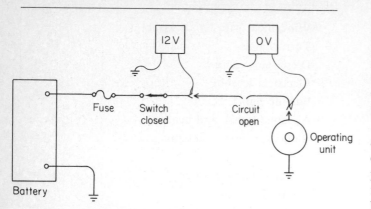

Figure 5–15   Locating an open in a circuit.

flows through the wires and ground to make a complete circuit. This cannot be repeated too many times. The battery or the alternator is the source of electrical current. Current flows from the positive source terminals through the conductor to the unit being operated, such as a light bulb, electric motor, solenoid, instrument, and so on, then through another conductor to the ground source terminal. Failure of electrical circuits results from three basic causes: opens, shorts, and grounds. Any one of these will keep an electrical unit from operating.

When a conductor in a circuit is disconnected or broken it will not conduct electrical current. This type of failure is called an **open** (Figure 5–15). It acts just like

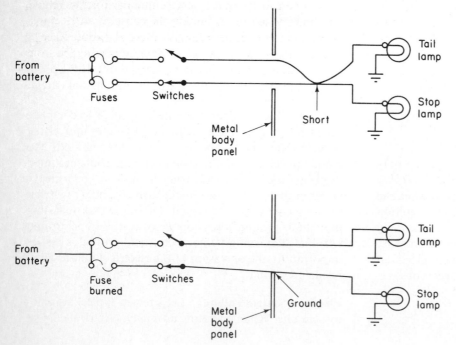

Figure 5–16   Example of a shorted circuit. Both lamps will light when either one of the switches is closed.

Figure 5–17   Example of a grounded circuit. Excess current going to ground has blown the fuse.

ments are connected. Any change in test indications during the wiggle test shows an intermittent connection at that point in the circuit.

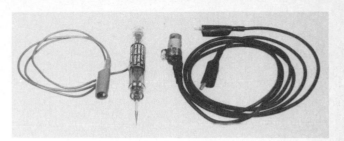

Figure 5-19 Commercial and homemade test lights.

5-3 ELECTRICAL TEST EQUIPMENT

You can find the cause of many electrical system problems using simple test equipment. First you will use the wiring diagrams to identify the most likely place in the circuit that could cause the problem. Once it is identified you still may have trouble locating the place in the circuit on the vehicle. This is especially true when it is under an instrument panel where there are a large number of wires. In other cases you will have to remove interior trim panels to reach the wires and junctions.

Simple Test Equipment. Jumper wires with a terminal on each end are the type of electrical test equipment most often used. They can be connected parallel with a part of a circuit. They get their name from being used to jump around part of the circuit. Jumper wires can also be used to connect other equipment into a circuit. Most automotive service technicians have a number of jumper wires of different lengths using different types of end terminals. Typical jumper terminals are illustrated in Figure 5-18. You can make the ones you need.

Jumper wires are often combined with a light bulb to make a simple 12 V **test light.** The test light is used to see if electrical power is reaching a terminal or junction. It can easily be made by fastening jumper wires to a bulb socket. Test lights can be purchased in auto and electrical parts stores. These testers usually have a probe tip. The light bulb is in the handle of the tester. A jumper wire from the handle of the test light has an alligator clip. Both types of test lights are shown in Figure 5-19. In use the clip is connected to ground. The bulb will light when the probe tip or second clip touches a hot wire or hot terminal (Figure 5-20).

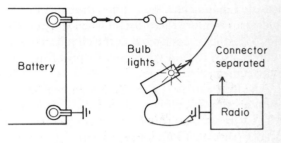

Figure 5-20 Using a test light.

Some test lights are self-powered. The **self-powered test light** is used when the circuit is not connected to the battery. They are made like the test light, but they also have a battery in the handle to power the bulb. Both types of test lights are shown in Figure 5-21. If the bulb turns on when the self-powered test light is connected between two points in a circuit, the circuit has an electrical connection between the two test points (Figure 5-22). We say that this circuit has **continuity.** If the bulb did not light, the circuit is open. The open circuit does not have continuity between the two test points.

Figure 5-18 Typical terminal ends used on test jumper wires.

Figure 5-21 Test light on the left and a self-powered test light, including self-contained battery, on the right.

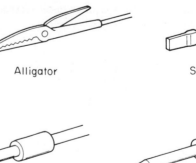

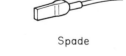

Alligator   Spade

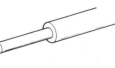

Pin   Probe

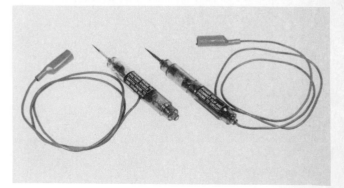

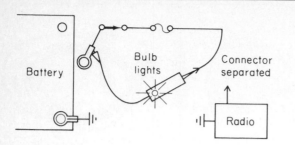

Figure 5-22 Using a self-powered test light.

Substitute Equipment.   Sometimes the cause of a circuit problem can be more easily found when an electrical part made for testing is connected in the circuit. This type of test can be used to find the cause of a problem in a resistive instrument circuit.

The lead wire is removed from an instrument sensor and a variable resistance is substituted for the sensor. The wire is connected to one terminal of a variable resistance (rheostat) with a jumper wire. The variable resistance is set at maximum resistance, then the other resistance terminal is connected to ground (Figure 5-23). The circuit can be checked by adjusting the variable resistance. The instrument reading will change as the resistance is changed. If there is no change, the resistor is connected at the instrument terminal and the system is retested. Some commercial testers are made to adjust to a specific resistance. You can use these testers to check the accuracy of the vehicle instrument reading. Be sure that the circuit is designed to operate with a variable resistance before you use one in testing.

Too much current flow in a circuit will cause a fuse to burn out. If the circuit is not fused, the electrical part or wire will burn out. The only thing that will cause too much current to flow in a vehicle circuit is a lower circuit resistance. This can be caused only by a short or

Figure 5-23 Connections made to test a vehicle instrument by substituting a variable resistance in place of the instrument sensor.

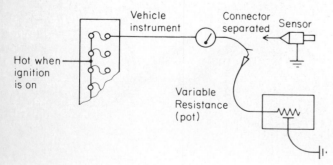

ground. A circuit breaker or turn signal flasher connected in place of the burned-out fuse will open the circuit when too much current flows. Current will turn back on when the circuit breaker or flasher cools. The off–on–off–on– . . . action of the circuit breaker puts a pulsing current in the circuit. You will be able to check the circuit during each pulse. A magnetic compass or a small hand-held inductive ammeter will help you find the place where the circuit is shorted or grounded. Move the compass or inductive ammeter along the faulty circuit as the circuit breaker puts an electrical pulse in the circuit (Figure 5-24). The magnetism around the conductor during each pulse will deflect the needle of the compass or inductive ammeter. The needle will move each time the pulse goes into the circuit and when the pulse stops. You will see the needle movement only when the compass or inductive ammeter is over the wire that has the pulsing current. Needle movement will stop when you reach the point in the circuit where the circuit is shorted or grounded. The needle stops pulsing at this point because there is no current flow in the circuit beyond the short or ground.

When you are testing a circuit by yourself it is sometimes hard to see the test instrument you are using. You

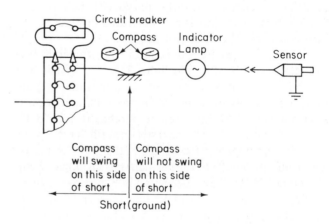

Figure 5-24 A circuit breaker is put in place of the fuse. A compass moved along the wire will swing each time the circuit breaker turns on or off until the compass is moved past the short.

Figure 5-25 Loud test light and short finder schematic adapted from Ford reference books.

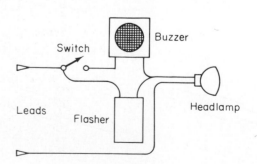

can build a loud test light as suggested in several Ford reference books. This tester is made by connecting a headlamp bulb, flasher, and buzzer, as shown in Figure 5–25. The light will flash and the buzzer will sound each time the flasher sends a pulse in the circuit. It can be used as a higher current draw test light by moving the switch position to open the buzzer circuit.

Basic Test Instruments. If you made the battery tests described in Chapter 4 you have used a voltmeter. You will need to use two other types of electrical test instruments: the ammeter and the ohmmeter. For many years these instruments used meters with dial and pointer readout. Most electrical test instruments are this type. Their operation was discussed in Section 1–7. This type of instrument is an analog-type instrument. In the late 1970s electrical test instruments with number readouts became popular in automotive service. These are digital-type instruments. The digital type will read only from one number to the next. It cannot give a reading between the two numbers. The analog-type meter can be read at any place on the dial, even between numbers.

The self-powered digital-type test instrument uses less current from the circuit being tested than does the analog type. As a result, digital-type test instruments must be used when measuring electrical properties of some automotive electronic parts. In these tests the analog-type instrument would draw so much current from the circuit that it will show readings which are not correct. In some cases measuring with an analog-type instrument could even damage the electronic part. Use only the type of test instruments that the test procedures specify.

An electrical test instrument may be made to measure a single electrical property, such as voltage. When it is designed to measure several properties it is

called a **multimeter.** Most multimeters are designed to measure volts, amperes, and ohms. Figure 5–26 shows analog- and digital-type multimeters.

All electrical instruments that you will use must be connected to the correct electrical polarity. The black test lead is always connected to the most negative polarity. The red test lead is connected to the most positive. In automobiles positive is the insulated circuit. Some test instruments are designed for special tests. They may use blue and yellow leads. These leads are connected to the positive voltage at specific test points in the electrical system of the vehicle.

When a voltmeter is connected to two points in the electrical system it will show the difference in voltage between the two points. Make sure you use the correct voltage range on the voltmeter. If you are not sure of the voltage, start with the highest range (Figure 5–27). A voltmeter will show battery voltage when it is connected to the battery terminals. It will show voltage drop when it is connected between two points on the same side of a circuit that is carrying a direct current. This was discussed in Sections 1–3 and 1–4. Notice that a voltmeter can be used without disconnecting any connector or junction. When it is used with the junction disconnected or across an open circuit, it will read battery voltage.

Ammeters measure the current flowing through a circuit. To use a typical ammeter a circuit is opened at a connector or junction. The ammeter leads are connected between the separated connectors. You can see this type of ammeter connection in Figure 1–12. When the circuit is turned on, the current flowing in the circuit will also

Figure 5–26 Analog multimeter on the left and digital multimeter on the right. They are both connected to the same fully charged battery and show the battery voltage.

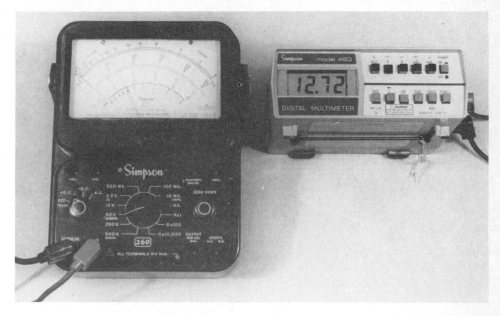

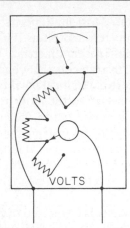

Figure 5-27 Simplified voltmeter wiring with resistances to set the range.

flow through the ammeter. Be sure to select the correct range before connecting the ammeter. The ammeter range is changed by switching to the correct shunt in the instrument case. The shunts are shown in Figure 5-28. If you do not know which range to use, start with the highest range, then adjust down to the range that will give a mid-range reading. If the range is too high, it will hardly move the meter pointer. If the range is too low, the pointer will hit the upper stop. This is called **pegging the meter.** It could actually burn out the shunt in the ammeter. Some ammeters have a fuse or a circuit breaker to protect the meter from too much current flow.

Inductive ammeters were developed in the 1970s as a result of emission controls and electronic engine controls. Disconnecting conductors in these systems sometimes caused a problem that was not there before. At other times a loose ammeter connection would cause a sudden voltage spike that could ruin the electronic parts.

The pickup lead of the inductive ammeter is clamped around the conductor that is carrying the current to be measured. The inductive pickup senses the magnetism around the conductor. This magnetism was described in Section 1-5. An electronic circuit in the ammeter increases the strength of the signal from the pickup to operate the readout. Large leads on the instrument are connected to the battery terminals to power the electronic circuit. You can see how this instrument is connected in Figure 1-13.

Ohmmeters are used to measure the resistance of circuits that carry small currents. The resistance of circuits that carry large currents is measured by the voltage-drop method. This was discussed in Section 1-2. The use of ohmmeters in testing automotive circuits has increased since electronic controls have been used on vehicles. The part of the circuit being measured for resistance with an ohmmeter is separated from the rest of the electrical circuit. The ohmmeter leads are connected together and the meter is adjusted to zero ohms. This is called **calibrating** the ohmmeter. One lead is then connected to each end of the circuit or part being measured. A small current from a standard cell battery in the ohmmeter flows through the circuit. The ohmmeter circuit is shown in Figure 5-29. With the known voltage from the cell you will notice that the ohmmeter is actually measuring the current flow through the instrument. Using Ohm's law, the resistance changes inversely with current flow when a constant voltage is used. This means that when the resistance is doubled, the current will be only half.

Specialized Test Instruments. Basic test instruments are put in an equipment box with electrical and electronic circuits. Two common instruments of this type are the tach-

Figure 5-28 Simplified ammeter wiring with shunts to set the range.

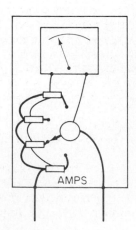

Figure 5-29 Simplified ohmmeter wiring. Notice that it has a self-contained battery.

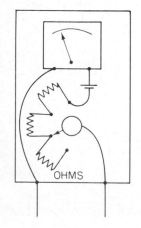

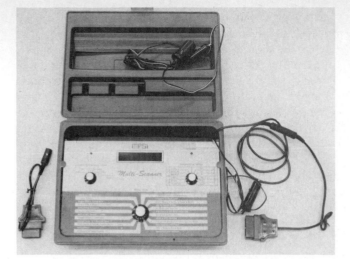

Figure 5-30 Specialized tester for computer engine controls.

ometer and dwell meter. You also use battery-starter testers and volt-amp testers to check the operation of electrical parts of vehicles.

Electrical test equipment may be even more specialized. One of the earliest pieces of special testers was made to test the General Motors automatic headlamp dimmer, called an electric eye. Since then specialized testers have been made to test electrical systems, such as solid-state regulators, alternators, electronic ignition systems, automotive air-conditioning circuits, electronic fuel injection, electronic instruments, and computer operation (Figure 5-30).

Late in the 1950s an oscilloscope was developed for testing the operation of the ignition system. The readout is a pattern trace shown on the face of a cathode ray tube (CRT). The face of this tube is the same as the face of a television screen. The ignition patterns shown on the

Figure 5-31 Test results shown on a specialized cathode ray tube. Notice the fault shown on the fourth cylinder in the firing order. It was caused by a burned exhaust valve in that cylinder.

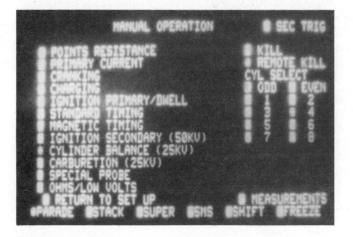

scope are discussed in Section 13-4. The scope can also be used to check the operation of the charging system parts while the charging system is in operation. Some newer scopes give the readout as letters and numbers. An example is shown in Figure 5-31. Printers can be connected to the computer to type out a record of the analysis. You can use this printed record as you discuss the condition of the vehicle with the customer.

5-4 ELECTRICAL PROBLEM DIAGNOSIS

Electrical circuit problems are usually hard to correct by trial and error. They can be found with test procedures using electrical test instruments and careful visual inspections. It may take a little while to find the cause of a problem with the correct use of simple test equipment. The correct use of specialized test equipment will help you pinpoint the problem more quickly.

The two most useful tools for electrical problem diagnosis are a 12 V test light and a voltmeter. Both can be used to see if there is voltage at any point in the circuit. The test light draws some current. The light is brighter when there is more voltage. The analog-type voltmeter draws a small amount of current and will give you a direct voltage reading. The current used by the digital-type voltmeter is so small that it does not affect the system being tested. You will need to know how much current the system should draw before you select the tester you will use. Any type of voltmeter can be used in most tests.

When an electrical unit fails to operate, the test light or voltmeter should be connected between the insulated wire at the unit terminal and a good ground. The black voltmeter test lead is connected to ground. When the switch for the circuit is turned on, the test bulb should light or the voltmeter show a voltage reading. If there is no electricity, the unit will have to be disconnected and the wire itself checked using the same test procedure. If the circuit has electricity at the terminal wire with the electrical unit disconnected, the unit itself is faulty or the unit has a poor ground. If there is no electricity at the terminal wire, the circuit is open. The circuit will have to be tested in small sections to pinpoint the place where it is open. This test procedure was shown in Figure 5-15.

The circuit is open if electricity goes into the circuit, but it does not get to the operating unit. It is also open if the operating unit is not properly grounded. The circuit is checked at the connectors, fuses, junctions, and switch terminals for voltage to pinpoint the problem. Move the insulated voltmeter lead from junction to junction along the circuit until you find the wire causing the problem. This principle is illustrated in Figure 5-32. When you find the wire causing the problem, loosen the harness and inspect the wire for damage. If the problem point cannot be seen, the harness will have to be opened at several places. Only when there is no other way to find the open point in the wire, push the test probe of the voltmeter or test light into the insulation of the problem wire to touch the metal of the wire. The probe is pushed into several points along the wire until the exact problem point is found. The openings made in the insulation by the probe should be wrapped with electrical tape to reduce the chance of corrosion in the wire.

Shorts between wires will put electrical power into two or more circuits. This was shown in Figure 5-16. For example, a short between filaments in a tail light bulb could cause the instrument panel lights to flash as the turn signal flashes. Shorts are difficult to locate. Follow both circuits on the wiring diagram to see where they might possibly be shorted together. The easiest way to find the short is to use a short finder, described in Section 5-3. The faulty electrical system should be separated at the junctions in the wiring harness to locate the specific shorted wires. The actual short can usually be seen. Each wire at the short should be wrapped with electrical tape to keep the wires from touching.

Grounds allow current to bleed from the insulated circuit to the automobile sheet metal. A slight ground acts as a short. A typical ground was shown in Figure 5-17. Grounds usually draw enough current to burn out the fuse or open the circuit breaker. Junctions should be disconnected to locate the specific wire that is grounded. Grounds may be located by lifting the harness away from the sheet metal and giving it a careful inspection. Grounds can be found most easily with a short finder described in Section 5-3. There is no magnetism around the circuit beyond the ground.

If a motor does not operate, the first thing to do

is check to see that the wire feeding the motor is electrically hot when the circuit switch is on. If it is not hot, the circuit should be checked. If the lead is hot, make sure that the motor has a good ground. The motor should be removed for service if it has power and a good ground. Many of the motors used in vehicles are low-cost, high-production units that are not repairable. Faulty motors are replaced. Motors that are repairable can be serviced.

When there is an electrical circuit problem, you should check the fuse, fusible link, circuit breaker, operating unit, grounds, and wiring diagram. Consider the possible cause of the problem and then systematically check the system causing the problem. If the service manual has a diagnosis procedure, it should be followed.

5-5 REPAIRING ELECTRICAL CIRCUITS

Once the specific electrical problem has been found, it can easily be repaired using standard electrical repair procedures. If a wire is shorted or grounded as a result of breaks in the insulation, it can be repaired by tightly wrapping the damaged wire with plastic electrical tape when there is no other damage. If the wiring is damaged or if the system is open, the faulty part will have to be repaired or replaced.

The damaged ends of a broken wire can be spliced together or a short piece of wire can be spliced between them. The splice must be mechanically strong and electrically sound. Splicing can be done by stripping a section of insulation from the wire. The bare ends of the two wires are wrapped around each other to make the joint mechanically strong. The joint is heated with a soldering iron. At the same time **rosin-core solder** is held against the joint. Keep heating the joint until the solder flows through the splice.

Using a crimp-type terminal, as shown in Figure 5-33, is a faster way to repair a wire. Enough insulation is stripped from the wires so that the bare wire fits the connector being used. An insulating sleeve is placed on one of the wires, then the connector is put on the wire. A special crimping plier is used to squeeze the connector around the wire. The second wire is placed in the other end of the connector and crimped. The splice is finished by centering the insulating sleeve over the splice. Use heat to shrink the sleeve over the connector. An alternative method is to finish the splice by wrapping it with plastic electrical tape. This makes a mechanically strong and electrically sound joint.

Wire end terminals are available in a number of different sizes and shapes. They may be connected to the wire by rosin-core solder or by crimping, depending on the terminal type. Terminals are usually held in a connector by a tab on the connector. A simple connector is shown in Figure 5-34. A group of terminals may be held

Figure 5-32 Typical test connections used to measure voltage along a circuit. The switch must be closed to measure voltage at V_3, V_4, and V_5.

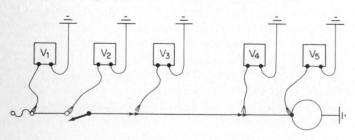

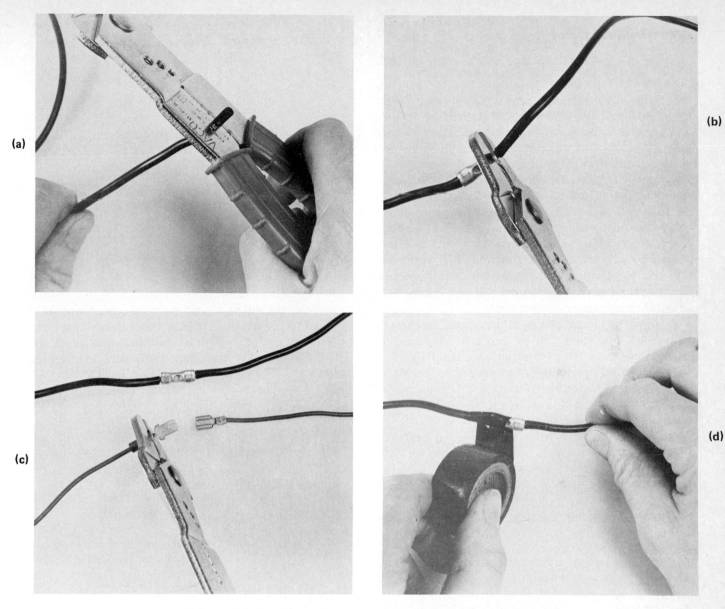

(a)

(b)

(c)

(d)

Figure 5–33 Steps in making a wire repair using crimp-type terminal: (a) stripping insulation; (b) crimping a connector; (c) crimping a terminal; (d) taping the terminal connection.

Figure 5–34 Terminals are held in connector blocks by a tab on the terminal. The tab must be released to remove the terminal from the connector. A small screwdriver can be used on some types of connectors. Other connector types require the use of special release tools.

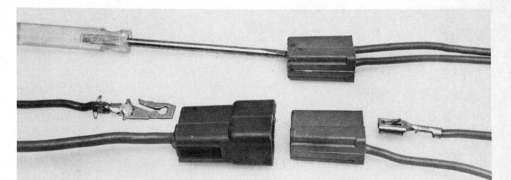

together in a junction block to interconnect the wiring between separate parts: for example, in the wiring junction at the body fire wall bulkhead (see Figure 5–4). At this point all the front-body wiring is connected with one junction block. This makes it easy to assemble the wires during manufacture. There is no chance of misconnecting the wires. The junction is a good place to separate the electrical circuits to check for opens, shorts, or grounds.

Be sure to use the correct-size wire. You should never use a wire smaller than the wire you are repairing. If you are installing an added accessory, such as a tape deck, driving lights, or trailer lights, you will have to select the correct size wire. The minimum wire size is based on the maximum current the system will use. Figure 5–35 shows the recommended wire sizes.

After the wires are repaired they should be checked for correct operation and be properly supported in brackets and clips. This keeps the wires from vibration damage or from contacting hot engine parts. The wiring

Minimum wire size		
Metric	AWG	Amps
0.5	20	12
0.8	18	16
1.0	16	20
2.0	14	30
3.0	12	40
5.0	10	50
8.0	8	60
13.0	6	80
19.0	4	100
32.0	2	200

Figure 5–35 Minimum wire sizes recommended for the amperage used by a circuit.

may be sound and have good electrical connections at the time of test or service. The only way you can be assured of continued good operation is to check visually and wiggle the wires and connectors to make sure that they are secure.

STUDY QUESTIONS

Section 5–1

1. Describe a vehicle electrical circuit in general terms.

2. How can you find a specific circuit wire in a wiring harness?

3. What must be done to disconnect a modern electrical connector?

4. Why is it important to connect electronic parts correctly?

5. Aluminum is not as good an electrical conductor as copper. Why do some automobiles use aluminum wires even when they have to be larger than the copper wires they replace?

6. What determines the size of wire used in vehicles?

7. Why is different-color insulation used on primary wiring?

8. Name three types of insulated conductors.

Section 5–2

9. What is the first thing you must do when the vehicle operator asks you to correct a problem?

10. What is the most common cause of electrical problems?

11. Why are connectors often filled with grease?

12. What do you know about a wire when you read that a wire is hot?

13. What protects wires in hot circuits?

14. What could cause failure of all units connected to one fuse?

15. How important is the ground connection?

16. List three common causes of electrical system failure.

17. How does an open circuit act?

18. What type of electrical problem is the most difficult to locate?

Section 5–3

19. What is the first thing you should check when you have an electrical problem?

20. How is a test light used?

21. How is a self-powered test light used?

22. In what direction does the instrument reading go when the circuit resistance is lowest?

23. What causes too much current to flow in a circuit?

24. What makes the compass needle swing when using a short finder?

25. How does the reading differ between an analog and a digital multimeter?

26. What reading would you expect to get if the voltmeter were connected across an open circuit?

27. How is the typical ammeter connected in a circuit?

28. How is an inductive ammeter connected into a circuit?

29. How is the resistance measured in circuits that carry small currents?

30. How is the resistance measured in a circuit that carries large currents?

31. How is an ohmmeter used?

32. Name five types of specialized test instruments.

Section 5–4

33. What are the two most useful tools for electrical diagnosis?

34. What is indicated when there is voltage at the lead wire going to an electrical unit but the unit does not operate?

35. When should a test probe be pushed through the insulation of a wire?

36. What type of problem usually indicates a short?

Section 5–5

37. How are shorts and grounds usually repaired?

38. Name three ways in which you can repair a broken wire.

MOTORS
AND STARTERS

Electric motors are used in vehicles to drive blowers used in heaters, defoggers, and air conditioners. They operate power seats, window lifts, power door locks, power antennas, headlight doors, windshield wipers, windshield washers, electric fuel pumps, and many other units. Most of these motors are not repaired when they fail. It is fortunate, however, that the motors seldom fail during the useful life of the vehicle.

The electric motor uses electricity to cause rotation. The rotation often goes through a gear train to operate a mechanism. Electric motors may be one-speed motors, two-speed motors, or variable-speed motors. They can also be made so that they can rotate in either direction or in both directions. Some motors are designed to produce a high turning force for a short time. Others are designed to operate at a constant speed for a long time. The difference in motors is primarily the difference in the design of the magnetic field, the size of the conductors in the motor, and in the method of switching the electrical power.

One motor used on all vehicles is the cranking motor. It has a pinion gear on the drive assembly that engages the teeth on the outer edge of the engine ring gear. The ring gear is on the flywheel or automatic transmission drive plate that rotates with the engine crank-

shaft. These gears produce a high rotating torque to crank the engine.

The pinion gear on the drive assembly of a cranking motor is engaged with the engine ring gear while the engine is being cranked. When the engine starts to run, the ring gear rotates faster than the cranking motor drive. The drive disengages the pinion gear from the ring gear to keep the cranking motor from overspeed.

Small motors are usually connected to electrical power directly through a switch. Motors that use high current, such as cranking motors, are connected to electrical power through a relay. Relay operation was discussed in Section 1–8.

6–1 MOTOR PRINCIPLES

Technical words in this section you will need to learn:

Armature	Laminations
Commutator	Series winding
Counter electromotive force (CEMF)	Shunt winding
Field	Torque
Free speed	

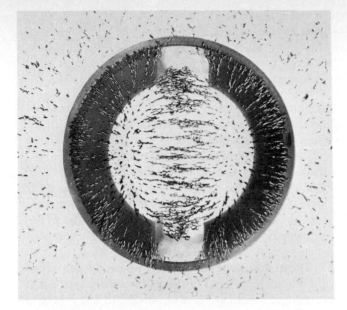

Figure 6-1 Iron filings on a plastic sheet over the end of a permanent magnet motor field that shows the magnetic field.

Figure 6-2 Armature placed in the center of the magnetic field.

A permanent-magnet motor is one of the simplest electric motor designs. The field of the motor is made of very strong permanent magnets fastened inside the motor case. Iron filings on a clear plastic sheet in Figure 6-1 show the magnetic field between the magnets. An armature supported by end bearings rotates between the pole shoes (Figure 6-2).

The **armature** is made of a stack of stamped soft iron pieces, called **laminations.** These are fitted on the armature shaft. Insulated wire is wound through slots in the iron laminations. The ends of the wire **winding** are soldered or welded to **commutator** bars. The commutator bars are insulated from the rest of the armature assembly. Electric current is sent to the armature windings through **brushes** that rub on the armature commutator bars. You can see an example of these armature parts in Figure 6-3.

Figure 6-3 The motor field has been removed to show the brushes, commutator, and laminated core of the armature in a windshield wiper motor.

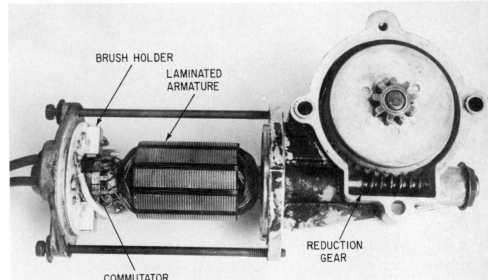

BRUSH HOLDER

LAMINATED ARMATURE

REDUCTION GEAR

COMMUTATOR

Current flowing through the armature windings produces magnetism around the armature. This magnetism reacts with the magnetic field to force the armature to rotate.

Field.   The field magnet can be considered to be made of two thin slices of a large bar magnet bent to the correct shape. You saw the effect of magnetism around the slices of magnets in Figure 1–20. This makes the inner surface of one field a north magnetic pole and the inner surface of the other field a south magnetic pole. The iron armature core, which almost touches both field magnets (see Figure 6–2) becomes a magnetic bridge between the fields. It will concentrate the magnet lines of force between the field magnets when no current is flowing in the armature windings. You will remember from Section 1–5 that reluctance is the resistance to magnetic lines of force. Iron has low reluctance. The iron case or motor frame on the outside of the fields forms the path to complete the magnetic lines of force around the outside of the fields.

Armature.   When voltage is applied across the motor brushes, current is carried from one commutator bar through the armature winding to another commutator bar that is under the second brush. Current flowing through the armature winding produces a magnetic field in the armature core. The magnetic field around the armature reacts with the magnetic field of the motor field magnets as shown in Figure 6–4. When both fields have the same

polarity they repel each other. When they have opposite polarity they attract each other. The magnetized part of the armature is repelled by one field magnet and attracted by the other. It is the repelling and attracting magnetic forces that rotate the armature.

Commutator.   As the armature rotates, another pair of commutator bars slide under the brushes. You can see brushes and commutator bars of a small motor in Figure 6–5. The new commutator bars magnetize another part of the armature that is now located in the most effective part of the magnetic field. This action keeps repeating to force the armature to rotate as the brushes keep switching to the next commutator bars. This keeps the armature magnetism in the most effective part of the magnetic field to give the motor the strongest rotating force.

The motor speed and rotating torque are controlled by the magnetic strength of the motor field magnets and the armature windings. It is important to know several electric motor characteristics to help you understand how motor speed and direction are controlled. This becomes important when you are diagnosing motor problems.

1. The stronger the magnetism of the field magnets and armature, the slower the motor will rotate.
2. The slower the armature turns, the more current the motor will draw and the stronger the turning torque will be.

These facts are based on the electromagnetic self-induction principle described in Chapter 1.

Keep in mind that the armature of the motor is rotating within a magnetic field. This forces the arma-

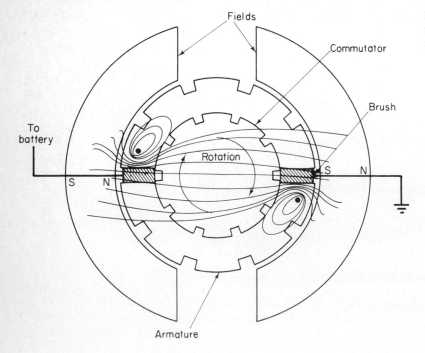

Figure 6–4   The armature is forced to rotate through the reaction of the magnetic fields.

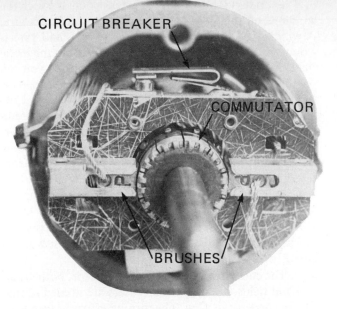

CIRCUIT BREAKER

COMMUTATOR

BRUSHES

Figure 6-5 Brushes on the commutator of a small motor. This motor has a circuit breaker to protect the motor if it is overloaded.

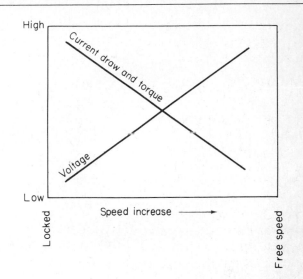

High

Current draw and torque

Voltage

Low

Locked

Speed increase ⟶

Free speed

Figure 6-7 Effect of motor speed on the voltage, current, and torque.

ture windings, which are conductors, to cut across the lines of magnetic force of the motor fields. This, in turn, develops a counter electromotive force within the armature windings. The counter electromotive force (CEMF) opposes the voltage being supplied to the motor. The starter motor CEMF opposing the battery electromotive force (EMF) or voltage is typical of all motors. It is shown in Figure 6-6. The faster the armature rotates, the more counter electromotive force is produced, and this slows the current flow through the armature windings. You will remember from Section 1-9 that this type of opposition to voltage is called inductance. With this principle in mind you can see that electric motor design affects motor operation. If the motor is slowed as it drives a heavy load, more current will flow in the armature to increase the turning torque to handle the increased load. When the load is lowered the motor will speed up, and this increases CEMF to reduce current flow. The graph in Figure 6-7 shows how inductance affects current flow, torque, and voltage in an electric motor.

Figure 6-6 The starter motor counter electromotive force reduces the flow of current through a motor that is rotating at a high speed.

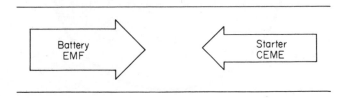

Battery EMF

Starter CEME

Motor Rotation. The permanent-magnet type of motor can be made to turn forward or backward by using a switch to reverse the direction of current flow through the armature. Power-window, power-door-lock, and power-seat adjusters are examples of this type of motor. They operate at two speeds in some windshield wipers. Two-speed permanent-magnet wiper motors have three insulated brushes. The brushes directly across from each other are used for low-speed operation. One brush is fed through a resistor. The other connects to ground. The motor will reverse when the polarity is reversed through these brushes. The third brush is fed directly through the motor-feed circuit to provide high-speed operation. One of the other brushes is connected to ground.

Many automotive electric motors have electromagnetic fields rather than permanent magnetic fields. You can see the difference in the field magnets by comparing Figures 6-2 and 6-8. The two types of motors operate the same way. Electromagnetic motor field magnets have a wire coil wound around a laminated soft-iron **pole shoe.** Low-speed high-torque motors have the field coils in series with the brushes and armature. The series-type motor winding is shown in Figure 6-9. The motors will rotate backward by reversing the direction of current flow through the fields. The current always flows through the armature in the same direction. Field current is reversed by the switch.

Electric motor speed will increase by weakening the field strength. This reduces the retarding effect of the motor caused by the counter electromotive force. The armature must rotate faster in the weak field before

Figure 6–8 Small motor with an electromagnetic field.

brushes and armature. All the current going through the windings on this field also goes through the armature. A winding of a large number of turns of small wire is wound in the opposite direction on the other magnetic field. It is connected to ground. In Figure 6–10 you can see that this winding is parallel across the brushes. This type of motor winding is called a **shunt winding.** Current is fed through the series coil when the motor operates at low speed. When the speed needs to be increased current is also sent through a resistor in the feed wire going to the shunt winding. An opposing magnetic field from the shunt winding causes the effective field strength to weaken. This weakened field allows the motor armature to rotate at higher speed. Fixed resisters located in the switch are used to feed the shunt winding for step-speed motors. A variable resistor is used in the shunt winding circuit in a variable-speed motor.

The conductors in the cranking motor, both armature and fields, are copper bars. Bars are needed so that a large current can flow. The turning effort or torque of the cranking motor, like other electric motors, is directly proportional to the current flow. This was shown in Figure 6–7. When the cranking motor is held so that it cannot rotate it will draw the most current and give maximum torque. Under these conditions the starter resistance may be as low as 0.01 Ω. As the engine begins to crank the armature will rotate. Rotation will increase the counter electromotive force, which, in turn, reduces cur-

Figure 6–10 Circuit in a shunt-wound motor. The series field with the heavy windings is connected in series with the armature. The shunt field with the small wire winding goes directly to ground.

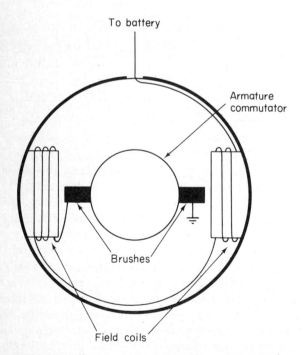

Figure 6–9 Circuit in a series-wound motor. The fields and armature are connected in series through the brushes.

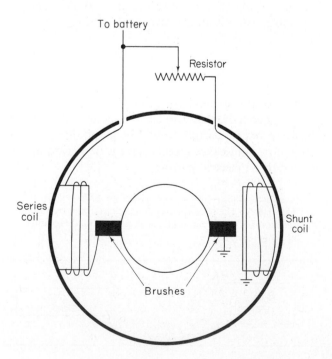

counter electromotive force is high enough to balance system voltage.

Field strength of multiple-speed and variable-speed small automotive electric motors can be controlled by using two different field coil windings. Heavy windings on one magnetic field are connected in series through the

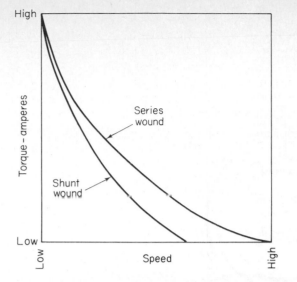

Figure 6-11 Speed and torque characteristics of series- and shunt-wound motors.

rent flow through the cranking motor. When a cranking motor runs without cranking the engine, it will rotate at maximum speed. This is called **free speed.** The starter will run at the free speed when the operator holds the start switch after the engine has started to run. At this speed the counter electromotive force will be highest and current draw will be lowest (Figure 6-11).

Torque and free-speed characteristics of a motor are controlled by the design of its field coils. Field coils may all be series wound; they may have three coil series wound and one coil shunt wound; or they may have two pairs of coils in parallel with each other and both pairs in series with the armature. Parallel field windings have many more coil turns using smaller wires than series field windings.

6-2 CRANKING MOTOR

Technical words in this section you will need to learn:

Field frame	Ramp
Hold-in coil	Relay
Overrunning clutch	Solenoid
Pull-in coil	

The cranking motor is usually referred to as the starter because it is used to start an engine. The 1984 *SAE Handbook* uses both terms: cranking motor and starting motor. The cranking motor is a specialized electric motor made to give a high turning force, called **starting torque,** at high speeds for a short period of time. It has a drive pinion assembly used to connect the motor armature to

the engine ring gear to crank the engine and an over-running clutch to disconnect it when the engine starts.

Cranking Motor Windings. The armature of the cranking motor is similar to the armature of small motors. Its major difference lies in its size and armature shaft design. The armature rotates in sleeve bearings or bushings. A steel shell housing, called a **field frame,** holds the field coil windings close to the armature windings to take maximum advantage of the magnetic field. A section view of a typical cranking motor is shown in Figure 6-12.

Most automotive cranking motors have four fields and four brushes. The polarity of the fields alternate, first north, then south, then north, then south, and so on.

Series-wound cranking motors (Figure 6-13) rotate at very high free speeds. As the counter electromotive force builds up, motor current draw is reduced. This reduces field strength, which, in turn, allows an increase in speed. In series-wound cranking motors the operating speeds are very high right after the engine starts, before the operator releases the "start" switch. A shunt winding coil on one of the fields helps to limit maximum speed. One end of the shunt winding is connected directly to ground (Figure 6-14). Its field strength is based on cranking-circuit voltage, not on counter electromotive force. As a result, its magnetic field remains strong. The

Figure 6-12 Section view of a typical cranking motor. (Courtesy Delco-Remy Division, General Motors Corporation.)

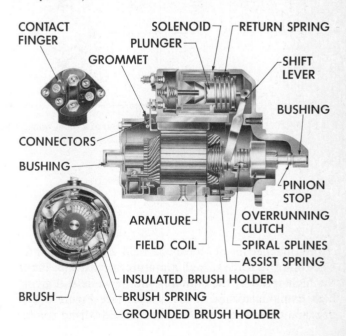

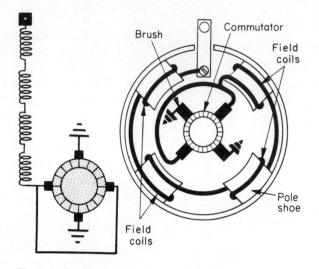

Figure 6–13 Circuit of a series-wound cranking motor. (Courtesy Oldsmobile Division, General Motors Corporation.)

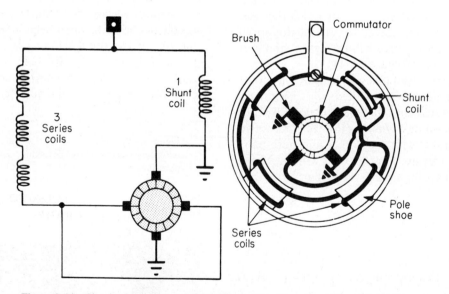

Figure 6–14 Circuit of a shunt-wound cranking motor. (Courtesy Oldsmobile Division, General Motors Corporation.)

strong magnetism of the shunt field increases counter electromotive force at high armature speeds. This limits the high speed of the cranking motor while still giving high cranking torque at low speeds (see Figure 6–11). Schematic drawings of three other field-wiring combinations used in current passenger-car cranking motors are shown in Figure 6–15.

The cranking motor armature has conductor windings made of copper bars to carry high amperage. Each winding makes a complete loop from one commutator

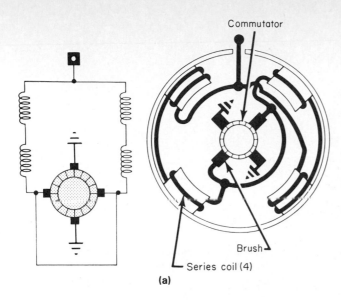

(a)

Labels in figure (a): Commutator, Brush, Series coil (4)

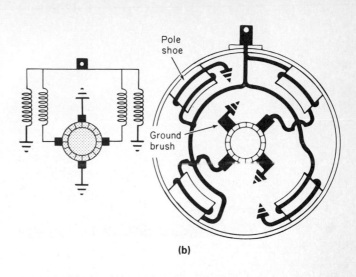

(b)

Labels in figure (b): Pole shoe, Ground brush

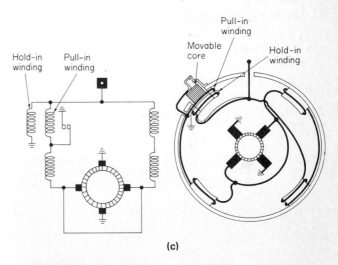

(c)

Labels in figure (c): Hold-in winding, Pull-in winding, Movable core, Pull-in winding, Hold-in winding

Figure 6-15 Alternate field connections used in automotive cranking motors. [Views (a) and (b) courtesy Oldsmobile Division, General Motors Corporation.]

Figure 6-16 A pointer shows where solder fastens two windings to a commutator bar.

bar to another. This is done all around the armature so that all windings are interconnected. The ends of two different windings are soldered to junctions on each commutator bar. You can see the soldered junctions in Figure 6-16.

Brushes are held against the commutator by a brush spring. The brushes are usually angled slightly so that they will have good contact, minimum arcing, and long service life. You can see the angle in Figure 6-17. Two opposite brushes are insulated from the frame. The other two brushes are grounded to the frame (see Figures 6-13, 6-14, and 6-15).

Drive Assembly. Cranking motor armatures are designed to rotate at high speeds to minimize amperage draw. To do this, drive ratios run from 15:1 to 20:1. Some Chrysler cranking motors have a built-in 3.5:1 reduction gear between the armature and the pinion drive gear. This allows these cranking motors to be built somewhat lighter

BRUSHES

BRUSH SPRING

Figure 6-17 Cranking motor brushes and leaf-type brush springs.

and to use a smaller crankshaft ring gear. The small ring gear allows a smaller clutch or transmission bell housing for reduced vehicle size and weight. This allows a smaller transmission hump in the floor pan. The small pinion drive gear meshes with a large ring gear mounted on the flywheel or torque converter drive plate (Figure 6-18).

The drive pinion will engage the ring gear **before** the cranking motor starts to rotate. It will release from the ring gear after the engine starts. Cranking motor

Figure 6-18 Small starter drive pinion in mesh with the engine ring gear on a torque converter drive plate.

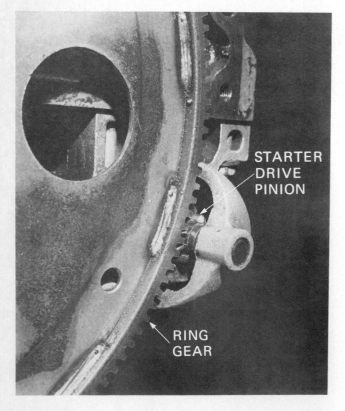

STARTER DRIVE PINION

RING GEAR

drives have evolved to one basic type of drive assembly. This is the **overrunning clutch drive.**

The overrunning clutch is an assembly made of rollers that wedge between a hub and outer race. You can see the end of the roller and spring in Figure 6-19. When the assembly is rotated in one direction it engages and when it is rotated in the opposite direction it releases. You can see how this works in Figure 6-20. The overrunning clutch assembly is splined to the armature shaft (Figure 6-21). A solenoid pushes the entire overrunning clutch assembly through a shift lever until the drive gear is in full mesh with the ring gear (Figure 6-22). The armature splines drive the overrunning clutch hub. Hub rotation and springs force the rollers up a ramp, jamming them between the hub and outer race. This pulls the outer race along to rotate the drive pinion gear. When the engine starts, the ring gear spins the drive pinion gear faster than

Figure 6-19 The cover is removed to show the roller and spring in an overrunning clutch of a cranking motor drive assembly.

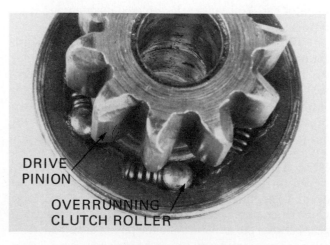

DRIVE PINION

OVERRUNNING CLUTCH ROLLER

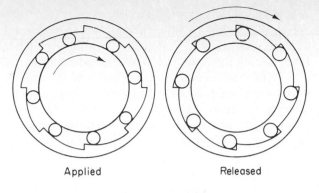

Applied   Released

Overrunning clutch

Figure 6-20 Overrunning clutch operation.

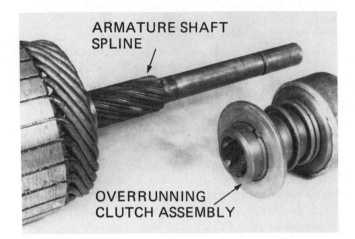

ARMATURE SHAFT
SPLINE

OVERRUNNING
CLUTCH ASSEMBLY

Figure 6-21 Curved splines on the armature shaft.

the free speed of the cranking motor. This rotates the outer race of the overrunning clutch ahead of the drive rollers. The rollers move down the ramp to release the clutch hub. The drive pinion gear will spin freely while being driven by the ring gear, causing no damage to the

armature of the cranking motor. At this time the cranking motor will rotate at free speed. This continues until the driver releases the start switch, allowing the solenoid return spring to pull the pinion gear from the ring gear.

Start Switches. The cranking motor draws a large current. Electrical cables between the battery and cranking motor need to be large and short to carry this current with minimum resistance. An electrical relay switch in the starter circuit allows the operator to control the cranking motor by using the start position in the ignition switch and still have low electrical circuit resistance in the cranking motor circuit.

The starter relay has a set of heavy-duty contacts. The contacts are closed by an electromagnet and opened by a spring. The electromagnetic circuit is fed through start contacts in the ignition switch. When the operator turns the ignition switch to the start position, current flows through the magnet coil of the relay. The magnetism will close the contact disc against relay contacts to engage the starter circuit. A relay circuit is shown in Figure 6-23. The cranking motor will crank as long as the relay coil is energized. When the operator releases the start switch the relay is demagnetized and a spring opens the relay contacts to stop the cranking motor operation. This type of starter relay is used on cranking motors engaged by the magnetic attraction of one starter field on an engaging lever. This type of cranking motor is used by Ford and some American Motors automobiles. The electrical circuit for this type of cranking motor is shown in Figure 6-15c.

There is also a relay built into the cranking motor solenoid. You can see the solenoid at the top of Figure 6-12. When the ignition key is turned to the start posi-

Figure 6-22 Typical shift lever that moves the overrunning clutch assembly.

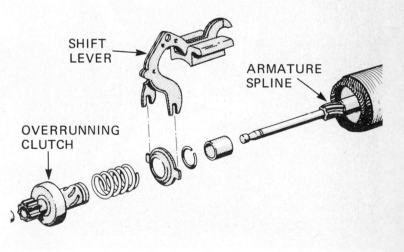

SHIFT
LEVER

ARMATURE
SPLINE

OVERRUNNING
CLUTCH

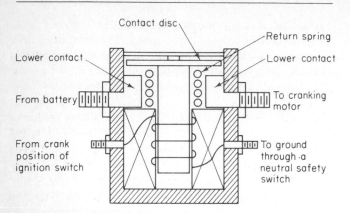

Figure 6-23 Section view of a cranking motor relay.

tion an electromagnet is energized. This pulls a core **plunger** toward the center of the coil. A **shift lever** connected to the plunger moves the pinion gear into engagement with the ring gear. As the plunger reaches its limit it moves the contact disk against battery and motor contact teminals in the relay assembly of the solenoid. This will close the cranking circuit and the engine will crank. You can see typical contacts of this switch in Figure 6-24.

The solenoid has two coil windings. The **pull-in** coil has a few turns of large wire. It is connected in series between the switch terminal (S) and cranking motor (M).

A **hold-in** coil has many turns of fine wire. It is connected between the switch terminal of the solenoid and ground. The two coils and the solenoid are shown in Figure 6-25. Look at this figure as you study the next paragraph.

When the operator turns the ignition key to the start position the switch circuit is complete. It magnetizes both solenoid windings. This strong magnetic field pulls the core plunger, shift lever, and drive assembly to move the pinion into engagement with the ring gear. The switch disc will hit the battery (B) and motor (M) contacts after the gears engage. When the disc is against the contacts, current will stop flowing in the pull-in winding because the voltage is the same on both ends of the pull-in winding. While cranking, the S, B, and M terminals have the same voltage. The magnetism of the hold-in winding is only strong enough to hold the core plunger in the engaged position.

When the operator releases the key from the crank position there is no current going to the coils in the solenoid. At this point the contact disk is still carrying current to the motor contact. Current goes from the motor contact backward through the pull-in winding to the start switch terminal, then forward to ground through the hold-in winding. This causes the coils to have opposite magnetic polarity to neutralize the effect of the magnetism. With no magnetic effect the spring pushes the core plunger from the solenoid. The plunger movement lets a small spring push the contact disc from the contacts. It will also pull the drive pinion from the ring gear through the shift linkage.

Figure 6-24 Parts of a cranking motor relay assembly.

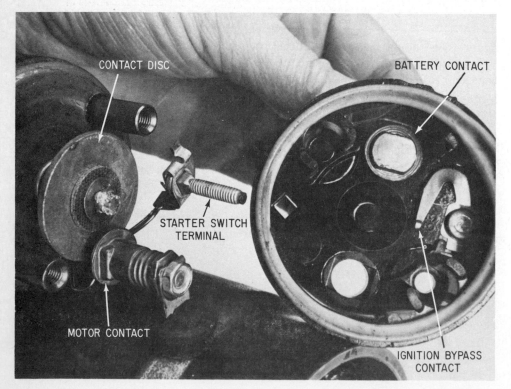

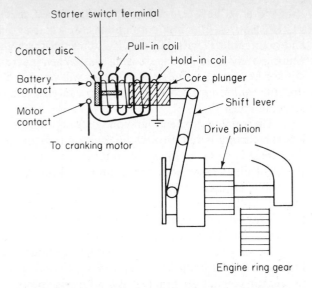

Figure 6-25 Schematic showing the pull-in and hold-in windings of a cranking motor solenoid.

6-3 CRANKING MOTOR CIRCUITS

The insulated half of the main cranking motor electrical circuit goes through a heavy cable connecting the positive battery post through a relay or solenoid to the cranking motor terminal. In the grounded half of the circuit the negative battery post is connected to the engine block with a battery ground cable. The cranking motor is bolted to the engine block or bell housing. The cranking motor circuit carries high current while the engine is being cranked, so that it must have minimum resistance.

The rest of the vehicle electrical system is connected to the battery-starter insulated circuit. This junction might be at the battery cable clamp, the battery junction at the relay or solenoid, or at a special junction block. In Figure 6-26 it is the 12 RED and 10 RED wires coming from the battery terminal of the solenoid through fusible links.

Figure 6-26 Complete circuit of a typical cranking motor.

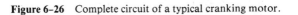
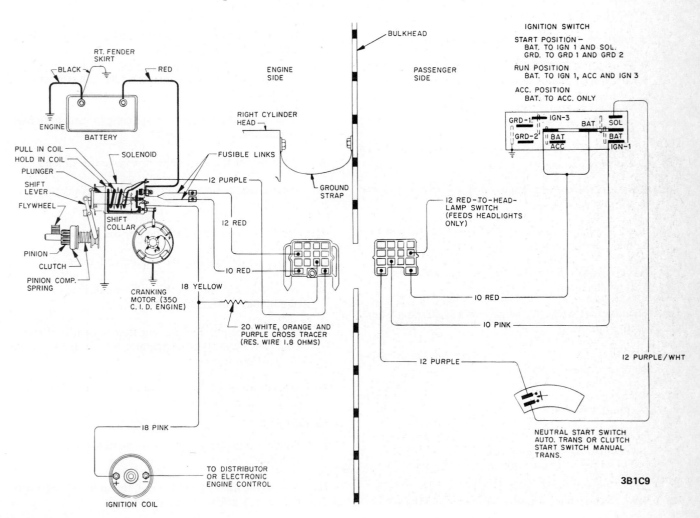

When the ignition switch is turned to the start position it energizes the relay or solenoid to operate the starter. This part of the electrical system is called the starter switch circuit. You may be able to see this easier on the simple cranking motor circuit in Figure 1–15.

For safety, vehicles equipped with automatic transmissions cannot be cranked while the transmission selector is in a gear range. A neutral safety switch or neutral start switch will allow cranking only while the automatic transmission gear selector is in neutral or park. It is located electrically in series with the ignition switch start terminal and the solenoid or relay switch terminal to keep the circuit open while the transmission selector is in any gear position. On the right half of Figure 6–26 the neutral start switch is between the 12 PURPLE/WHT and 12 PURPLE wires. Chrysler automobiles use a starter relay and a solenoid. The relay coil is connected through a neutral safety switch in the transmission. When the transmission is in park or neutral the relay will be closed so that the ignition switch start position can energize the solenoid coils.

There will not be enough voltage for ignition when ignition current is fed through an ignition resistor while the engine is being cranked. An ignition resistor bypass is used while the starter is being cranked. Two methods are used to bypass the ignition resistor. In one system the bypass contacts are located in the ignition switch. They feed from the Ign. 2 terminal. In the other system the bypass contacts are located at the solenoid disc contact. You can see this type of bypass contact in Figure 6–24. In Figure 6–26 it is the 18 YELLOW wire coming from the motor contact terminal of the cranking motor.

STUDY QUESTIONS

Section 6–1

1. Name the parts of an armature.

2. What forms the path for magnetic lines of force from motor fields?

3. What causes a motor armature to rotate?

4. What effect does the commutator bars have on the power of the motor as they slide under the brushes?

5. What happens to the motor speed as the fields get stronger?

6. How does the current change when the motor is slowed by a heavy load?

7. What is done to reverse the direction of rotation of a permanent-magnet motor?

8. What is done to reverse the direction of rotation of a motor with an electromagnet field?

9. What is done to change the speed of a small shunt-wound electric motor?

10. How does increasing the current flow through the shunt winding weaken the effective field strength?

11. What type of windings are used to carry the large current in cranking motors?

12. How does the design of shunt windings in a cranking motor differ from series windings?

Section 6–2

13. What does a shunt winding do for a cranking motor?

14. How many windings are connected to each commutator bar in a cranking motor?

15. Give three reasons why cranking motor brushes are angled slightly.

16. When does the drive pinion engage the ring gear when an engine is cranked?

17. What keeps the engine from spinning the armature back through the drive assembly?

18. What moves the shift lever to engage the pinion?

19. What closes the relay contact disk in a cranking motor solenoid?

20. Where do the ends of the pull-in coil connect?

21. Where do the ends of the hold-in coil connect?

22. What stops current flow through the pull-in coil when the motor starts to crank?

23. In what direction does current flow in each of the solenoid coils right after the operator releases the key from the start position?

24. What moves the plunger out of the solenoid when the coil magnetism is neutralized?

Section 6–3

25. Where is a neutral start switch connected in the starting system?

26. What is the number and color of the ignition bypass wire in Figure 6–26?

7

ELECTRIC MOTOR SERVICE

When an automotive electric motor does not run the system must be checked to identify the cause of the problem. To do this you will check the electrical system voltage, the condition of the conductor, and the operating units. Wires in the electrical circuit are checked for minimum resistance. The wires must not touch vehicle metal. Switches must open and close the circuit. Motors must run at the proper speeds drawing minimum electrical current. If the circuit is tested using correct procedures, the cause of the problem can be identified. The part causing the problem must be either repaired or replaced. After service the system should be retested to make sure that the problem has been corrected.

The minimum size of the battery cables is very important. An oversize cable will not affect the starter circuit operation. It is not used because it costs more, weighs more, and takes more room than the correct-size cable. Undersize cables have high resistance. This would reduce the flow of electrical current. The starter motor would not receive enough electrical power to crank the engine properly if they were used.

The resistance is very low in the cranking motor circuits, so it is measured using the voltage drop test. This test method was discussed in Section 5–4. If the current flows easily there is little voltage drop because there is little resistance. If the circuit has high resistance there will be a large voltage drop. Remember that current will flow only when there is a voltage drop.

7–1 CRANKING-SYSTEM TESTING

Technical words in this section you will need to learn:

> Amperage draw
> Cranking voltage
> Remote control

Cranking problems are caused by a defective battery, circuit resistance, switches, cranking motor, drive assembly, or engine resistance. The battery should always be checked first when there is any electrical problem. The battery must be at least 75% charged for cranking system testing. This is a hydrometer reading of 1225, an open-circuit voltage of 12.4 V, or a green charge indicator. The battery state of charge was discussed in Section 4–2.

Cranking Voltage. The cranking system can be given an overall check by measuring the cranking voltage. Several things can be done to keep the engine from starting during this test. The coil secondary cable can be removed from the distributor cap center tower and placed against the engine block. This will ground the secondary voltage coming from the ignition coil. An alternative method is to connect a jumper wire from the negative side of the coil primary to ground. This keeps the primary current flowing in the coil so that there is no collapsing magnetic field (see Section 1-9). It would be still better to remove the wire from the coil BAT or positive terminal. On Delco-Remy HEI distributors the wire connected to the BAT terminal is removed to keep the engine from starting. This opens the primary circuit so that no current can flow. The negative voltmeter lead (black) is connected to the negative battery terminal. The positive voltmeter lead (red) is connected to the positive battery terminal. The voltage should be above 9.6 V when a warm engine is cranking at normal speeds. Cranking should be limited to the shortest cranking time you need to get a steady voltage reading. Manufacturers' specifications should always be followed. In a normal warm engine in good operating condition, the cranking voltage will usually be 10.0 V or slightly more.

Amperage Draw.   This test is run with the voltmeter connected to the battery terminals. One way is to connect a battery-starter tester (BST) to the battery as shown in Figure 7-1. The voltmeter is connected like it is for the cranking voltage test. The large amperage leads are con-

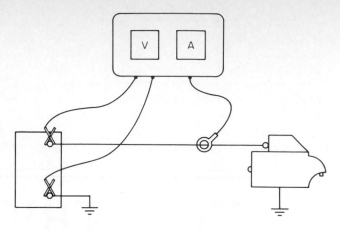

Figure 7-2 Inductive ammeter being used to check the cranking voltage and amperage draw of a cranking motor.

nected parallel to the voltmeter leads. Some testers have internal connections to connect the voltmeter to the large amperage leads. Adjust the carbon pile to get the same voltage you found when you measured the cranking voltage. While holding this voltage, quickly read the ammeter, then open the carbon pile. Do not keep current flowing any longer than necessary because it will discharge the battery and heat the carbon pile. Amperage draw can also be measured directly using an inductive ammeter pickup around one of the battery cables. The connection is shown in Figure 7-2. The voltmeter is connected across the battery. Connect the inductive ammeter to its power source. The cranking voltage and amperage draw can then be measured at the same time as the engine is cranked. Small automotive engines may have as little as 100 A draw, while cranking motors on large engines may draw over 225 A.

The lower the amperage draw, the better. High amperage draw is caused by slow rotation of the cranking motor. Slow rotation is caused by a faulty motor, low cranking voltage at the cranking motor, or a hard-cranking engine. You will have to compare all the test results and the way the parts look to determine the cause of high current draw.

Voltage Drop.   Most starter problems occur because resistance forms in the battery cables, cable junctions, and electrical contacts within the solenoid. They may look bad and still work normally. On the other hand, they may look normal but not work correctly. The starting circuit can be accurately checked using the voltage-drop test procedure.

You will remember from Section 1-2 how voltage drop is used to measure resistance of a circuit carrying current. It is handy to use a remote-control starter switch to crank the engine. Any time you use a remote-control starter switch you should make a habit of placing the transmission in neutral and setting the parking brake.

Figure 7-1 Starter-battery tester connected to make an amperage draw test on a cranking motor.

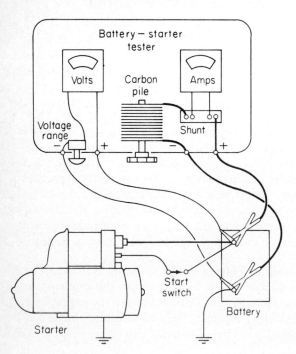

The remote-control starter switch is a heavy-duty pushbutton switch with two leads. Each lead has a clip at its end. One clip is connected to the S terminal of the relay or solenoid switch. The other clip is connected to a hot terminal (with battery voltage). When the remote-control switch is closed, the engine will crank. Keep the engine from starting by using one of the methods described in the section on cranking voltage.

With the voltmeter set on the 16 or 20 V range the red voltmeter lead is connected on the positive battery terminal. The black voltmeter lead is connected to the cranking motor M terminal (Figures 7-3, 7-4, and 7-5).

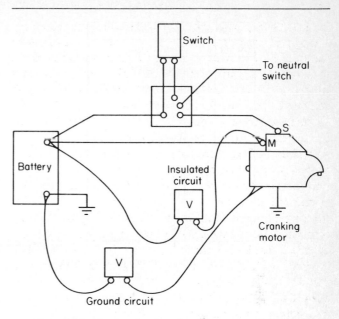

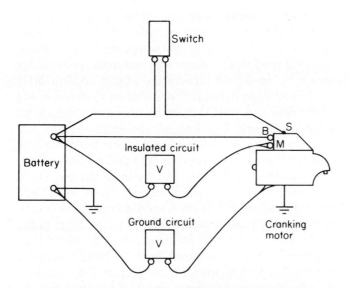

Figure 7-3 Starter circuit voltage-drop test connections typical of GM vehicles.

Figure 7-4 Starter circuit voltage-drop test connections typical of Ford vehicles.

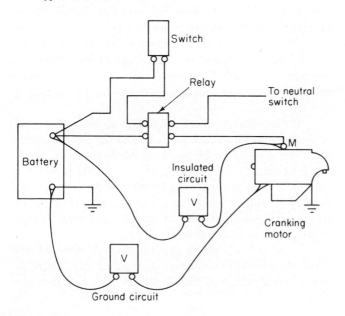

Figure 7-5 Starter circuit voltage-drop test connections typical of Chrysler vehicles.

This is on the motor side of the solenoid. It is very difficult to make this connection on some vehicles.

While the engine is cranking, switch the voltmeter to the lowest voltage range and observe the voltage. Immediately return the voltmeter scale to the 16 or 20 V range **before you release the starter switch.** The voltage drop of the insulated starting circuit should be less than 0.2 V.

If the voltage drop is greater than 0.2 V, the individual parts of the circuit will have to be checked. This test method was described in Section 5-4. Leave the red voltmeter lead on the battery post. Move the black voltmeter lead to the battery side of the solenoid. You could also connect the black voltmeter lead to the 10 RED or 12 RED wires on the left side of Figure 6-26. If the vehicle has a GM Diagnostic Connector (Figure 7-6), you can use the number one cavity for this connection. The voltage drop reading taken at this point (solenoid B terminal) shows the resistance in the insulated circuit to the solenoid. If the voltage drop is more than 0.2 V, there is too much resistance in the insulated battery cable or in its connections. A general rule allows a maximum voltage drop of 0.2 V for each battery cable and each switch. Voltages slightly higher than this indicate that a problem is developing.

The grounded side of the cranking circuit is just as important as the insulated side. It is checked by first placing the black voltmeter lead on the negative battery post. Connect the red voltmeter lead on the metal case

mobiles. The major difference will be the difference in the wire color codes.

GM diagnostic connector	
Cavity	Identification
1	Solenoid "BAT"
2	Ignition switch "BAT"
3	Light switch "BAT"
4	Blank
5	Distributor "BAT"
6	Ignition switch "Ign"
7	Blank
8	Solenoid "S"
9	Ignition switch "S"
G	Ground

Figure 7-6 Cavity identification for GM diagnostic connectors.

of the cranking motor. Remember that the red voltmeter lead is connected to the most positive end of the conductor being checked. The maximum allowable voltage drop of 0.1 V is normal with the engine cranking. A larger voltage drop indicates too much resistance. The point causing the high resistance can be found by bringing the red voltmeter lead toward the negative post, a junction at a time. Crank the engine as the red voltmeter lead is held at each point; first on the engine block, then on the engine end of the battery ground cable, and finally on the negative battery connector. The resistance point is between the last high-voltage reading and the next low-voltage reading.

Switch Circuit. You will remember that the starter switch circuit uses contacts in the ignition switch to energize a coil in the starter relay or solenoid. If the starter solenoid does not move the pinion into engagement with the ring gear it may be the result of faulty start contacts in the ignition switch, a faulty relay or solenoid, or the connecting wiring. Each can be checked by placing the black voltmeter lead on a good ground and the red voltmeter lead on the small relay or solenoid S terminal. Use cavity 8 in the GM Diagnostic Connector. In a normally operating starter switch circuit you should see the normal cranking voltage on the voltmeter. If the starter does not crank and there is no voltage, the switch circuit is at fault. If you read battery voltage, the solenoid is open. If you see a very low voltage, the solenoid is shorted or the starter cannot rotate.

Figure 7-7 is a typical block diagram flowchart for diagnosing starting circuits. It applies to most auto-

7-2 BENCH TESTING

The cranking motor will have to be removed when electrical checks of the starting system indicate that it is faulty. The ground cable is first removed from the battery to prevent dangerous sparks. Place the vehicle on jack stands or on a hoist if it is necessary to work under it. The wires are removed and the two or three mounting bolts removed from the cranking motor. It can then be taken from the engine.

The **free-speed test** is used to check a cranking motor after it has been removed from an engine. Specifications use voltage, amperage, and motor speed. You will need a tachometer that can measure armature speed. A hand-held tachometer with a friction drive works well when the end of the armature shaft comes out of the motor. A strobtachometer also works well on all cranking motors. A carbon-pile rheostat is used to control the voltage. The battery-starter tester is usually used to make this test. The ammeter and carbon pile are connected in series so you can read the amperage being used by the cranking motor during the test. The heavy red lead from the carbon pile in the battery-starter tester is connected to the positive battery post and the other heavy lead is connected to the cranking motor BAT terminal. A ground cable is connected from the battery negative post to the cranking motor frame (Figure 7-8). Connect the voltmeter leads between the BAT terminal and the motor frame.

You will need to look up the specifications to know the test voltage, amperage, and motor speed. Connect a remote starter switch or a jumper wire on the solenoid to energize the coils. Hold the cranking motor as you adjust the carbon pile until you have the test voltage. Read the tachometer and amperage while the motor is operating at this voltage. Open the carbon pile just as soon as you get the readings. Speed and amperage of the starter are compared to specifications. Low-speed and high-amperage readings indicate problems in the cranking motor.

If the cranking motor is found to be faulty, it should be disassembled and each part checked for correct operation. This is called **bench checking.** Many shops exchange cranking motors for rebuilt units when tests show that the motor does not meet the specifications. It is a good practice to run the free-speed test on any replacement cranking motor to see that it operates correctly *before* installing it on the engine.

A relay has a single coil winding. A solenoid has a pull-in and hold-in windings (see Figure 6-25). The relay and solenoid windings should also be tested. If they are

STARTING CIRCUIT DIAGNOSIS

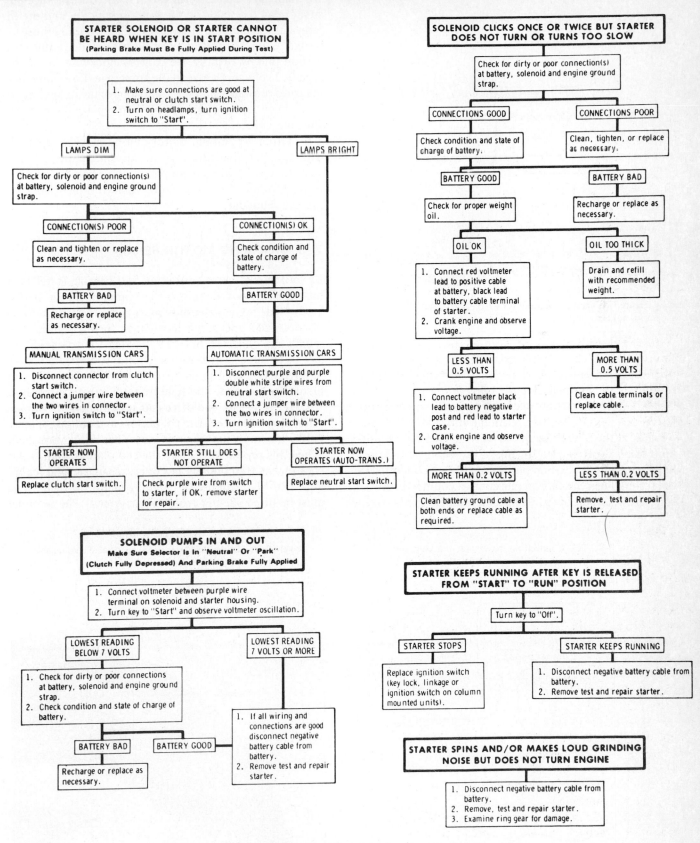

STARTER SOLENOID OR STARTER CANNOT BE HEARD WHEN KEY IS IN START POSITION
(Parking Brake Must Be Fully Applied During Test)

1. Make sure connections are good at neutral or clutch start switch.
2. Turn on headlamps, turn ignition switch to "Start".

LAMPS DIM

Check for dirty or poor connection(s) at battery, solenoid and engine ground strap.

CONNECTION(S) POOR

Clean and tighten or replace as necessary.

CONNECTION(S) OK

Check condition and state of charge of battery.

LAMPS BRIGHT

BATTERY BAD

Recharge or replace as necessary.

BATTERY GOOD

MANUAL TRANSMISSION CARS

1. Disconnect connector from clutch start switch.
2. Connect a jumper wire between the two wires in connector.
3. Turn ignition switch to "Start".

AUTOMATIC TRANSMISSION CARS

1. Disconnect purple and purple double white stripe wires from neutral start switch.
2. Connect a jumper wire between the two wires in connector.
3. Turn ignition switch to "Start".

STARTER NOW OPERATES

Replace clutch start switch.

STARTER STILL DOES NOT OPERATE

Check purple wire from switch to starter, if OK, remove starter for repair.

STARTER NOW OPERATES (AUTO-TRANS.)

Replace neutral start switch.

SOLENOID PUMPS IN AND OUT
Make Sure Selector Is In "Neutral" Or "Park" (Clutch Fully Depressed) And Parking Brake Fully Applied

1. Connect voltmeter between purple wire terminal on solenoid and starter housing.
2. Turn key to "Start" and observe voltmeter oscillation.

LOWEST READING BELOW 7 VOLTS

1. Check for dirty or poor connections at battery, solenoid and engine ground strap.
2. Check condition and state of charge of battery.

BATTERY BAD

Recharge or replace as necessary.

BATTERY GOOD

LOWEST READING 7 VOLTS OR MORE

1. If all wiring and connections are good disconnect negative battery cable from battery.
2. Remove test and repair starter.

SOLENOID CLICKS ONCE OR TWICE BUT STARTER DOES NOT TURN OR TURNS TOO SLOW

Check for dirty or poor connection(s) at battery, solenoid and engine ground strap.

CONNECTIONS GOOD

Check condition and state of charge of battery.

CONNECTIONS POOR

Clean, tighten, or replace as necessary.

BATTERY GOOD

Check for proper weight oil.

BATTERY BAD

Recharge or replace as necessary.

OIL OK

1. Connect red voltmeter lead to positive cable at battery, black lead to battery cable terminal of starter.
2. Crank engine and observe voltage.

OIL TOO THICK

Drain and refill with recommended weight.

LESS THAN 0.5 VOLTS

1. Connect voltmeter black lead to battery negative post and red lead to starter case.
2. Crank engine and observe voltage.

MORE THAN 0.5 VOLTS

Clean cable terminals or replace cable.

MORE THAN 0.2 VOLTS

Clean battery ground cable at both ends or replace cable as required.

LESS THAN 0.2 VOLTS

Remove, test and repair starter.

STARTER KEEPS RUNNING AFTER KEY IS RELEASED FROM "START" TO "RUN" POSITION

Turn key to "Off".

STARTER STOPS

Replace ignition switch (key lock, linkage or ignition switch on column mounted units).

STARTER KEEPS RUNNING

1. Disconnect negative battery cable from battery.
2. Remove test and repair starter.

STARTER SPINS AND/OR MAKES LOUD GRINDING NOISE BUT DOES NOT TURN ENGINE

1. Disconnect negative battery cable from battery.
2. Remove, test and repair starter.
3. Examine ring gear for damage.

Figure 7-7 Typical block diagram flow chart for diagnosing starting circuits.

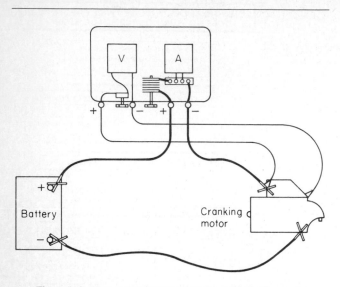

Figure 7-8 Test connections for a free-speed test of a cranking motor.

faulty, the part can be replaced without replacing a good operating cranking motor. Use the following test setup to check the windings (Figure 7-9).

Connect a carbon pile and ammeter in series between the battery positive terminal and one end of the winding at the S terminal of the relay or solenoid. A volt-amp tester is often used for this. You will have to know how the ammeter, carbon pile, and leads are connected in the tester. Turn the carbon pile control counterclockwise to keep the circuit open. Connect a jumper wire between

Figure 7-9 Test connections to test a cranking motor solenoid.

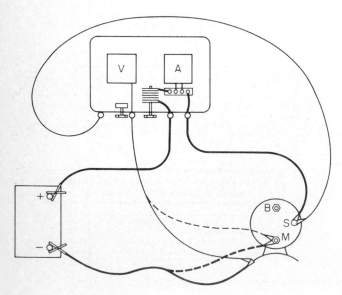

the battery negative terminal and the other end of the winding. This would be the metal relay cover or a second small relay terminal for the hold-in winding and the M terminal for the pull-in winding. Each winding must be tested. When the test connections are made, adjust the carbon pile by turning the control clockwise to set the specified voltage, then read the amperage. Low amperage indicates resistance and high amperage indicates a shorted field. In either case you will have to replace the relay or solenoid coil.

Often a cranking motor can be quickly repaired. This may save time and save the customer money. At the same time you will increase your income because you will be paid for rebuilding the motor yourself rather than paying the rebuilder.

7-3 CRANKING MOTOR REPAIR

By looking at the solenoid you will be able to tell if it has to be removed before the cranking motor is disassembled. Some solenoids must have their shift forks disconnected and some must have their electrical terminals disconnected before removing the solenoid.

The direct-drive cranking motor is disassembled by removing two long assembly through-bolts from the end plate. The end plate and field frame can then be removed from the armature and drive-end subassembly. If you see solder thrown on the field connectors and housing (Figure 7-10), you know the cranking motor has been overheated. When this problem is found the end plate is usually put back on and the cranking motor is exchanged for a rebuilt unit. In the reduction-gear cranking motor the field frame must be lifted slightly from the drive end. The terminal

Figure 7-10 Solder thrown from an overheated commutator onto the field winding.

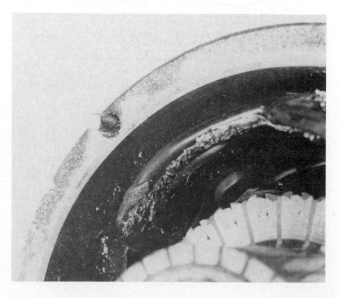

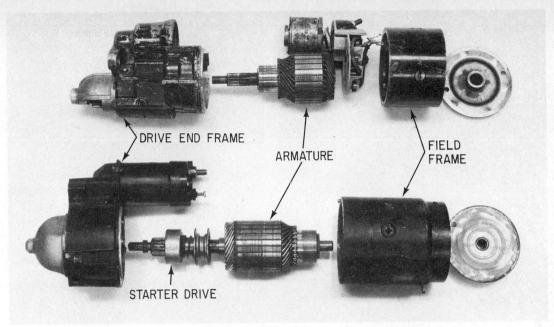

Figure 7-11 Major cranking motor subassemblies. Chrysler gear drive type (upper) and Delco-Remy direct-drive type (lower).

screw can then be removed. The field frame can be lifted off (see Figure 7–11). Following this, the shift-lever mechanism and solenoid are removed to free the drive end from the armature. Each part is cleaned, inspected, and tested for proper operation, then repaired as required.

Cleaning. The electrical parts of the cranking motor should not be soaked in or flushed with cleaning solvents. Cleaning solvents will damage the protective insulating varnish. Vapors from solvents that remain in the parts become a fire hazard after the starter is put back into use. Electrical parts should be wiped with a clean shop towel. Stubborn surface soil can be removed with a shop towel dampened with cleaning solvent. Remove the surface solvent with a clean dry shop towel. Mechanical parts, with the exception of the overrunning clutch, can be cleaned with degreasers in the normal way you clean automotive parts. The overrunning clutch has a sealed-in lubricant for the rollers that will wash out if the clutch is soaked in cleaning solvent.

Inspection. The shift levers and forks are mechanical. They should operate freely without binding or sticking. They should not be bent or show signs of wear. The drive assembly with the overrunning clutch and pinion is the part most likely to need replacement. The overrunning clutch slips when it becomes worn and the teeth of the starter pinion wear and sometimes break. The drive assembly is not repairable. It is replaced as a complete unit.

Current flows through the fields, insulated brushes, armature, and grounded brushes when the starter is cranking. Poor connections in any of these parts can cause high resistance and loss of cranking ability. Most of the starter resistance is at the brush-to-commutator contacts. The solder in the joint connecting the armature winding to the commutator will melt if the starter is cranked so long that it overheats. An example of thrown solder from an overheated starter was shown in Figure 7–10.

Starter brushes slide on the commutator, causing the brushes to wear (Figure 7–12). The commutator will

Figure 7-12 Badly worn brushes in a cranking motor.

Figure 7-13 Scored commutator from a cranking motor.

Figure 7-14 Test lead connections to test a cranking motor armature for grounding.

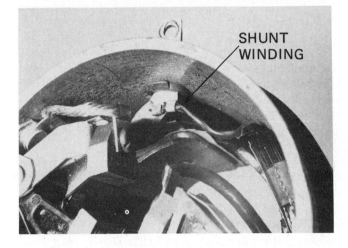

SHUNT WINDING

Figure 7-15 Shunt coil winding connection going to the M terminal.

wear too. Figure 7-13 shows a commutator scored from brush wear.

Brush spring tension should be checked. This can be done using a small spring scale, but it is usually done by feel. Pay special attention to the normal tension of the brush springs so that you will develop the ability to identify weak springs. Spring tension that is too light will allow the brush to float, causing an arc that will burn the commutator. Too much spring tension will cause excessive brush and commutator wear. Weak brush springs should be replaced.

Electrical Tests. Each electrical part of the cranking motor can be tested. Faulty parts can be rebuilt in specialized automotive electrical shops. The part that is faulty can be exchanged for a new or rebuilt part. Most service technicians exchange the complete faulty cranking motor for a reconditioned one. The simplest electrical test on a cranking motor part is to check it with a 110 V test light for continuity and electrical ground. If electricity can pass through the part, it has **continuity**. If an electrical system is insulated for 110 V, it can keep 12 V from leaking to ground. To check the armature windings for **grounding** one test light probe is put on the commutator bars and the other on the armature metal core, as shown in Figure 7-14. If the light comes on, the armature is grounded. Grounded armatures are replaced.

Disconnect the shunt winding on both ends (Figure 7-15). The terminal on the battery end is in a slot next to the M-terminal on the series winding. The ground end of the shunt winding is usually held on the field frame

with a rivet. The rivet will have to be removed to test the shunt winding. Test the winding for continuity and grounding with a 110 V test light. Replace the rivet if the fields are normal.

The test probes of the 110 V test light are placed on both ends of the field windings. The light should come on. If the bulb does not light, the field is open. One probe is then switched to the field frame, while the other probe is kept on one end of the field winding. If the light comes on the field is grounded. The field frame assembly is replaced if any of the fields are open or grounded.

The brush holders can be checked by placing one 110 V test light probe on the housing and touching the other probe to the brush holder. Two opposite holders cause the bulb to light (grounded brush holders) while

Figure 7-16 Using a growler to test an armature for a short.

the other two should not (insulated brush holders). If the insulated holders allow the bulb to light, the insulated brush holders are grounded.

Armature shorts can be checked by placing the armature in a growler (Figure 7-16). The growler puts a 60-cycle alternating magnetic field around the armature. A blade is placed across the armature as the armature is rotated by hand on the growler. A shorted armature will cause the blade to vibrate at some point on the armature. Shorted armatures must be replaced.

Opens in an armature are difficult to find. The windings are heavy and there are only a few. While in the magnetic field of the growler they will not produce enough voltage to be measured easily with automotive service-type test equipment. However, armature opens can usually be seen where the windings are soldered to the commutator (see Figure 6-16). If the motor is overheated, this solder will melt and be thrown into the housing (see Figure 7-8). When the solder is thrown out of the winding, the commutator connection will loosen to cause an open. In time, vibration may cause a soldered joint to harden and break. Sometimes you may be able to resolder armature opens with rosin-core solder to repair the armature. You will have to be careful not to loosen other solder joints or to burn the commutator insulation.

Reconditioning. You will find the parts that are faulty when you make the bench test, the visual inspection, and electrical tests. In general, electrical motor parts that have opens, shorts, or grounds are replaced with new or rebuilt parts. Some service manuals show how to replace fields, for example, but parts departments seldom stock these parts. Many service technicians run the free-speed test on a questionable cranking motor. If it does not operate properly, they exchange it for a rebuilt starter. This will

get the customer's automobile on the road as soon as possible.

Some manufacturers recommend the replacement of armature shaft bushings when they are worn. It is easy to press the old bushing out and a new one in when the bushing bore is open at both ends of the bushing. End-plate bushings are open at only one end. When the bushing is worn, the usual procedure is to replace the end plate. The new end plate has a new bushing already installed.

Insulated brushes in most starters are soldered to the field. These junctions must be heated enough to loosen the solder to release the old brush lead. The lead of each new brush is soldered in place using rosin-core solder. Ground brushes are usually bolted or riveted in place. In some cases the brush is bolted to a spring-loaded arm. These brushes can be replaced easily by bolting a new brush on the arm.

A retainer and snap ring must be removed from the armature shaft to remove the drive assembly from Delco-Remy and Ford cranking motors. Place a sleeve of the right size over the drive end of the armature shaft (Figure 7-17). Tap the sleeve to drive the retainer toward the armature. This will free the snap ring (Figure 7-18). Slide the snap ring and retainer from the shaft. The old drive assembly can then be removed. Clean the shaft and install the replacement drive assembly. Put the retainer on the shaft with its open side away from the clutch assembly. Lay the snap ring on the end of the shaft. Place

Figure 7-17 Using a sleeve to remove the snap ring retainer to allow removal of the starter drive assembly.

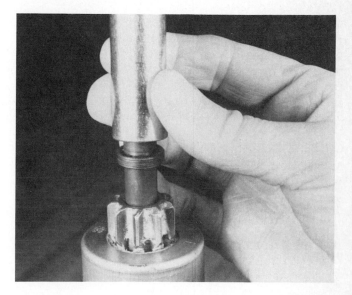

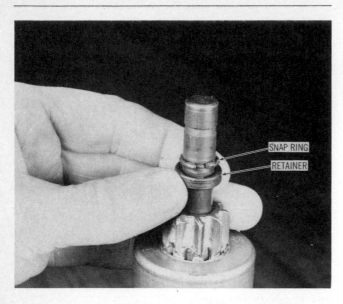

Figure 7-18 Retainer is removed to free the snap ring.

a block of wood on the snap ring. Tap the wood with a hammer to force the snap ring over the end of the shaft, then slide it into the groove. Pull the retainer up and force it over the snap ring (Figure 7-19). Special tools are available from tool companies that make it easy to remove and install the snap ring and retainer.

You can buy solenoid switch repair kits. They contain new switch contacts and a disc so that the switch

can be repaired without replacing the solenoid. The solenoid is removed and the switch disassembled. New parts are installed (see Figure 6-24) and the switch reassembled. It should be done carefully. The cranking motor is mounted under the engine where it gets road splash that can corrode the switch contacts. On these engines it is necessary to have a good seal on the switch cover. Drive assembly movement should be checked anytime the solenoid is serviced. This is necessary to make sure that it has the correct pinion clearance. With the solenoid fully engaged, the pinion should not touch the end of the starter-drive housing. If the clearance is not correct, some parts are worn. They will have to be replaced.

Shifting forks are assembled in the drive end frame. When the solenoid is mounted on the drive end frame, it must be connected at the same time the fork is assembled. When mounted on the field frame, the solenoid is installed after the rest of the starter is assembled.

The bearing journal ends of the armature are lubricated with high-melting-point grease. You can get this grease at most automotive parts departments. After lubrication, the armature is installed in the drive end bushing. In reduction gear cranking motors the armature must be fitted through the brush holder. You can see this type as the upper cranking motor in Figure 7-11. Brushes are held back against the spring for assembly using a special bracket (Figure 7-20). The field frame is then fitted over the armature. In many direct-drive cranking motors the brushes are held in the field frame. You can see this type of brush holder in Figures 7-12 and 7-15. They are lifted over the commutator as the field frame is installed. In some reduction-gear cranking motors it

Figure 7-19 Using pliers to force the retainer over the snap ring for assembly.

Figure 7-20 A special bracket holds brushes against the brush springs for assemblying a Chrysler gear drive cranking motor. The bracket stays inside the assembled starter motor.

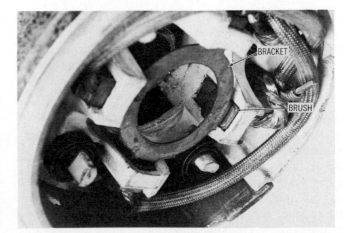

is necessary to make electrical connections at this time by bolting or soldering. Field frames are properly positioned over an alignment pin. The end plate is finally installed, making sure it is aligned on the pin.

The whole motor is held together by installing and tightening the long assembly bolts. Where required, the solenoid is installed. The pinion clearance is checked. If it is not correct, the motor will have to be disassembled and the worn parts replaced. After assembly the cranking motor is rechecked using the free-speed test. If it operates normally, it is ready to be installed on the engine.

The drive end of the cranking motor is placed in the bell housing and the mounting screws are installed and tightened. Torque specifications are usually given for the screws. The battery lead, switch lead, and ignition bypass, where used, are connected to the solenoid. When this is complete the battery ground cable is installed. To finish the job, make sure that the engine cranks normally.

STUDY QUESTIONS

Section 7–1

1. What is the first thing to check when there is an electrical problem?

2. What is the minimum state of charge the battery must have for testing the cranking system?

3. List three ways the engine can be kept from starting when testing the cranking system.

4. How is the voltmeter connected to the battery to make a cranking voltage test?

5. What cranking voltage should you expect on a warm engine with all systems working normally?

6. How is the voltmeter connected when making a starter draw test?

7. How long should the current be kept flowing through the carbon pile when making a test with a battery-starter tester?

8. What are the advantages of an inductive ammeter over a battery-starter tester?

9. How is a remote-control starter switch used?

10. What indicates that a problem is developing in the cranking motor circuit?

11. What is the general rule for connecting voltmeter leads during a voltage-drop test?

12. How can you recognize high resistance when measuring the voltage-drop of a circuit?

13. What do high- and low-voltage readings taken while cranking indicate to you when you have the red voltmeter lead connected to the solenoid S terminal and the black lead connected to ground?

Section 7–2

14. What is the first part to remove when you are taking the cranking motor off an engine?

15. What readings indicate problems when you are running a free-speed test on a cranking motor?

16. What should be done to a rebuilt cranking motor before it is installed on an engine?

17. Where are the leads connected to measure the current draw of the pull-in and the hold-in solenoid coils?

Section 7–3

18. How should the parts of a cranking motor be cleaned?

19. What part of a cranking motor is most likely to need replacement?

20. What part of a cranking motor should be checked by looking and feeling?

21. What is the simplest electrical test you can make on a cranking motor part?

22. Why is a 110 V test light used to check parts of a 12 V cranking motor?

23. What two things must be checked on electrical parts of a cranking motor?

24. What fault is indicated when a blade vibrates as it is held on top of an armature when the armature is in a growler?

25. What must be done to get the drive assembly off from the armature shaft?

26. What is the last thing you should do after repairing a cranking motor?

8

INTRODUCTION TO ELECTRONICS

You will not need to know much about electronics to service automotive electronic parts. All that you will need to do is to make sure that they are working correctly. Automotive technicians have been doing this for a number of years. Radios and tape decks are electronic parts. If you had one that did not work correctly, you would remove it for repair in an electronic shop or you would replace it with one that works correctly. Electronic parts have been used on production automobile alternators since 1960. By the mid-1970s nearly all domestic passenger cars used electronic ignition systems. You see, all experienced automotive service technicians have been working with electronics for a number of years. When you understand the fundamentals of electronics you will find that it will help you locate and correct problems caused by faulty electronic parts. If electronic automotive parts are faulty, they will need to be replaced. You may replace the faulty part with a reconditioned part or a new one. Faulty electronic parts that you exchange for reconditioned parts are serviced at specialized electronic repair shops.

Electronics use the characteristics of electricity, conductors, and insulators that you studied in Chapter 1. Electronics were first recognized in 1907 with the development of the vacuum tube. The vacuum tube used a great deal of electricity and this caused the tube to become quite warm. Forty years later, in 1947, scientists in the Bell Laboratories developed the first solid-state electronic parts. Solid-state electronics have no moving parts to wear out. They replaced vacuum tubes in electronic circuits. They were much smaller and they operate on very little electricity, so they operate much cooler than vacuum tubes. They have no hot parts to burn out. About the only problem they have is from vibration, high-voltage spikes, and poor connections. The technology in the design and use of solid-state electronics grew rapidly. It is used for all radio and sound equipment, as well as electronic controls and computers. By the early 1980s automotive engine ignition and fuel metering were operated with solid-state electronic sensors, computers, and controls. By the mid-1980s a separate computer, called a body control module, was introduced to control the air conditioning, dashboard fuel center, suspension self-leveling, and other body systems.

The following discussion will give you enough understanding of the fundamentals of electronics to help you intelligently find faulty electronic parts in automobiles.

Technical words in this section you will need to learn:

Diode	*P*-type material
Doped	Reverse bias
Forward bias	Semiconductor
Junction	Wafer
N-type material	

Complex solid-state electronic parts use the same principles as those used by diodes. We will look at the diode first because it is the simplest solid-state electronic part. It is called a diode because it has two electrical leads.

It was stated in Section 1–1 that metallic atoms with less than four electrons in the outer orbit are good conductors. Atoms with more than four electrons are good insulators. Atoms with exactly four electrons are not good conductors or good insulators. Silicon and germanium are metals that have four electrons in their outer orbit. In pure crystalline form, atoms in the metal share each other's four electrons of their outer orbits. In effect, they each have eight electrons in their outer orbit, as shown in Figure 8–1. This makes this material a good insulator.

Let us see what happens when a very small amount of metal that has five electrons in its outer orbit is added to silicon. When a very small amount of different material is mixed into metal it is said to be **doped**. Phosphorus, arsenic, or antimony have five electrons in their outer orbit. When silicon is doped with phosphorus there is not enough space in the shared outer orbit for nine electrons, so a free electron is left. You can see this in Figure 8–2. This type of doped metal would be called negative or **N-type material** because it already has extra electrons. The *N*-type material will repel negative charges and electrons.

Boron or indium have only three electrons in their outer orbit. When a very small amount is added to silicon,

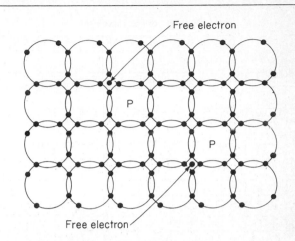

Figure 8–2 *N*-type material with two atoms of phosphorus that leaves two free electrons in the structure.

a gap or **hole** is left because there are only seven atoms in the outer orbit of the combined atoms. This is illustrated in Figure 8–3. A hole is a place where an electron is missing. Doped metal that has holes in the outer orbit is called positive or **P-type material**. The *P*-type material attracts a negative charge and electrons.

Movement of electrons and holes can be compared to heavy, slow-moving traffic. The cars are shown by the rectangles in Figure 8–4. Assume that the cars are in a line of traffic and that the first car (A) moves up one space. Each following car (B, C, D, etc.) in turn moves into the space ahead. The cars progress toward the left

Figure 8–3 *P*-type material with two atoms of boron. Two electrons are missing to leave two holes in the structure.

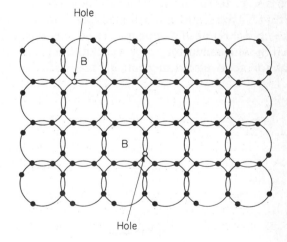

Figure 8–1 Atoms with four electrons in their outer orbit share the eight electrons in a structure.

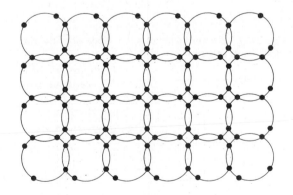

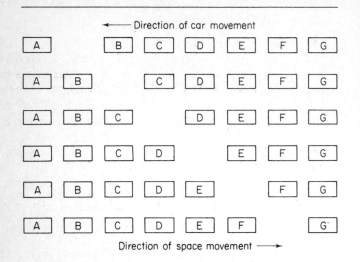

←— Direction of car movement

Direction of space movement —→

Figure 8-4   Electron and hole movement compared to vehicle movement in traffic.

Figure 8-6   The arrow shows a diode in a heavy metal case.

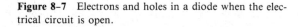

while the space moves toward the right. Electrons can be compared to the car and holes can be compared to the space. Electrons and holes move in opposite directions.

Semiconductor Material.   The *P*-type and *N*-type materials are called semiconductors. Semiconductors will conduct current in some circuits. In others, they will act as insulators. Semiconductors in automobile electronics are used in diodes and in transistors.

The diode semiconductor, shown in Figure 8-5, is made from a thin slice of crystal silicon called a **wafer**. The crystal wafer is about 0.007 in. (0.175 mm) thick. Boron is painted on one side and phosphorus on the other side of the crystal wafer. The doped wafer is put into a high-temperature furnace. It is heated until the doping materials are fused into the silicon. The place where *P*-type and *N*-type semiconductor materials come together in the crystal is called a **junction**. Following this, each side of the semiconductor wafer is plated with conducting metal for good electrical contact. The wafer is then

broken into chips about 3/16 in. (4.6 mm) square. The wafer is then put in a case for easy assembly into electrical circuits. One type of diode in a heavy metal case that was used in older alternators is shown in Figure 8-6.

Diode Operation.   Within the diode, the holes in the *P*-type material attract electrons from the *N*-type material toward the junction between the *P*-type and *N*-type materials. As the electrons move toward the junction they form negative ions along the junction. They leave holes in positive ions behind. Remember that negative ions are atoms that have an extra electron. Positive ions are missing an electron. The positive ions keep the electrons from crossing the junction into the *P*-type material. Figure 8-7 shows this movement. Notice that electrons are shown as small squares and holes are shown as small circles. Some electrons do drift across the junction. However, so few cross the junction that it does not affect the operation of the diode.

If the negative side of the diode in a circuit is connected to the *N*-type material and the positive side is connected to the *P*-type material, a current will flow

Figure 8-5   Symbol and section view of a diode.

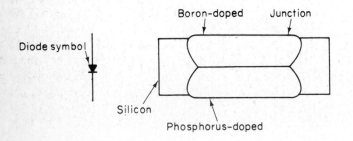

Boron-doped   Junction

Diode symbol

Silicon

Phosphorus-doped

Figure 8-7   Electrons and holes in a diode when the electrical circuit is open.

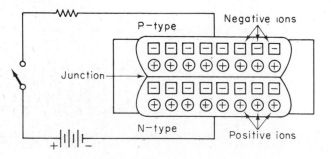

P-type   Negative ions

Junction

N-type   Positive ions

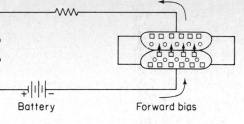

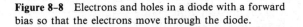
Electrons flow across junction

Figure 8-8 Electrons and holes in a diode with a forward bias so that the electrons move through the diode.

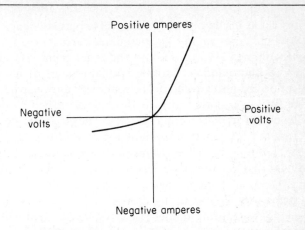

Figure 8-10 Curve showing how a diode conducts current as the voltage changes.

across the diode. This is called a **forward bias**. It is shown in Figure 8-8. Diodes have a resistance of about 5 to 10 Ω when connected in forward bias. Electrons from the circuit put more electrons into the N-type material. These electrons will satisfy the holes in the positive ions that had been holding electrons from crossing the junction. As a result the holes no longer hold the electrons from crossing the junction. The electrons at the junction will then move across the junction. Electrons that move across the junction are continually replaced with new electrons from the battery. This lets the forward bias current flow through the diode.

If the diode connections are reversed, a **reverse bias** will be formed. Holes in the P-type material are attracted by the negative side of the circuit. The electrons in the N-type material are attracted by the positive side of the circuit. This causes both the electrons of the N-type material and the holes of the P-type material to move away from the junction as shown in Figure 8-9. There is almost no current flow across the junction when the holes and electrons move away from the junction. Diodes have a reverse bias resistance of 1 million ohms or more.

The diode is used as a **one-way electrical check**. It works like the check valves in the fuel pump and oil filter. The diode will allow current to flow when there is a forward bias by acting as a conductor. It will keep the current from flowing backward when it has a reverse bias by acting as an insulator. This is shown on the graph in

Figure 8-10. You can see why this material is called a semiconductor. It conducts current only when it is connected with a forward bias.

Too much voltage, either forward or reverse biased, will force too much current across the semiconductor junction. This will overheat the semiconductor. If the voltage is high enough, the current will melt the semiconductor. This will open the circuit.

Some special diodes are heavily doped so that they can carry reverse currents without damage. When diodes are made in this way, they are called **zener diodes**. The reverse-biased voltage at which the zener diode conducts is called the zener point. This is shown in Figure 8-11. Zener diodes are used in electronic systems for voltage control (see Section 9-4). At less than the designed reverse-biased voltage, they act as a normal diode conducting only when they have a forward-biased voltage.

Figure 8-11 Curve showing how a zener diode conducts current as the voltage changes.

Figure 8-9 Electrons and holes in a diode with a reverse bias.

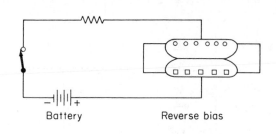
No electrons flow across junction

They act as insulators when the reverse-biased voltage is below the zener point. They conduct current when the reverse-biased voltage is above the zener point voltage.

A photodiode is another special type of diode. It is connected into an electrical circuit with a reverse bias. The light energy that hits the diode is absorbed by the silicone to form electrons and holes. The electrons move across the *PN* junction to allow the reverse-biased current to flow. The current is proportional to the amount of light that hits the diode. Photo diodes are about 0.020 in. (0.05 mm) square. They are often used as sensors in systems with light-emitting diodes.

Light-emitting diodes (LEDs) give off light when they conduct a forward-biased current. The *N*-type material of these diodes is gallium arsenide and the *P*-type material is gallium phosphide. The ratio between the arsenide and phosphide controls the color of the light emitted.

The LED gives a small spot of light. The light is expanded with reflectors and lenses for electronic displays. Seven LEDs are often used to make number readouts. Light from a LED can be carried through fiber-optic light pipes to control a photodiode. A mechanical shutter can be used between the LED and photodiode to turn the photodiode on and off. This type of system was used in place of contact points in some early electronic ignition systems. The LED–photodiode system is used for a sensor in some speedometers to let the engine control computer know the vehicle speed. These systems are also used inside some air-level shock absorbers to sense the correct vehicle height. The sensor controls air valves to readjust the vehicle height when it is too high or too low.

8–2 TRANSISTOR SEMICONDUCTORS

Technical words in this section you will need to learn:

Analog	Integrated
Base	Linear
Bipolar	Masking
Chip	*NPN*
Collector	*PNP*
Emitter	Proportional
Encapsel	Transistor
Field effect	Variable resistor
Heat sink	

Diodes used in automobiles are usually made of doped silicon crystals. Transistors are usually made from germanium crystals using indium to dope *P*-type material and antimony to dope *N*-type material. A diode is made of two materials, *P* type junctioned to *N* type. It has two electrical leads. Transistors add another junction to the diode, forming either *PNP* or *NPN* transistors. They have three electrical leads, so they are sometimes called triodes. Transistors have at least two semiconductor junctions.

Transistor Construction.   In large transistors a metal ring is connected to the outer edge of the center *N*-type material, as illustrated in Figure 8–12. An extension from the ring is used to connect to the conductor. This center *N*-type material of the transistor is called the **base**. The transistor is placed in a copper case with the larger *P*-type area pressed tightly against the inner surface of the container. In this way the case becomes an electrical connection called the **collector**. The container also acts as a heat sink. The **heat sink** removes heat from the transistor to help keep it cool. A strip of metal connected to the smaller size *P*-type material is an electrical connection called an **emitter**. This transistor assembly is brazed

Figure 8–12   Typical transistor construction.

PNP transistor schematic

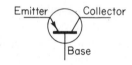

PNP power transistor construction

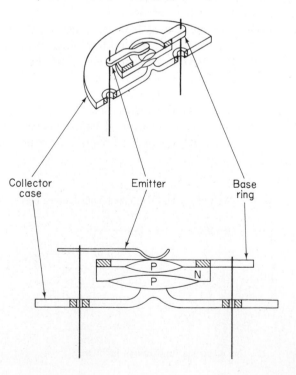

together and sealed into the case to form a large transistor. Plastic is poured around small transistors to seal them. This encapsulates the transistor so that it is not affected by moisture or vibration. Wire leads from the encapsulated transistor are used to connect the emitter, collector, and base to the electrical circuit. In each of these transistors the actual transistor is only a very small wafer crystal. Connections and case make up most of the size of the transistor assembly.

Some transistors are integrated into a complete electronic circuit. **Integrated** means that the transistor and circuits are made together in a single part. The integrated electronic circuit starts with a silicon or germanium crystal wafer about 3 in. (75 mm) in diameter. The wafer is coated with a ceramic insulation. The insulation is masked where insulation is needed. Masking is like covering a window before an automobile is painted. Where it is not masked, the ceramic insulation is removed with chemicals to clean the wafer material. Doping material is fused into the clean wafer material. The wafer is again coated with ceramic coating, masked and cleaned in other places, and then another doping material is used. In some places conductors are formed. In other places resistors and capacitors are made. This process builds many complete and duplicate electrical circuits with transistors, diodes, conductors, insulators, resistors, and capacitors within a single large wafer. The wafer is scribed between the circuits and is then broken into **chips**. Each chip is a complete circuit with all of the operating parts of the circuit. Complex integrated circuits are formed in chips made for microcomputer engine controls, as shown in Figure 8-13. These complete circuit chips are encapsulated with electrical leads for connection to the engine sensors and controls.

Figure 8-13 Many integrated-circuit chips are made from one crystal wafer.

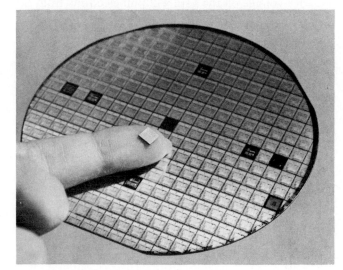

Transistor Operation. A *PNP*-type transistor will be used to describe the operation of a transistor. The *N*-type base in the middle of the transistor is made as thin as possible. *P*-type material on the outside forms the emitter and collector. The emitter is connected through the electrical load to the positive side of the battery. The collector is connected to the negative side of the battery. The transistor base circuit is used to control transistor operation. It is connected through a control switch to the negative side of the battery.

In Figure 8-14 the base circuit control switch is open. Electrons are always trying to fill holes to make neutral atoms in the transistor. Holes supplied by the battery positive terminal form along the emitter side of the emitter–base junction. Electrons supplied by the negative side of the battery form along the collector–base junction. The open base keeps the holes in the emitter from crossing the junction into the collector.

When the base circuit switch is closed, as illustrated in Figure 8-15, the base and collector are both negative.

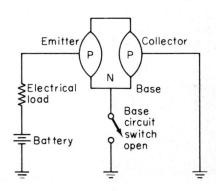

Figure 8-14 Transistor circuit with an open base circuit.

Figure 8-15 Transistor circuit with the base circuit conducting.

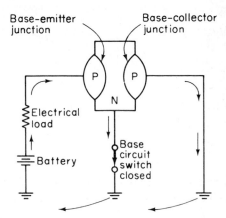

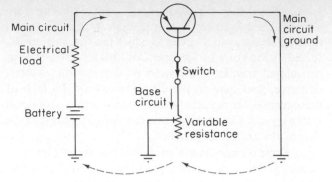

Figure 8–17 Schematic drawing of a basic transistor circuit.

The negative base attracts the holes across the emitter–base junction. From the base the holes go through the base circuit switch to the negative side of the battery. As holes from the emitter cross the junction to the base, their energy carries most of them on across the base–collector junction through the collector and on to the negative terminal of the battery. The emitter–collector current carries the current through the electrical load. This type of transistor is called a bipolar transistor. It uses two poles, positive (holes) and negative (electrons), for its operation.

Hole movement across the emitter–base junction stops when the base circuit control switch is reopened. The charges within the transistor become neutral and hole movement from the emitter to the collector stops. This also stops current flow through the electrical load. A transistor used in this way is a solid-state switch or relay. It still requires some way to start and stop current flow through the base.

The transistor works similar to the relay, shown as Figure 1–27. When the control switch (like the base circuit switch) is closed, magnetism closes the contact points. This lets a large amount of current flow from the battery through the relay to carry current through the electrical load (like the emitter–collector current). A small current continues to flow through the magnetic coil while the points carry a large current.

Current flowing from the emitter to the collector in a transistor is nearly proportional to the base *current*. This means that when the base current is doubled, the emitter–collector current is nearly doubled. The proportional change can be plotted as a line on a graph similar to Figure 8–16. A circuit with this type of proportional change is called a linear circuit or an **analog** circuit. Let us look at this proportional change using the transistor circuit shown in Figure 8–17. This figure is a schematic

drawing of Figure 8–15, with a variable resistance added to the base circuit. A variable resistance acts like the volume control on a radio. When the volume control is turned up (less resistance) more current flows. As more current flows in the base circuit, proportionally more current will flow in the emitter–conductor circuit. The base current carries only about 2.0% of the total current flowing from the emitter. The rest of the current flows to the collector.

You should remember that we have been looking at the operation of a *PNP* transistor. A great many transistors used in automobiles are *NPN* transistors. You can follow their operation in the same way we have just done. The only changes you will need to make are to replace holes with electrons and reverse the polarity put on each connection.

In addition to the bipolar transistor just described, automotive electronics use **field-effect transistors.** They are metal-oxide semiconductors (MOS). A simplified illustration of a field-effect transistor is shown in Figure 8–18. This type of transistor has three connections: source, gate, and drain. The source and drain contact N-type material and the gate contacts P-type material. A strong positive voltage on the gate will pull electrons from the

Figure 8–16 Curve showing how the transistor emitter-collector and base currents change with changes in voltage.

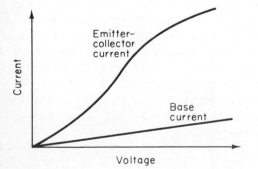

Figure 8–18 Simplified drawing of a field-effect transistor.

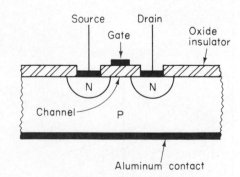

P-type material so rapidly that the area under the gate, called the **channel,** becomes negative. The electrons in the channel form an electrical bridge between the source and drain materials. Current can flow from the source to the drain through the electrons in the channel. The amount of current flow between source and drain in a MOS is proportional to the *voltage* on the gate. More voltage on the gate will put more electrons in the channel. This forms a better conductor so that more current can flow. Notice that the current flow of the field-effect transistor is controlled by voltage on the gate. Remember that the current flow of the *PNP* and *NPN* transistors is controlled by the current flow through the base circuit.

A floating gate has been added to some field-effect transistors, as shown in Figure 8–19. Electrons collect in the channel when there is a positive-charge on the upper gate. This acts the same as the transistor in Figure 8–18. When the upper gate is charged it will charge the floating gate. The charge stays in the floating gate when the charge is removed from the upper gate because the floating gate is insulated from the rest of the connections. The action is something like the way a condenser holds a charge. The floating gate holds its charge until a negative charge is put on the transistor gate. This will discharge the floating gate. As long as the floating gate has a charge it will hold electrons in the channel so that the transistor can conduct current from the source to the drain. You could say that the transistor had a **memory** to continue to conduct the way it had been charged.

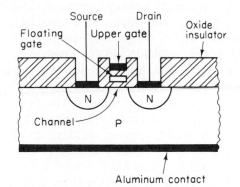

Figure 8-19 Simplified drawing of a floating-gate field-effect transistor.

8–3 AUTOMOTIVE COMPUTERS

Technical words in this section you will need to learn:

Actuator	Gate
Computer	Logic circuit
Flip-flop	Sensor

Computers in automobiles use thousands of transistors in integrated microchips, along with conductors, insulators, resistors, and capacitors. **Sensors,** for engine rpm, engine temperature, manifold vacuum, atmospheric pressure, oxygen in the exhaust, and so on, are wired to the computer. The computer compares the signal it gets from the sensors to directions stored in the **memory** of the computer. It then computes the action needed. The action signal is sent to **actuators.** The actuators make the adjustments needed. Engine idle-speed control, cruise control, ignition timing advance, and carburetor mixture control are examples of computer-controlled actuators.

As an automotive service technician, you will not be expected to repair computers, sensors, or actuators. If a computer, sensor, or actuator is faulty, you will replace it. Most computer-related problems are caused by poor electrical connections, faulty sensors, and faulty actuators. We will discuss only enough about computers to help you to know what the symbols on circuit drawings mean and how the computer fits into the electrical system of the automobile. This should help you diagnose computer-related problems.

Transistors used in analog computers have outputs that change as the current in the base circuit changes (see Figure 8–17). Transistors used in digital computers are either off or on. The OFF position is called **logic zero.** ON is called **logic one.** You see that this logic system uses a base of two numbers, 0 and 1. It is called a **binary logic** system because it has only two positions (off and on). The decimal logic system, including the metric system, has a base-numbering system of 10 (numbers 1 through 10). When measuring time we use a base of 12 (1 o'clock through 12 o'clock).

Low voltage on a transistor turns the transistor OFF (logic 0). High voltage (5 V in automotive computers) turns the transistor ON (logic 1). Transistors are assembled together to form specialized logic circuits. These logic circuits are called gates. Logic symbols for typical gates are shown in Figure 8–20. When two signals must work together to allow current to flow, the gate is called an AND gate. When either one or the other of two signals will allow current to flow, the gate is called an OR gate. Sometimes it is necessary to reverse the input logic signal to the opposite output logic signal (1 to 0 or 0 to 1). Reversing the output signal logic from the input signal logic is called inverting. A NOT gate inverts the incoming logic signal to the opposite output logic signal. The NOT gate is usually called an inverter.

A more complex gate is called a NAND gate. This gate is an AND gate followed by an inverter. A NOR gate

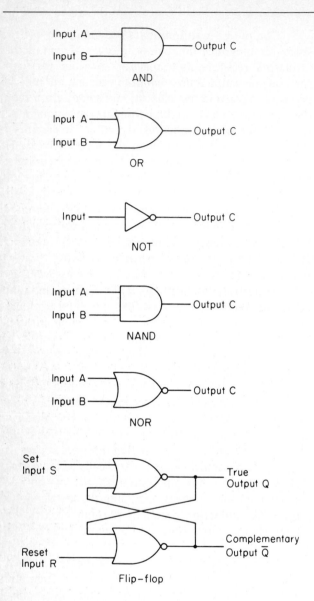

Figure 8-20 Logic symbols for typical gates.

is an OR gate followed by an inverter. Two OR gates can be cross-connected to form a **flip-flop**. Once the logic of a flip-flop is set with an input signal, it holds the same logic until it is reset by the opposite input. It is an important part of the memory. As a result, flip-flops have become the building blocks for computers.

You have little use for these logic symbols unless you are in a specialized shop that repairs computers. It is more practical to use block diagrams to show complex assemblies used in computers. This is done in the following discussion.

In many computers a series of flip-flops are connected together as a binary counter. This is illustrated in Figure 8-21. In this binary counter the "complementary output" $\overline{Q}$ terminal of a flip-flop is fed back into the flip-flop "set input" S terminal. Connected in this way, each output pulse of the flip-flop reverses its logic. The output of each flip-flop in the series is used as a clock signal to the "reset input" $\overline{R}$ terminal of the next flip-flop in the series. The flip-flop reverses on each clock pulse.

Figure 8-22 shows how the string of flip-flops acts as a binary counter. Look at the first column. Notice that the flip-flop 1 reverses between logic 0 and logic 1 each time the clock pulses. You can see in the second column that flip-flop 2 reverses on each logic 0 signal from flip-flop 1. As a result, flip-flop 2 counts only half as fast as flip-flop 1. Again, flip-flop 3 gets its input signal from the logic 0 pulse from flip-flop 2, as shown in column 3. Flip-flop 3 switches logic half as fast as flip-flop 2. As a result, flip-flop 1 has to switch logic four times for each time flip-flop 3 switches logic. Flip-flop 4 switches half as fast as flip-flop 3. This requires eight 0 logic pulses of flip-flop 1 to switch the logic of flip-flop 4. This is shown in the fourth column. Because flip-flop 4 has two positions, a binary counter with four flip-flops has 16 positions (0 through 15). Each of these positions is called a **bit**. A group of 8 bits is called a **byte**. Adding a fifth flip-flop would make a binary counter of 32 bits. A binary counter with six flip-flops would have 64 bits. Many automotive digital computers have a seven flip-flop binary counter with 128 bits (16 bytes).

Have you ever thought about how you do a math problem? You first see or hear the problem. You are using your eyes and ears as sensors. You have learned to recognize symbols and to write problems. You have also learned how to add, subtract, multiply, and divide. You learned to do this by memory. If the problem is complex, you use a scratch pad on which to work the problem. You keep the notes on the scratch pad until the problem is finished, then you throw it away. Your answer is given by the numbers you write or the words you speak.

A calculator (which is a simple computer) works in a similar manner. The keys are the sensors. First, you push the function key. This tells the calculator which part

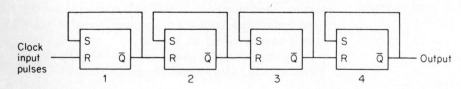

Clock input pulses

Output

1   2   3   4

Figure 8-21 Flip-flops connected together to form a binary counter.

Number of clock pulses	Flip - flop			
	1	2	3	4
0	0	0	0	0
1	1	0	0	0
2	0	1	0	0
3	1	1	0	0
4	0	0	1	0
5	1	0	1	0
6	0	1	1	0
7	1	1	1	0
8	0	0	0	1
9	1	0	0	1
10	0	1	0	1
11	1	1	0	1
12	0	0	1	1
13	1	0	1	1
14	0	1	1	1
15	1	1	1	1

The next clock pulse would switch back to zero and start the sequence over again.

Figure 8-22 How a string of four flip-flops acts as a binary counter.

of the built-in memory it must use (add, subtract, multiply, or divide). The built-in memory is called the ROM (read-only memory). Second, you push the number keys in the correct order. The calculator has a scratch pad where it can work the problem. It is called the RAM (random access memory). In a calculator the information on the scratch pad shows up on the display. These numbers can be put into a temporary memory to be used at a later time. When the power is turned off, all the temporary memory and the information in the RAM scratch pad is lost. Many automotive computers are always connected to battery power, even when the ignition switch is off,

so they do not lose the information in the temporary memory.

Automotive computers are designed to control vehicle actuators correctly. They need to have different calibration in memories when the automobile has different engines, transmissions, weight, gear ratios, tire sizes, and so on. It would be very costly to have separate computers designed with each of the different calibrations needed. To solve this problem, computers are built with common ROMs and RAMs. Automotive computers have an added memory that calibrates the computer for the specific vehicle being used. This calibration microprocessor is called a PROM (programmable read-only memory). Programming the memory of the PROM can be compared to recording on a cassette tape. The pickup in the microphone or record player sends a signal to an amplifier. The amplifier processes the pickup signal. The processed signal is sent on to the tape. The metal oxide on the tape is changed so that it will always reproduce the same signal when it is played back. Flip-flops and floating-gate metal-oxide semiconductors (MOS) hold their logic like a cassette tape when they are programmed. We call this programming the memory. The MOS transistor must have a positive voltage on the upper gate to change the floating gate to program its memory. It will always conduct at the same rate until it is reprogrammed. The program built into the computer ROM and the PROM tells the computer what to do when it receives certain signals from the sensors. The computer reads the memory, follows the program, and outputs the results.

You know that you can normally erase the signal from a cassette tape. After you have broken the tabs off the cassette, the tape can only be played; it cannot be re-recorded. The computer PROM is also made in this way. When the PROM has been programmed, small connections are removed so that the program cannot be changed.

STUDY QUESTIONS

Section 8-1

1. What makes a semiconductor material *N*-type?

2. What makes a semiconductor material *P*-type?

3. How do holes in the *P*-type material affect electrons in the *N*-type material?

4. When is a semiconductor said to be connected in forward bias?

5. Where do the electrons come from to replace the electrons that move across the semiconductor junction?

6. What keeps electricity from flowing through a semiconductor when there is a reverse bias?

7. Why are materials called semiconductors?

8. What happens to a semiconductor when the voltage is too high?

9. How does a zener diode differ from a normal diode?

10. What causes a photodiode to conduct?

11. What causes a light emitting diode to give off light?

Section 8-2

12. Why can a transistor be called a triode?

13. What part of a transistor is called the base?

14. What makes up the largest part of the transistor assembly?

15. What is an integrated circuit?

16. What makes current flow from the emitter to the collector?

17. What happens to the emitter-collector current when the base current is doubled?

18. What connection on a MOS transistor has the same effect as the base of a normal transistor?

19. Base current causes current to flow through a normal transistor. What causes current to flow through a MOS transistor?

20. What is the advantage of a floating gate on a MOS transistor?

Section 8-3

21. Make a list of engine sensors.

22. Make a list of engine actuators.

23. What three things cause most computer problems in vehicles?

24. What is binary logic?

25. What does an AND gate do?

26. What does an OR gate do?

27. What does a NOT gate do?

28. What does a flip-flop do?

29. How many computer bits are in a byte?

30. Why are automotive computers connected to the battery all the time?

THE CHARGING
SYSTEM

The charging system has a belt-driven generator, a regulator to limit maximum voltage, and electrical wiring to connect it into the vehicle electrical system.

The generator is large enough to supply all the electrical current required in normal vehicle operation and still charge the battery. The battery supplies electricity to the vehicle's electrical system when more electricity is needed than the charging system can deliver. This electricity is needed when the engine is idling and when many accessories and lights are turned on. The battery also supplies the high electrical demand of power windows, horns, power antennas, and so on.

9–1 CHARGING PRINCIPLES

Technical words in this section you will need to learn:

Alternator	Rotor
Pole shoe	Slip ring
Rectified	Stator

The alternator (diode-rectified generator) makes use of electromagnetic induction principles described in Section 1–9. Motion between magnetic lines of force and a conductor in the alternator will force the electrons to drift in one direction. This forced drift is caused by EMF (voltage) in the conductor. The strength of this voltage is based on the number of lines of magnetic force cutting the conductor each second.

You will remember that more magnetic lines of force can be made to cut a conductor in three ways:

1. By increasing the speed at which the lines cut the conductor
2. By increasing the number of windings in the conductor
3. By increasing the magnetic field strength

The alternator is belt driven, so its speed is based on the engine speed. Therefore, speed cannot be used for controlling the output of the alternator. The number of conductor windings is part of the alternator design. It cannot be used to control voltage in the electrical system of an operating vehicle. Alternator voltage is very effectively limited in a charging system by changing the strength of the magnetic field. Alternators are made so that they will produce maximum output (amperes) when maximum electrical system voltage is placed across the field winding. This causes maximum current to flow in the field winding and this will produce maximum magnetic field strength. *The voltage regulator controls the field strength by reducing the amount of current going through the field.* This will limit the voltage produced by the alternator to the maximum voltage needed by the electrical system.

A section view of an automotive alternator is shown in Figure 9–1. The main conductor is wound in a frame. This assembly is called a **stator**. A field winding is wound around an iron hub in the **rotor** assembly. It is supported on a shaft and bearings. Pole shoes on the rotor concentrate the magnetic lines of force from the field windings. The rotor spins inside the stator assembly.

Each end of the rotating field coil within the rotor is brought to a copper **slip ring**. Both slip rings are insulated from the shaft. Carbon brushes ride against the rotating slip rings (Figure 9–2). The brushes connect the field windings to the voltage regulator circuit.

In operation, current flows in series through the voltage regulator and the field windings in the rotor. This current magnetizes the rotor pole shoes. One pole shoe has a north pole and the other a south pole. By holding a screwdriver close to the rear alternator bearing you can feel the rotor magnetism while the alternator is charging. As the rotor turns, the magnetism around the pole shoes cuts across the stator windings, as shown in Figure 9–3. This induces voltage in the windings of the stator. Voltage in the stator windings will do nothing unless two other conditions are met. The stator must be connected

Fig. 9–2 Brushes ride against rotating slip rings.

Fig. 9–3 Alternating polarity of the pole shoes.

Fig. 9–1 Section view of a typical alternator. (Courtesy Delco-Remy Division, General Motors Corporation.)

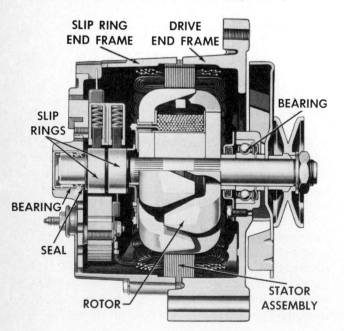

into a completed electrical circuit and the stator voltage must be greater than circuit voltage.

Stator. Alternator stators are made with three separate windings. A number of separate coils are connected in series within each winding. The coils in each winding are spaced so that the magnetic field polarity is the same on each coil at the same time. Each coil adds voltage to the winding. In this way each complete stator winding is able to produce the designed voltage.

All three windings are connected together. The most common connection used in automobile alternators is a Y (wye)-connection; however, some alternators use a delta connection. Alternators with Y-connection stators start charging at lower speeds and have lower maximum output than alternators with delta connection stators. Both

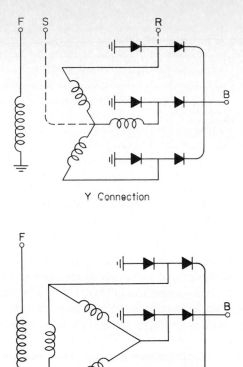

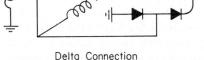

Fig. 9-4 Y and Δ stator winding connections.

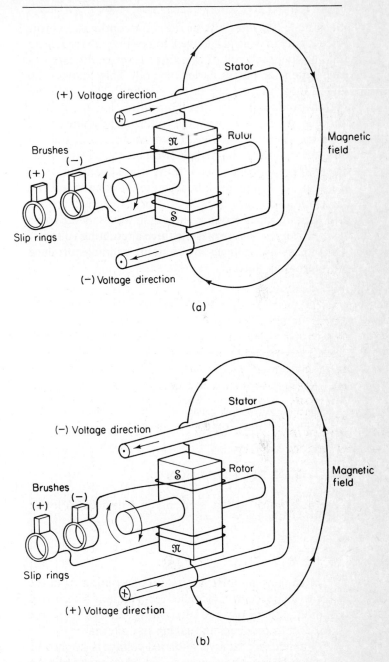

Fig. 9-5 How alternator voltage is produced in the stator.

are illustrated in Figure 9-4 and they operate in a similar way. The three windings in a Y-connection type used in most automobiles are connected together at the Y-junction. The other end of each winding goes to one pair of diodes. The opposite side of the diodes are connected to the charging system. In the Δ (delta)-connection the ends of the three windings are connected to form a triangle. A conductor goes from each of the three winding connections to a pair of diodes.

Rotor. The pole shoe fingers of the alternator rotor are spaced N–S–N–S–N–S, and so on, around the rotor (see Figure 9-3). North and south magnetic fields from the rotor pole shoes keep alternating as they cut through the stator windings as the rotor turns. The alternating fields cause the electrons in the stator windings to be forced one way, then back the other way. This produces an alternating voltage in the stator windings as shown in Figure 9-5. If the stator was connected directly to an outside circuit, the alternating voltage would make an alternating current (ac). Automotive electrical systems, however, require the voltage and current to be in one direction. This is called direct current (dc). Alternating current needs to be **rectified** to become direct current.

The voltage gets stronger as more magnetic lines of force cut the winding each second. The magnetic field

starts from zero when the center of the pole shoe finger is centered under the stator coils. As the rotor turns, the number of magnetic lines of force cutting the winding increases until it reaches a maximum. This happens when the fingers of the pole shoe are on each side of the coils. Voltage again drops to zero when the rotor shoe finger is centered under the next stator coil. The following pole shoe finger has the opposite polarity. Its polarity causes the voltage to go negative as the rotor continues to turn. Then it goes to neutral and back to positive. The magnetic field cutting each coil of the stator reverses direction as each pole shoe passes under the coil. This changes the direction of the voltage in the winding. The continual buildup and reduction, first in one direction and then in another, produces a sine-wave voltage. The name comes from the trigonometric function called sine. In Figure 9-5 a single conductor and a single two-pole magnet are used. The voltage is proportional to the trigonometric sine of the angle of the magnet in relation to the conductor. The three stationary windings in a rotor are equally spaced and their voltages produce three sine waves as the rotor turns. Figure 9-6 illustrates the three alternating voltages. The alternating voltages in the stator windings produce an alternating current.

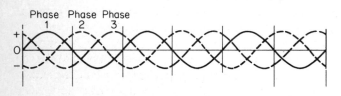

Fig. 9-6 Alternating voltage from the three phases of a stator. (Courtesy The Prestolite Company.)

9-2 DIODE RECTIFICATION

Technical words in this section you will need to learn:

> Full-wave
>
> Half-wave

Changing an alternating current coming from the stator to a direct current is called rectification. Alternators use diodes to rectify the alternating current from the stator to a direct current leaving the alternator.

Remember that reverse-biased voltage is stopped by a semiconductor. Only forward-biased voltage can push current through a semiconductor. With one diode the forward-biased half of the stator output would flow in the circuit and the reverse bias would be blocked. This is called half-wave rectification. The maximum electrical output from alternators would be low with half-wave rectification.

Full-wave rectification converts both halves of the sine wave to the forward direction, as shown in Figure 9-7. This is done with one positive and one negative diode connected in parallel at each stator junction. The output

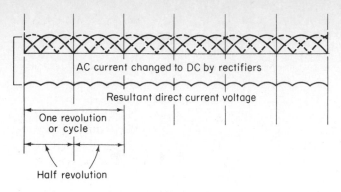

Fig. 9-7 Full-wave rectification. (Courtesy The Prestolite Company.)

side of one diode goes to the charging system (BAT terminal). The output of the other diode goes to ground. You can see this connection in Figure 9-4. The electrical circuit only senses maximum voltage from the three windings. The result is a voltage ripple in the forward (positive) direction.

The voltage reverses within the stator windings, but the outside circuit from the alternator battery (BAT) terminal is always in the forward direction. This one-way voltage is the force that moves a direct current through the charging system when the circuit is completed.

Battery current cannot flow through the diodes when the engine is not running because the battery puts a reverse-biased voltage on each of the diodes. The alternator voltage has to increase above battery voltage to put a forward-biased voltage on the diodes. This causes them to conduct current so that the alternator can charge the battery and supply current to operate electrical accessories.

9-3 CHARGING SYSTEM

The main part of the insulated charging circuit is a wire between the alternator BAT terminal and a junction point where the alternator can send electricity to the vehicle electrical system and the battery. Vehicle manufacturers use a number of different junction points. These include the BAT terminal of the starter solenoid, a junction block on the radiator support or inner fender pan, and the positive battery terminal. The ground side of the charging circuit is the metal-to-metal contact between the alternator case and the engine. Sometimes a ground wire is added. The engine is connected to the negative battery post by the battery ground cable.

The voltage regulator is an important part of the charging system. It is connected in series with the field winding in the rotor. The voltage regulator controls electrical current going through the field to limit the voltage supplied by the alternator. Mechanical regulators are connected to feed current into the rotor field. This is the positive side of the field coil. The other end of the field is grounded inside the alternator. This type of field circuit is an internally grounded B circuit. In most systems with solid-state regulators one end of the field is fed from the electrical system. The other end of the field is grounded through the regulator on the negative side of the field coil. This type of field circuit is called an externally grounded A circuit.

A switch in the regulator field circuit opens the circuit when the engine is not running. It closes the circuit when the engine starts. Chrysler vehicles use a heavy-duty ignition switch to feed electrical power into the regulator field circuit. Ford and General Motors vehicles use a standard-duty ignition switch to energize a field relay in the voltage regulator case. The field relay connects the regulator field circuit to the electrical circuit of the vehicle.

The charging circuit includes an indicator to show battery charge or discharge. It may be a charge indicator light, an ammeter, or a voltmeter. The charge indicator light will turn on when the alternator is not charging. The ammeter shows the amount of charge or discharge. The voltmeter shows the electrical system voltage, normally this is regulator voltage. The battery is discharging as it supplies electricity when the voltmeter shows a system voltage of 12.5 V or less.

Mechanical regulator operation is used in the following discussion because it is easier for you to see how regulators work with switches than with transistors. An indicator lamp is connected parallel to a resistor in the circuit between the ignition switch and the regulator. It connects to the Delco-Remy terminal 4 and the Ford terminal 1 on the mechanical regulators. It is connected to the number 1 terminal of integrated-circuit Delco-Remy alternators. When the ignition switch is turned on, field current is supplied through the parallel-wired resistor and indicator lamp. You can see this in the schematic drawing of a mechanical regulator Delco-Remy circuit in Figure 9–8. A schematic diagram of a Ford mechanical regulator would be almost like this regulator, but it has different terminal numbers. The external wiring of a Ford alternator is shown in Figure 9–9. If the indicator lamp bulb burns out, the resistor will still feed field current. When the alternator starts to charge, the Delco alternator R or Ford alternator S terminal feeds a small amount of current to the field relay winding through the Delco regulator 2 terminal or Ford regulator S terminal. This small current energizes the coil of the field relay to close the relay contact points. The closed points connect the Delco regulator 3 and 4 terminals and the Ford regulator I and A+ terminals to battery voltage. The closed field relay points effectively connect both terminals of the indicator lamp. The voltage is equal on both lamp terminals so no current will flow through the lamp bulb. As a result the charge lamp goes out. It stays out as long as the alternator is charging, even when part of the electrical power is being taken from the battery.

Fig. 9–8 Schematic diagram of a Delco-Remy mechanical regulator.

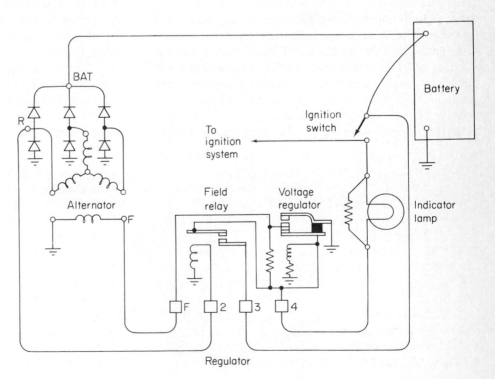

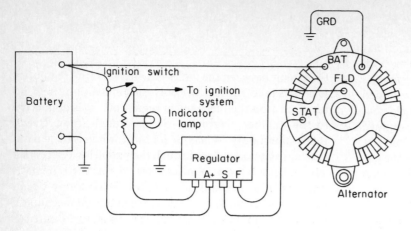

Fig. 9-9 External wiring of a Ford alternator.

The ammeter, as used in Chrysler charging systems, is connected between the hot lead on the starter relay and the junction going to the fusable links feeding the vehicle electrical system. You can see in Figure 9-10 that this makes the ammeter parallel to part of the electrical system. The ammeter actually indicates current by checking the polarity and amount of voltage drop across a fixed resistance in the electrical system. This section forms the ammeter shunt. The ammeter shows charge when the alternator is producing more output than the vehicle electrical system can use. This makes the alternator more positive than the battery. This extra electricity is used to charge the battery. It shows discharge when the alternator cannot supply enough electrical current by itself. This makes the alternator less positive than the battery. During discharge the battery is supplying some of the current that the electrical system needs.

Import automobiles have used voltmeters for a number of years as charge indicators. Domestic vehicles started to use them in the late 1970s. The voltmeter is connected to the instrument or gauge fuse so that it will measure voltage when the ignition switch is turned to the run position. The battery open-circuit voltage can be checked by turning the ignition switch on without cranking the engine. Remember, the open-circuit battery voltage will indicate the battery state of charge. The voltage while cranking indicates the condition of the cranking circuit. Once the engine is running the voltmeter is used to indicate the condition of the charging system. With all accessories turned *off* and the engine running, the voltage should be near 14 V. With all accessories turned *on* and the engine running at a moderate speed, the voltmeter should read 13.5 V or more.

9-4 CHARGING-SYSTEM REGULATION

The battery regulates the voltage in the charging system any time the voltage is below the regular voltage setting. The regulator limits the maximum charging-system *voltage* to the regulated voltage. If the voltage would go too high, it would try to overcharge the battery. This would ruin the battery. High voltage would also burn out the electrical accessories by forcing too much current through them.

The maximum *current* produced by the alternator is limited by inductance built into the alternator. Inductance was discussed in Section 1-9. The current being produced by the alternator (output) depends on the voltage in the charging system and the current flowing in the field.

Fig. 9-10 External wiring of a Chrysler alternator.

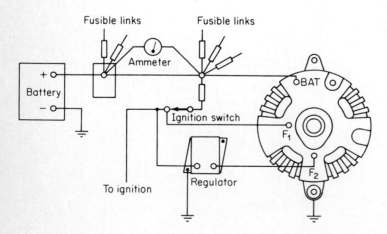

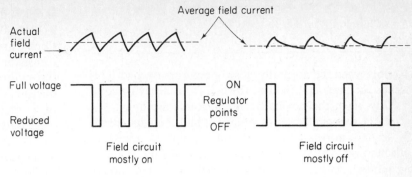

Fig. 9-11 Graph illustrating how the on-off periods of the regulator control the average field current.

Actual field current

Average field current

Full voltage

ON

Reduced voltage

Regulator points

OFF

Field circuit mostly on

Field circuit mostly off

Battery Regulation. The battery supplies electrical power to crank the engine. If the starter cranks a long time, quite a bit of electrical energy is taken from the battery. This causes a lower battery voltage. As soon as the engine starts, the charging system begins to supply electricity to the vehicle accessories and to recharge the battery. While the battery CEMF (counter electromotive force) is low, the battery accepts a high charging current. As the battery becomes charged, its CEMF increases. This decreases the charging current. The higher battery CEMF causes an increase in the voltage of the entire charging system. When battery CEMF reaches the regulator voltage setting, the regulator begins to take control to keep the voltage from going any higher (see Figure 3-7).

Voltage Regulation. Maximum electrical system voltage is controlled by adjusting the magnetic strength of the rotor field. This is done by changing the amount of current flowing in the coil windings of the rotor. The regulator does this by switching the field voltage on and off. The longer it is **on** compared to being **off**, the stronger the average field current will be. The timing of the on-off cycle is changed by the regulator to limit maximum charging-system voltage produced by the alternator. This is illustrated in Figure 9-11.

Mechanical regulators. The first alternators used mechanical voltage regulators. Solid-state regulators were introduced in the early 1970s. By 1980 nearly all automobiles were using solid-state regulators.

The mechanical voltage regulator has breaker points mounted on an armature above a voltage-sensitive coil (Figure 9-12). The normally closed points of the voltage regulator are connected in series with the field. They put **full** electrical system voltage across the field coil to make the strongest possible magnetic field.

The voltage regulator points are held closed with an adjustable point spring. The magnetic force of the coil pulls the regulator armature down to open the points when system voltage reaches the set voltage.

The magnetic strength of a coil is described as **ampere-turns**. A coil with a few turns carrying high current would have the same magnetic strength as a coil with many turns carrying a little current. The voltage regulator

coil is connected between the charging circuit and ground. The coil has a large number of windings (turns) of fine wire. This gives the coil a high resistance so it draws little current. The amperage or current flow in the coil windings is greatest at a high charging-system voltage. This makes the magnetism of the coil strong enough to pull on the spring-held armature. The **normally closed** points will separate to break field current flow. The graph in Figure 9-11 shows how the field current drops when the regulator points open. The points stay open until lower field current reduces the voltage put out by the alternator. The reduced charging system voltage weakens the magnetism of the regulator coil so that the armature spring closes the points. They stay closed until a higher system voltage increases the magnetic strength of the alternator field enough to open the regulator points again. This rapid open-close cycle continues all the time the regulator is controlling the voltage in the electrical system. An oscilloscope trace of the field current and voltage being controlled by a regulator is shown in Figure 1-36. When the points work in this way the action is called **dither.** You will use this term again when you study electronic engine control.

A resistor is used parallel with the regulator points to form a bypass so that some field current will continue

Fig. 9-12 Schematic diagram of a mechanical voltage regulator.

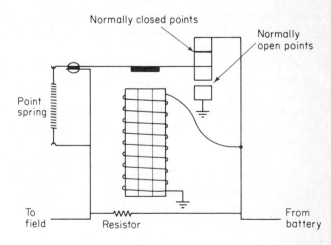

Normally closed points

Normally open points

Point spring

To field

Resistor

From battery

105

to flow when the normally closed points are opened. This keeps the magnetic field of the coil from decaying completely when the normally closed points are open.

To prevent excessive voltage at higher engine speeds a second **normally open** contact point is added to mechanical voltage regulators. This second point is grounded. At high alternator speeds more than enough current will flow through the resistor so that the voltage begins to go above the regulated voltage. This high-voltage forces more current through the voltage regulator coil winding. The stronger magnetism pulls the armature far enough to close the normally open voltage regulator points. The normally open points then direct all the current flowing through the resistor to ground. As a result, no current flows through the alternator field. This stops alternator output and the electrical system voltage begins to drop. When the voltage drops the spring opens the normally open grounding points, again allowing current to flow through the resistor to the field coil in the alternator. This action recycles, as the points vibrate (dither) on the normally open grounded point while there is high alternator rpm and little need for electricity.

Regulators are temperature compensated. They let the voltage go higher when they are cold. They lower the maximum voltage when they are hot. This helps to charge a cold battery and it prevents overcharging a hot battery.

Solid-state regulators. Mechanical regulators are being replaced by solid-state regulators. These regulators are made with no moving parts by making use of semiconductors, resistors, capacitors, and conductors. In some regulators, these parts are assembled from individual solid-state parts. Other regulators use a small single integrated circuit. The solid-state regulator parts work the same way regardless of how they are made.

The solid-state regulator has several advantages over the mechanical regulators. It can control higher field currents with improved durability and reliability. It is almost foolproof; it is smaller in size; and when manufactured at high production rates, it costs less than a mechanical regulator.

The solid-state regulator controls the alternator in the same way that the mechanical regulator controls maximum voltage. It turns the field current on and off. A power transistor in the solid-state regulator switches the alternator field circuit on and off. The power transistor is controlled by other small transistors, diodes, and resistors. You studied about these in Chapters 1 and 8.

It is important for you to understand the basic principles of transistor regulation to help you to understand how to test and trouble shoot solid-state regulators. A simplified solid-state regulator circuit is shown in Figure 9–13. Follow it as you study the description of its operation. Current comes from the battery to the emitter of transistor T_1. The base of T_1 is connected to the ground through resistor R_1, so it conducts. With the base conducting, current can go from the emitter to the collector of T_1 to supply full alternator field current.

Battery voltage is also at the emitter of transistor T_2. The base of T_2 is connected to the zener diode D_z, which is reverse biased. This does not allow base current to flow, so transistor T_2 is turned off. Battery voltage is at resistor R_2. A small current flows through R_2, variable resistor R_3, resistor R_4, and thermal resistor R_t to ground. There is a voltage drop across each resistor as current flows.

The zener diode is the voltage-sensing part in the solid-state regulator. When the reverse-biased voltage across the zener diode reaches its zener point, it will conduct current in the reverse direction. The reverse-biased voltage at the zener point is equal to the voltage drop across R_2 and part of R_3. Changing the connection point of the zener diode on variable resistance R_3 is used to adjust regulator settings, when solid-state regulators are adjustable.

When the zener diode conducts a reverse current, the base of transistor T_2 is turned on and T_2 conducts from the collector to ground through R_1, R_t, and R_4. The collector of T_2 places battery voltage on the base of transistor T_1. This is the same voltage as on the emitter of T_1. Therefore, there is no voltage drop between the T_1 transistor emitter and base, so T_1 is turned off. This stops the flow of field current. The alternator voltage drops when the field current stops. The lower alternator voltage reduces the reverse-biased voltage on the zener diode, so the diode stops conducting the base current of transistor T_2, turning T_2 off. The base current of transistor T_1 restarts current flow through R_1, turning T_1 back on. Then transistor T_1 begins to supply field current to the alter-

Fig. 9–13 Simplified basic solid-state regulator circuit.

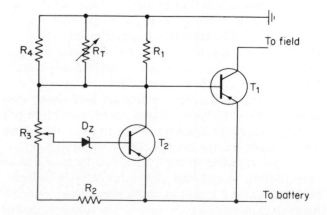

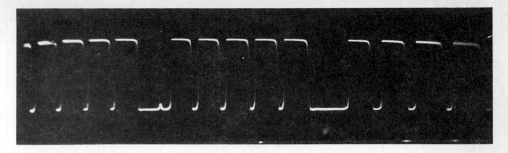

Fig. 9-14 Oscilloscope trace of the on–off switching of a solid-state regulator.

nator again. This cycle is repeated at a very high rate, controlling the voltage of the alternator. An oscilloscope trace of T_1 turning the field voltage on and off is shown in Figure 9–14.

The resistor R_t is sensitive to temperature. It is called a **thermister**. At low temperatures, it has high resistance. This reduces current flow through the series resistances R_2 and R_3. A higher charging circuit voltage is required to force the zener diode to conduct because the resistance in R_t is high. This causes the charging system to operate at a higher voltage when the regulator is cold and at a lower voltage when it is warm. The change in charging voltage matches the operating characteristics of the battery.

The basic operating circuit of the solid-state regulator is smoothed out and speeded up using resistors and capacitors. A schematic drawing of a complete solid-state regulator is shown in Figure 9–15. Voltage spikes and leakage are controlled with additional diodes, resistors, and capacitors. Note the **diode trio**. It is used to supply electricity to the regulator when the alternator starts to charge. The diode trio puts the same voltage on

terminal 1 as the battery supplies through the ignition switch and charge indicator lamp. The lamp goes out when it has the same voltage on each side. If the diode trio fails, the regulator will not send current to the alternator field, the alternator will not charge, and the indicator lamp stays on.

Current Regulation.   The current flowing in the alternator stator reverses itself, increasing and decreasing as it alternates in the same way voltage alternates. A magnetic field forms around the winding as the current flow increases and decreases as it alternates directions. This expanding and contracting magnetic field cuts across conductors of the stator coil windings to induce a counter voltage in the side-by-side conductors (as described in Chapter 1). The induced counter voltage opposes the voltage being produced in the stator. Maximum alternator current output is limited by the induced counter voltage. As counter voltage becomes nearly as great as the output voltage, the alternator output stabilizes at a maximum safe amperage. You can see that the maximum output is self-limiting by the design of the alternator.

Fig. 9-15 Schematic diagram of a regulator used inside a Delco-Remy 10-SI alternator.

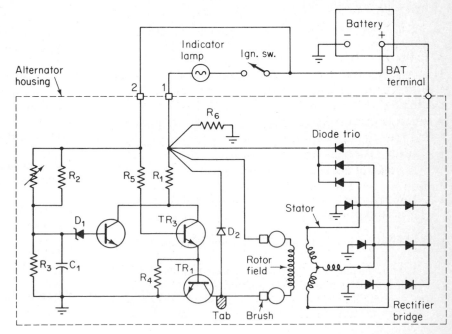

Reverse Current. When the engine is stopped the alternator voltage is zero. The battery tries to discharge through the alternator, but it cannot. Remember, all six alternator diodes are reverse biased with the battery voltage so that they prevent a flow of reverse current through the alternator. If you look carefully at Figure 9–15 you will see that a very small current will always be flowing through this type of solid-state regulator. The small current will very slowly discharge a battery of a stored vehicle.

STUDY QUESTIONS

Section 9–1

1. How is alternator voltage limited?

2. When will an alternator put out maximum current?

3. What is the name given to the main conductor assembly in an alternator?

4. What is the name of the alternator assembly that includes the field winding?

5. What do the brushes do in an alternator?

6. What conditions must be met before stator voltage can do anything?

7. What happens to the alternator voltage as each finger passes under a stator winding?

Section 9–2

8. What is done when current is rectified?

9. What do you call the shape of the maximum voltage from full-wave rectification?

10. What keeps the battery from discharging through the alternator?

11. What puts forward bias on alternator diodes?

Section 9–3

12. What does the voltage regulator do to limit voltage?

13. What is the field circuit called when one end of the field is grounded inside the alternator?

14. How does the location of the mechanical and solid-state regulators differ in the field circuit?

15. What three indicators are used to show discharge?

16. What is the purpose of a resistor connected parallel to the indicator lamp in a regulator circuit?

17. What makes the charge lamp go out when the alternator begins to charge?

18. How can a voltmeter show you that the alternator is charging?

Section 9–4

19. What regulates the charging system voltage when it is below maximum system voltage?

20. What limits the maximum alternator charging voltage?

21. What limits maximum alternator charging amperage?

22. What causes the charging-system voltage to increase as the battery becomes charged?

23. In an alternator, what controls maximum electrical system voltage?

24. What do the normally closed regulator points do to the alternator when they remain closed?

25. What term is used to describe the strength of a magnetic coil?

26. What do you call the rapid open–close cycle of the regulator points?

27. What keeps the magnetic field from completely decaying when the normally closed points of a mechanical regulator are open?

28. Why do mechanical regulators have normally open points?

29. List four advantages of solid-state regulators over mechanical regulators.

30. What is the voltage sensitive part of the solid-state regulator?

31. What part of solid-state regulators causes them to control at a higher voltage when cold?

32. What does the diode trio do in Delco-Remy alternators?

10

CHARGING-SYSTEM SERVICE

Many automotive service technicians do not understand charging systems. When there is a charging-system problem, these technicians change parts until the system operates. Using this method to correct problems takes a lot of time and the parts are expensive for the customer. Service technicians who correct problems in this way have helped to give the automotive service trade a poor name. Modern test equipment can be used to test the charging system quickly and simply. When you have a good understanding of the charging system and you use test equipment correctly, you will be able to diagnose the problem quickly. Only the malfunctioning part will need to be repaired. This will save time, parts cost, and a "comeback" that results from incorrect repairs. Let us review the operation of the charging system.

The battery is part of the charging system. In addition to supplying electrical power when the alternator does not have enough output, the battery acts as an electrical reservoir. As the battery becomes charged its voltage (CEMF) increases so that it begins to resist further charging. This raises the voltage in the electrical system and causes the alternator charging rate to drop. Let's again use an air pressure system to help understand the charging system. The compressor fills an air tank while it supplies air to operate a spray gun. As air is forced into the

tank the pressure increases. The air compressor cannot put air into the tank as fast when the pressure is high as it can when the pressure is low. Less and less air can be put into the tank at higher and higher pressures.

In a compressed-air system the maximum amount of air being compressed is based on the compressor size and its operating speed. In an alternator, the maximum output (amperes) is based on the alternator size and the rotating speed. In a charging system the alternator speed depends on the engine operating speed, and the alternator design limits maximum amperage output.

A compressed-air system has a pressure switch to turn the air compressor off when the air pressure has reached a safe maximum limit. The charging system uses a voltage regulator to limit maximum charging-system voltage. Like the switch in the air pressure system, the voltage regulator does not affect output (amperes) until voltage reaches the voltage setting of the regulator. The only purpose of the regulator is to keep voltage from going above a safe maximum limit. High voltage will shorten the life of the battery, ignition points, light bulbs, radios, electrical motors, and so on. It is best to have the voltage regulator set so that the maximum voltage is just high enough to charge the battery fully without overcharging it.

Voltage of the charging system is controlled by the battery counter voltage whenever the electrical system voltage is below the voltage setting of the regulator. A charging system operating with a partly charged battery will have low voltage. The voltage in the charging system and the whole electrical system will rise as the battery charges. When the voltage reaches regulated voltage the regulator will stop any increase in system voltage.

10-1 CHARGING-SYSTEM MAINTENANCE

The charging system will provide long useful service with minimum maintenance. For long life all electrical junctions must be kept clean and tight. The insulation on the wires should be kept clean and the wires should be properly supported to minimize the chance of their becoming shorted or broken. The battery must be kept clean and the cells filled with pure water.

The charging-system part that wears out most rapidly is the drive belt. Its condition should be checked at each oil change (Figure 10-1). The belt tension should be readjusted any time it seems to be loose or when it becomes glazed and shiny.

Belt tension is adjusted by first loosening the alternator mount bolt and the belt adjuster cap screw in the slotted adjuster. A typical example of this is shown in Figure 10-2. A special tool is often used to tighten the alternator belt. If you do not have the special tool you can tighten the belt with a pry bar. Place the pry bar against the drive end frame of the alternator to tighten the belt. Correct tension is set with a belt tension gauge. One type of belt tension gauge is shown in Figure 10-3. Hold the tension while you retighten the belt adjuster cap

Fig. 10-2   Alternator bolt to be loosened for belt adjustment.

Fig. 10-3   One type of belt tension gauge.

Fig. 10-1   Three alternator drive belts. A normal belt is shown on the top, a glazed belt in the middle, and a cracked belt on the bottom.

screw. Finally, tighten the alternator mount bolt to complete the belt adjustment.

A check to make sure that the charge indicator works correctly is part of the charging-system maintenance. The charge indicator lamp should be off when the ignition switch is off. It should glow when the ignition switch is on and the engine is not running. The indicator lamp should be off when the engine is running. Check it in each condition. The vehicle ammeter should show discharge with the headlamps turned on and the engine not running. It should move to charge when the engine runs. The vehicle voltmeter charge indicator should show battery voltage when the ignition switch is turned on and the engine is not running. The voltage should increase to regulated voltage when the engine runs. If the charge indicator does not operate normally, the charging system should be tested to find the cause of the problem.

10-2 TESTING THE CHARGING SYSTEM

A red charge indicator warning light or ammeter discharge shows that there is a problem in the charging system. A weakness in the charging system will usually show up when you check the electrical system. Many technicians check the charging system as a routine service operation during a tune-up.

A simple test can be used to see if the alternator and regulator are working normally. To make this test connect a voltmeter to the battery terminals. Battery voltage is noted before starting the engine. After starting, the engine speed is increased and held at 1500 rpm. All electrical systems, except the ignition, are turned off. The voltage should gradually increase and stay at 14.0 to 14.5 V while holding this engine speed. With the engine still held at this speed, all the electrical accessories that are often used together are turned on. For example, the lights, radio, wipers, air conditioner, and defroster may be used at the same time. This should cause the voltage to drop to no lower than 13.0 to 13.5 V. If you do not have these voltages, the charging system requires diagnosis to determine the cause of the problem.

As in all electrical test work, the first thing to check is the battery. It should be tested to see that it is in good condition and charged (see Section 4-2). If the battery is faulty, it should temporarily be replaced with a good battery before further tests are run. The alternator belt tension should be checked and adjusted as necessary.

Alternator Tests. The battery test is followed by an alternator **output test**. In this test, a test ammeter is connected in the charging circuit, either at the alternator or at the battery (see Figure 10-15). The best test ammeters use an inductive pickup that clamps around the wire coming from the alternator BAT terminal. This type of pickup is pictured in Figures 10-4 and 10-14. The alternator field wire is removed at the regulator or at the alternator. This disconnects the regulator. A jumper wire is connected to put full system voltage across the alternator field. The jumper wire is connected between the field terminal and BAT terminal on B-type circuits (Figure 10-5). The internal wiring of a B-circuit alternator is shown in Figure 10-6. On externally grounded field A circuits, the jumper wire is connected between the field terminal and ground (Figure 10-7). The internal wiring of an A-circuit alternator is shown in Figure 10-8. The jumper can be connected at the alternator or on the connector removed from the regulator on both A and B circuits as

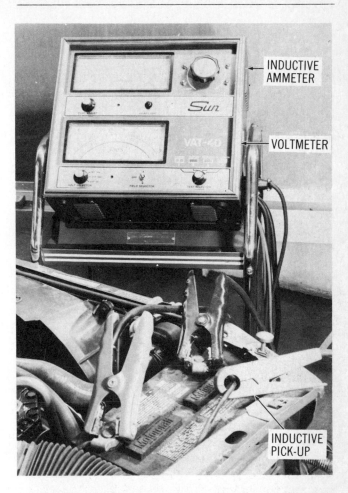

Fig. 10-4 Inductive ammeter connected to measure charging amperage.

Fig. 10-5 Jumper connections made when testing the output of alternators with B-circuit fields.

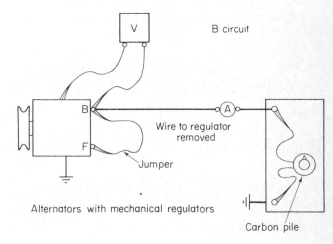

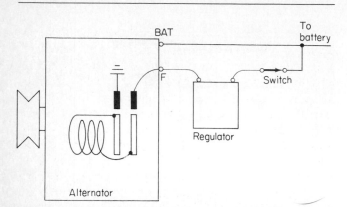

Fig. 10-6 Internal wiring of an alternator with a B-circuit field.

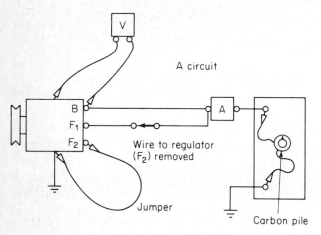

Alternators with external solid–state regulator

Fig. 10-7 Jumper connections made when testing the output of alternators with A-circuit fields.

Fig. 10-8 Internal wiring of an alternator with an A-circuit field.

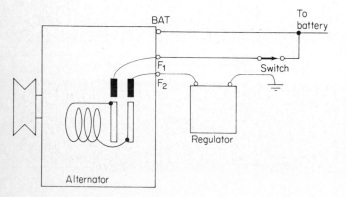

shown in Figure 10-9. The jumper on a B circuit connects the mechanical regulators: Ford A+ and F cavities, Delco-Remy mechanical regulators F and 3 cavities, and Chrysler F cavity and BAT terminals. Solid-state regulators use A circuits. The jumper connects the field directly to ground. You will notice in Figures 10-5 and 10-8 that a heavy carbon pile is connected across the battery. This is the carbon pile built into battery-starter testers. It is adjusted, as necessary during the test, to keep the charging system voltage at the specified voltage, between 14 and 15 V. The engine is started and adjusted to the required speed, about 1500 rpm. The carbon pile

Fig. 10-9 Jumper connected between cavities of a regulator when checking alternator output. Jumper connects F and electrical power cavities of an A circuit in view (a). Jumper connects F cavity and ground of a B circuit in view (b).

(a)

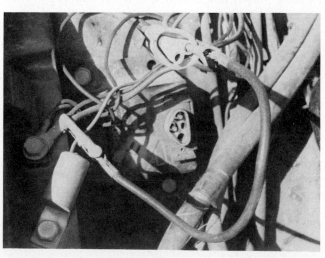

(b)

is tightened just enough to limit the maximum charging voltage to the specified voltage. Alternator output is read on the ammeter while the engine is running at the correct speed and voltage is being held at the specified setting. Be sure to loosen the carbon pile when the engine speed is reduced to idle.

Regulators built inside the alternator case (integral regulators) have their fields connected like externally grounded regulators (A circuit). In these alternators you bypass the regulator by putting the blade of a screwdriver through a hole in the alternator case. The screwdriver blade should touch a tab on the grounding brush at the same time that it touches the edge of the case hole. A typical case hole is shown by the arrow in Figure 10-10. The grounding tab is on the terminal from the bottom brush in Figure 9-15. Grounding the tab completes the field circuit to ground, to produce maximum current through the field winding in the rotor.

Some service manuals do not recommend separating a junction of the charging circuit to connect the test ammeter. The charging system test ammeter leads could accidentally separate from the junction connection during an output test if the ammeter were carelessly connected. Separation would cause high voltage to surge through the electrical system. This voltage surge could be high enough to damage solid-state control units used in other vehicle systems. These charging systems are checked while they are fully connected. They can be checked with an inductive ammeter (see Figures 10-4 and 10-14). The inductive ammeter is also easier to connect to systems with side terminal batteries than an ammeter that must be put in series in the circuit.

Fig. 10-10 The grounding tab inside the alternator can be seen through a hole in the rear alternator case.

The best test instrument for alternator problem analysis is the oscilloscope. Many engine scopes have connections and circuits that you can use for alternator testing. The ignition primary test leads will usually work for this. The trace displayed on the scope, similar to Figure 10-11, indicates a normal alternator. If the trace is not normal, the alternator will have to be removed for repair or replacement. Figure 10-12 shows three abnormal scope traces that result from alternator problems. The alternator will have to be disassembled, no matter what the abnormal trace looks like. Serious alternator malfunctions will show up on test meters.

Fig. 10-11 Oscilloscope trace of normal alternator operation.

Fig. 10-12 Abnormal alternator operation shown by oscilloscope traces: (a) open diode; (b) partly shorted diode or stator; (c) shorted diode or stator.

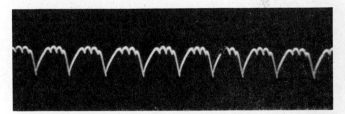

(a)

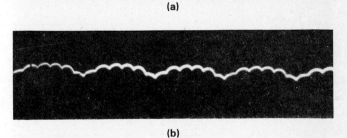

(b)

(c)

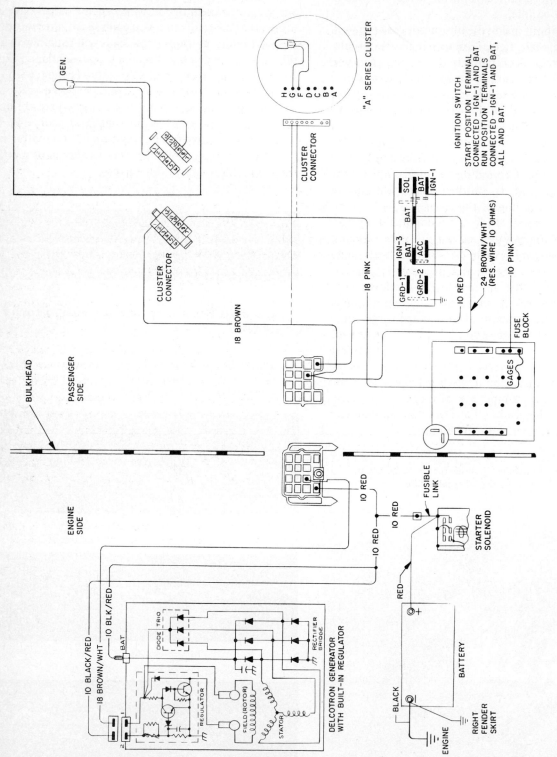

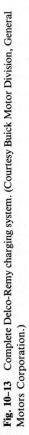

Fig. 10-13 Complete Delco-Remy charging system. (Courtesy Buick Motor Division, General Motors Corporation.)

114

Voltage-Drop Tests. All conductors must be free of abnormal resistance if the charging system is to operate correctly. Figure 10–13 shows the complete electrical circuit of a typical Delco-Remy charging system. Voltage-drop tests are made to check for resistance in the charging circuit while the alternator is producing 20 A. The test is run using the same test connections that you used to check alternator output. The engine speed is changed or the carbon pile is adjusted so that there is a 20 A charging rate. The insulated charging circuit should have a voltage drop of less than 0.7 V on charging systems with a vehicle ammeter. There should be less than 0.3 V drop on systems with a charge indicator lamp or voltmeter. The voltmeter connections may confuse you when you first make the voltage-drop tests on charging systems. You know that the alternator voltage is higher than battery voltage. The positive battery terminal is less positive than the alternator BAT terminal. In the test of the insulated circuit voltage drop, the positive voltmeter lead connects to the alternator BAT terminal. The negative lead of the voltmeter connects to the positive terminal of the battery. The grounded side of the circuit should have a voltage drop of less than 0.1 V. It is tested by connecting the negative voltmeter lead to the alternator case and the positive voltmeter lead to the battery negative terminal. Voltage-drop test connections are shown in Figure 10–14.

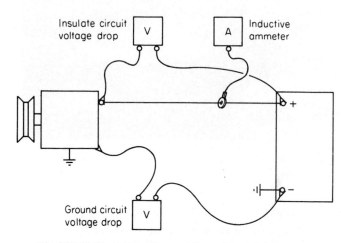

Fig. 10–14 Test connections used to measure voltage drop in the charging system.

When the alternator operates properly and the charging circuit resistance is normal, the jumper wire used to bypass the regulator or grounding screwdriver can be removed. The regulator is reconnected so that it will operate normally.

Voltage Regulator Setting. The voltage regulator limits the maximum voltage *at the battery*. This is why a regulator often has a separate lead that connects close

to the positive terminal of the battery. If the regulator setting is too low, the battery will not fully charge. A high voltage regulator setting will shorten the service life of the battery, ignition points, electronic controls, electric motors, radio, lights, and so on, by forcing too much current through them. High-voltage regulator settings may be first recognized as an unusual amount of headlight flare when the engine accelerates from idle. The battery will also use too much water, as charging turns the electrolyte water into oxygen and hydrogen gases. The gases leave the battery through vents.

Charging-system voltage increases when there is little demand for electricity and there is no place for the current to flow. The voltage decreases when there is a demand for electrical current and there are many places for current to flow. There must be enough resistance in the vehicle electrical system to limit current and raise the voltage to make the voltage regulator control the voltage. The system voltage can usually be increased by increasing the engine speed to 1500 rpm with all accessories turned off. If the voltage still does not go high enough for the regulator to control, a 1/4-Ω series resistor can also be put in the charging circuit. It will add enough circuit resistance to force the voltage up to the regulating range. Most volt-ampere testers have a 1/4-Ω fixed resistance built into the tester, as illustrated in Figure 10–15. Specific test settings and specification procedures are given by each vehicle manufacturer. These should be followed when comparing the measured voltage to the specified voltage regulator settings. The settings of voltage regulators range between 13.8 and 14.5 V. Remember that regulators are temperature compensated. They will con-

Fig. 10–15 Test connections used to measure the voltage regulator setting with a $\frac{1}{4}$-Ω resistance in the charging circuit.

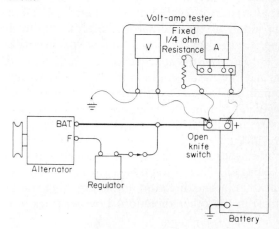

trol at a higher voltage when cold [15 to 16 V at -20°F (30°C)] and a lower voltage when warm [13 to 14 V at 140°F (60°C)].

Charging systems that fail the test will have to be repaired. Make sure that the connecting terminals are clean and tight before removing any parts. Faulty regulators are replaced.

10-3 ALTERNATOR REPAIR

It is a good safety practice to remove the battery ground cable before working on the alternator to prevent grounding that would cause a spark. Disconnect the wires from the terminals of the alternator. The wire removed from the BAT terminal is hot because it is connected directly to the battery. After it is removed from the alternator it should be insulated. Temporarily cover the terminal with electrical tape, to prevent a spark if someone should happen to reconnect the battery ground cable. The alternator mounting bolts are loosened, the alternator is tipped, and the drive belt is removed. The mounting bolts can then be taken off so that the alternator can be lifted from the engine.

It is a good practice to check the field circuit on an alternator that uses a separate regulator before the alternator is disassembled. This is done to check the operation of the brushes, brush holders, and slip rings, as well as the field coil.

Chrysler alternators are checked to measure field current draw before disassembly. One test lead of a low-range ammeter is connected to a battery terminal. Use the correct polarity. The other test lead from the ammeter is connected to the field terminal. A jumper from the second battery terminal is connected to the other field lead. This is shown in Figure 10-16. The amperage is measured as the alternator is rotated. It will range from 2.0 to 6.5 A, depending on the alternator rating. Be sure to check the specification for the alternator that you are servicing.

Ford alternators are checked for rectifier assembly shorts and internal grounds before they are disassembled. An ohmmeter is used for this test. It is calibrated before it is used. The ohmmeter leads are connected to the field terminal and the BAT terminal of the alternator, as shown in Figure 10-17. The meter reading is checked. Then the leads are reversed and the meter reading is checked again. There should be a low resistance reading (about 6 Ω) in one direction and a very high resistance (infinite) in the other direction. Low readings in both

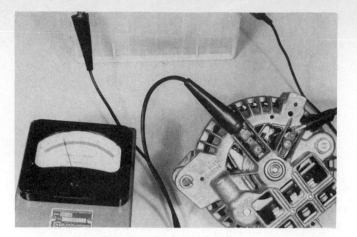

Fig. 10-16 Measuring field current draw on a Chrysler alternator.

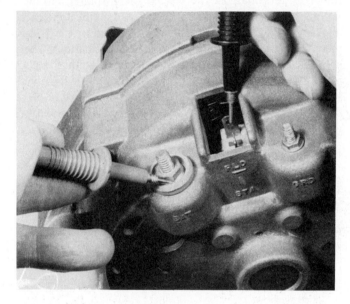

Fig. 10-17 Connections to measure rectifier shorts and grounds on a Ford alternator.

directions indicate a shorted diode. High readings in both directions indicate an open rectifier bridge.

The ohmmeter lead is switched from the BAT terminal to ground (Figure 10-18). The resistance is measured as the alternator is rotated. The resistance should be between 2.5 and 100 Ω. A reading of less than 2.5 Ω indicates a grounded brush or stator. No meter movement indicates an open. The open can be caused by a poor brush contact or an open rotor coil.

Check the service manual to make sure that the amperage or resistance values are correct for the alternator you are checking. If any tests show abnormal readings, the alternator will have to be disassembled for further testing and repair.

Fig. 10-18 Connections to measure resistance in the field of a Ford alternator.

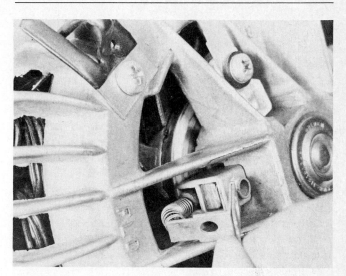

Fig. 10-19 Field brushes are removed from Chrysler alternators before disassembling the alternator.

Disassembly. Alternators that do not operate correctly will have to be disassembled for repair. The field brushes in Chrysler alternators must be removed before the alternator case is separated (Figure 10-19). This will keep you from damaging the brushes or the brush holders. In other makes of alternators, the brushes are not removed until the two halves of the alternator case are separated. Mark the two halves of the alternator so that they can be reassembled correctly. Remove the assembly through-bolts that hold the case together. Carefully separate the front case and rotor assembly from the stator and rear case as-

sembly. The two alternator halves will look like those in Figure 10-20 after they have been separated. The stator is connected to the diodes in the rear case. Nuts can be removed from the diodes in Chrysler and Delco-Remy alternators to remove the stator. The diode rectifier assembly is soldered to the stator leads in Ford alternators,

Fig. 10-20 Typical alternators separated for testing. (a) The rotor pole shoes and slip rings can be seen in the front case assembly. (b) The stator is part of the rear case assembly.

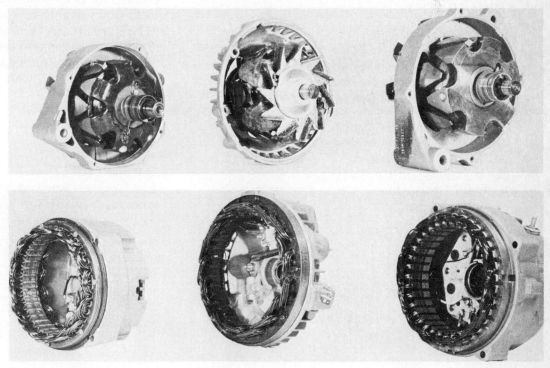

Fig. 10-21 The rectifier assembly is soldered to the stator leads of a Ford alternator.

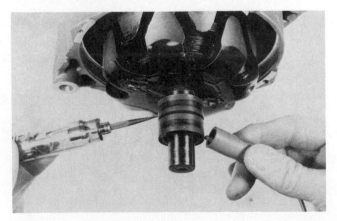

Fig. 10-23 Checking the stator winding ground with a self-powered test light.

so the diode rectifier and stator are removed from the rear case as a subassembly (Figure 10-21). With the alternator disassembled this far, all electrical checks can be made.

Stator Tests. To test stator winding continuity, the self-powered test light should glow when one test lead is connected to each pair of the free stator ends. This test is shown in Figure 10-22 (test lights are discussed in Section 5-3). The test light is connected between each of the three stator terminals in the delta-type stator. The stator is not grounded and the test light does not glow when one test lead is connected to a stator terminal and the other test lead touched to the stator core, as shown in Figure 10-23. Stator shorts are not easy to find because they normally have low resistance. A short would not lower the resistance enough to measure with an ohmmeter. Ford recommends a voltage-drop test to check for stator shorts. Generally, stator shorts show up as overheated discolored insulation at the short.

Rotor Tests. Field coil *continuity* in the rotor is checked by placing one lead of a continuity test light on each slip ring (Figure 10-24). An ohmmeter can be used in place of the test light. The light should glow or the ohmmeter should show very little resistance for normal continuity. Field coil *grounds* are checked by placing one lead of the self-powered test light on one of the slip rings and the other test lead on the rotor pole piece, as shown in Figure 10-25. The test light should not glow.

Fig. 10-22 Checking the stator winding continuity with a self-powered test light.

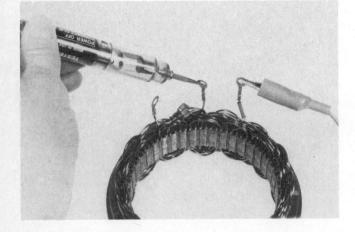

Fig. 10-24 Checking the continuity of rotor windings by placing one lead of a self-powered test light on each slip ring.

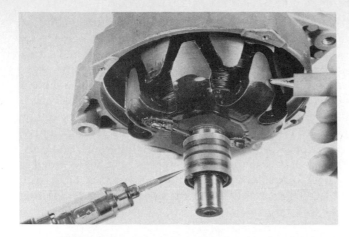

Fig. 10-25 Checking field coil grounds by placing one lead of a self-powered test light on one slip ring and the other on the rotor pole piece.

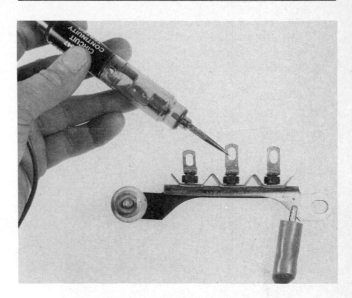

Fig. 10-27 Checking a diode with a self-powered test light.

Fig. 10-26 Measuring the field current draw with an ammeter connected in series between the battery and one slip ring. A jumper is used to connect the other slip ring to the second battery terminal.

Fig. 10-28 Ohmmeter used to check the condition of alternator diodes. (Courtesy Delco-Remy Division, General Motors Corporation.)

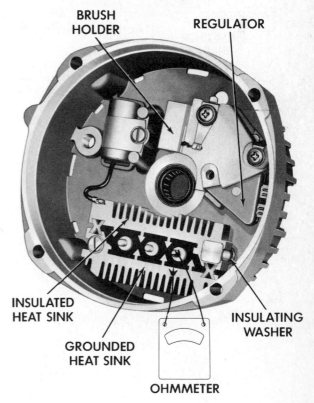

A field coil is tested for a *short* by measuring the current flow through the field at 12 V. This is usually called current draw. If there is too much current flow, the field coil is shorted. This test is shown in Figure 10-26.

Any shorted, grounded, or open stators or field coil in the rotor will have to be replaced. Stators and rotors are repaired only in specialized rebuilding shops. Most technicians exchange the faulty stator or rotor for a rebuilt one.

Diode Tests. A diode that is disconnected from the circuit can be checked with a self-powered continuity test light (Figure 10-27). The light bulb should glow when one test lead is connected to the diode case and the other test lead is connected to the diode lead wire (forward bias). The bulb should not glow when the test leads are reversed (reverse bias). The diode is faulty if the bulb stays on or off with both connections. An ohmmeter can also be used to check diodes (Figure 10-28). Normal diodes have high resistance one way (reverse bias) and low resistance the other way (forward bias). Faulty diodes are not repairable and must be replaced.

Diodes in some of the first alternators (like the one shown in Figure 8–6) could be replaced individually using the correct removal and installation tools. Late-model Chrysler alternators have a separate positive and negative rectifier bridge assembly. The bridge assembly with a faulty diode is replaced if any one of the three diodes in the bridge is faulty. Ford and Delco-Remy alternators are designed so that the entire rectifier bridge assembly with six diodes is replaced when any one diode is faulty.

Delco-Remy alternators with internal regulators have a diode trio to supply power to the regulator (Figure 10–29). The alternator will not charge if the diode trio fails. It is checked the same way the other diodes are checked, as shown in Figure 10–30.

Bearing Replacement. A faulty rear needle bearing can be pressed from the frame. Care must be taken so that the aluminum case or frame will not be broken. The frame is supported by a tube with an inside diameter slightly larger than the bearing. The bearing is pressed with a pin that has an outside diameter slightly smaller than the bearing but large enough to press near the edge of the bearing. A new needle bearing can be pressed in with the same tools used to remove the old bearing. A soft plug and seal are installed where they are used in specific alternator types.

To replace the front ball bearing it is necessary to remove the pulley. Ford and Delco-Remy pulleys are held on the shaft with a nut and drive the shaft through a key. The nut is removed (Figure 10–31); then the pulley can be tapped to free it. In some alternators it is necessary to remove a shaft key. Chrysler alternators have the pulley held on the shaft by a press fit. A puller is used on a pulling ring that is part of the pulley. One type of puller is shown in Figure 10–32. Do not pull on the edge of the pulley because the edge-type puller will bend the pulley.

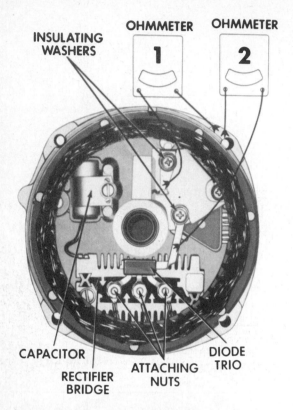

Fig. 10–29 The diode trio location is shown in this view. The ohmmeter connections measure grounding. (Courtesy Oldsmobile Division, General Motors Corporation.)

Fig. 10–30 Checking the condition of a diode trio with an ohmmeter.

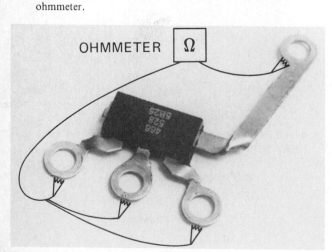

Fig. 10–31 Tools used to remove the nut from the drive pulley on Delco-Remy and Ford alternators.

Fig. 10-32 A Chrysler alternator drive pulley is removed with a puller connected to a pulling ring.

Fig. 10-34 Removing the clip-type bearing retainer from a Chrysler alternator.

This is what happened to the pulley shown in Figure 10-33. With the pulley off and a ring spacer removed, the bearing can be freed from the end frame. In Chrysler alternators the bearing is held in place with a clip-type retainer (Figure 10-34). The retainer is loosened from the frame, then the rotor with the bearing can be pulled from the frame. Ford and Delco-Remy alternators have a bolted-type retainer (Figure 10-35). The parts are then cleaned and thoroughly inspected for physical damage.

The ball bearing must be pulled off the shaft of Chrysler alternators with a special pulley. One type is shown in Figure 10-36. The bearing will be discarded, so the bearing can be pulled using its outer race. The Chrysler clip-type retainer must be put on the rotor shaft before the new bearing is installed. The new bearing is pressed on the shaft on Chrysler alternators using a sleeve that fits against the inner race. It is pressed on the shaft before the rotor is put in the case. This allows you to press against the back end of the rotor shaft. The outer race

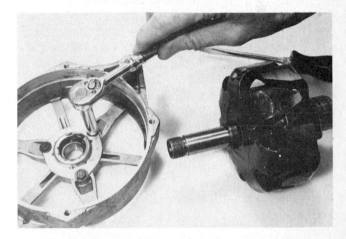

Fig. 10-35 Removing the bolted-type bearing retainer used in Delco-Remy and Ford alternators.

Fig. 10-36 Special puller being used to remove the front bearing from a Chrysler alternator.

Fig. 10-33 Drive pulley damaged with a puller connected to the edge of the pulley instead of the puller ring.

is a push fit (not a press fit) in the drive end case of Chrysler alternators.

Bearings in Ford and Delco-Remy alternators are a push fit in the housing and on the shaft so a puller or press is not used. These bearings are installed in the case, then the rotor shaft is slipped through the bearing. The front ball bearing is prelubricated and sealed, so it requires no attention. In some cases a small amount of special bearing grease, such as Delco-Remy lubricant part 1948791, should be placed in the bearing retainer cavity.

Assembly. Assembly starts by installing the rotor and its ball bearings in the front-drive end frame as described. The ring spacer and drive pulley are installed next. The pulley is pressed on the shaft when this holding method is used. All of the pressing force is put on the end of the rotor shaft. If a pulley-retaining nut is used, it should be tightened to 70 to 80 lb-ft (1022 to 1168 N/m).

Reassemble the alternator stator, rear frame, diode bridge, internal regulator, and condenser. The brushes of Delco-Remy and Ford alternators are installed inside the case. They should be held in place during assembly with a temporary pin like the one shown in Figure 10-37. The rear needle bearing should be lubricated with the special bearing grease. The rotor shaft is wiped clean and

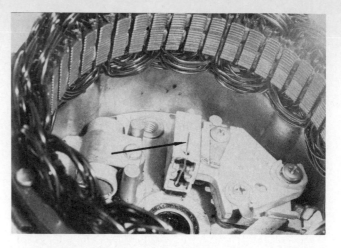

Fig. 10-37 Pin used to hold the brushes in Delco-Remy and Ford alternators for assembly.

slid into the needle bearing. With the case halves properly aligned, the through-bolts are installed and tightened. The pin that temporarily holds the brushes is removed. The external brushes are put in place in Chrysler alternators. The alternator is ready to be tested and then to be put into service.

It is wise to retest the alternator output and voltage regulation on a generator test bench or immediately after it has been reinstalled on the engine. This will assure you that the repaired alternator is working properly.

STUDY QUESTIONS

Section 10-1

1. What charging-system part wears most rapidly?

2. How can you check the operation of the charge lamp?

Section 10-2

3. What basic test instrument can you use to see if the alternator and regulator are working normally?

4. What should be done with a faulty battery before checking the charging system?

5. What type of ammeter is best for checking charging systems?

6. What is done to the field circuit when running an alternator output test?

7. Why is a heavy carbon pile connected across the battery when running an alternator output test?

8. Give two reasons why inductive ammeters are preferred over an ammeter that must be connected into the circuit.

9. What is the best instrument to use for alternator problem analysis?

10. What scope patterns indicate that the alternator will have to be disassembled for repair?

11. What test connections are made to measure the voltage drop in the charging circuit?

12. How much current should flow through the charging system when checking the voltage drop of the system?

13. Which voltmeter lead is connected on the battery positive terminal when running the voltage drop test?

14. What two problems indicate that there is a high-voltage regulator setting?

15. What is necessary in the charging system to make the voltage regulator operate?

Section 10-3

16. What should you do before removing wires from the alternator?

17. Why do you tape the terminal of the wire you removed from the BAT terminal?

18. How is a test ammeter connected to measure field current draw on a Chrysler alternator?

19. What ohmmeter reading should you expect to see when you are checking the rectifier of a Ford alternator?

20. What should be done before you start to separate the alternator case?

21. What two stator tests can be made with a self-powered test light?

22. Why are stator shorts difficult to find?

23. A test light is used to measure continuity and grounds in rotors. Which of these tests is not necessary if the field current draw is normal?

24. What should be done to correct alternators with faulty stators or rotors?

25. What should be done to correct faulty diodes?

26. How can you tell if a diode is normal?

27. What tools are needed to remove and replace the rear needle bearing?

28. Name an alternator and list the steps you will need to follow to replace the front bearing.

29. How does the fit of the drive end bearing differ between the Chrysler and the Ford or Delco-Remy alternators?

11

THE IGNITION SYSTEM

The ignition system forces a spark or an electrical arc across the spark plug electrodes to ignite the air/fuel charge in the combustion chamber. Older ignition systems have a point-type design. Newer systems use high-energy transistor switching. The spark is delivered to the spark plug with enough energy to ignite the charge.

It is not only important for the charge to ignite, but it must ignite at the correct instant during each cycle so that combustion will produce maximum useful energy. The spark is timed so that the combustion chamber will reach its maximum pressure when the crank pin is from 5 to 10° after top center. Ignition timing must change during engine operation for efficient engine operation under all operating conditions.

11–1 IGNITION REQUIREMENTS

Technical words in this section you will need to learn:

| Carbon monoxide | Mass |
| Hydrocarbon | Turbulence |

Lean air/fuel mixtures need a higher ignition voltage to fire the spark plug than rich mixtures. Higher-voltage ignition systems were, therefore, required on emission-controlled engines that used lean mixtures. Contact points could not carry enough primary current to develop the high secondary voltage needed on these engines. It was necessary to replace the contact point in the ignition with solid-state electronic controls. In addition, the resulting higher secondary voltage made it necessary to increase the electrical insulation in the high-voltage parts of the ignition system. The Delco-Remy HEI ignition system and the large-diameter blue distributor cap used by Ford are examples of this change. Larger-diameter 8-mm spark plug cables used in these systems have more insulation than the smaller 7-mm cables used in other systems.

In operation the ignition timing requirements of an engine keep changing. Timing must change as the engine speed and temperature change. The throttle must be moved to keep the engine operating at a constant speed when the load on the engine changes. Any change in the position of the throttle or engine speed requires a change in the ignition timing.

Ignition Timing and Engine Speed. The ignition timing must be advanced as the engine speed increases. This is the *same* for both mechanical and computer-controlled timing because it is the timing that the engine needs. The ignition timing is advanced in a mechanical distributor with a centrifugal advance mechanism that is sensitive to engine speed. As the engine speed increases, the crankshaft rotates through more degrees while the charge is burning in the combustion chamber. Because of this, it is necessary to advance the ignition timing so that the burning will be complete at the same point after top center. **Turbulence** or mixing of the charge in the combustion chamber increases as the engine speed increases. The turbulence causes the rate of burning to increase just like a draft increases the burning rate of a fire. As a result, the timing advance does not increase in direct proportion to the increase in engine speed. At high engine speeds the burning speed is so fast that more advance is not needed.

Ignition Timing and Engine Load. The mass of the intake charge taken into the combustion chamber results from the throttle position and engine load. **The mass is the amount of intake charge.** You can think of it as the weight of the charge. With a light throttle there is a vacuum in the intake manifold. Only a small amount of intake charge can be drawn into the combustion chamber from this vacuum in the manifold. Compression of this small intake charge will be less dense, have low pressure, and its burning rate is slow. This slow-burning charge requires a large ignition advance to be able to complete combustion at the same point after top center.

A wide-open throttle lets the maximum amount of air enter the intake manifold. The largest amount of intake charge will enter the combustion chamber at a low engine speed and full throttle. When compressed, this charge is dense and has high pressure. Compression of this dense charge forces more gas molecules between the electrodes of the spark plug. It also has a higher turbulence that burns fast. As a result timing is retarded so that combustion will not be complete before the required point after top center.

A vacuum advance mechanism is used to change ignition timing for throttle position and engine load. It is sensitive to manifold vacuum. Timing is advanced under high-vacuum, light-load operation when the burning rate is slow. It is retarded under low-vacuum, heavy-load operation when the burning rates are fast. The vacuum advance fully retards at full throttle because there is no manifold vacuum. It also fully retards at idle because the sensing port is opened to atmosphere. The primary reason for having a vacuum advance is to give fuel economy during part throttle operation. Many of the emission controls on the engine modify the timing of the vacuum advance to minimize controlled exhaust emissions.

Ignition Timing and Emissions. The engine exhaust emissions are greatly affected by the timing. Some hydrocarbons and carbon monoxide are left in the exhaust when

the combustion of the fuel is not complete. Oxides of nitrogen form when oxygen and nitrogen in air combine at high combustion temperatures. The maximum amount of energy in the fuel is changed into useful work when combustion is complete. This leaves less heat to be exhausted from the combustion chamber. As a result the exhaust gases have a lower temperature. Exhaust gases will contain more hydrocarbons and carbon monoxide when the engine runs rich with the throttle closed—at idle and especially during deceleration. By retarding the timing, engine efficiency is reduced. To maintain the same idle speed the throttle must be adjusted further open. The idle mixture can be leaned when using this larger throttle opening. These engine operating conditions result in higher exhaust temperatures. Increased exhaust heat helps to complete the burning of hydrocarbons and carbon monoxide in the exhaust gas as it flows through the exhaust system. Rapid ignition advance as the engine speed increases gives the engine normal ignition advance for economy cruise and for high-speed operation.

To make sure that the vacuum does not cause the ignition to advance during acceleration some manufacturers have a transmission spark control (TSC) system connected to the transmission to allow vacuum advance only in direct drive. Other manufacturers allow vacuum advance only when the vehicle is operating over 30 mph.

During deceleration the engine has a high intake manifold vacuum. If the throttle were only partly closed during deceleration manifold vacuum would cause the distributor timing to advance and produce more hydrocarbons and carbon monoxide. Emission controls adjust the vacuum advance to minimize the emissions.

A computer in modern automobiles adjusts the ignition advance so that the engine always has the correct advance for its engine speed, fuel economy, and low emissions.

11-2 IGNITION SYSTEM OPERATION

Technical words in this section you will need to learn:

Cathode ray oscilloscope	Primary
Corona	Rise time
Eddy currents	Secondary
Electronic control	Signal
Engine scope	Timer
Laminations	
Leakage	

Point-type and solid-state ignition systems operate the same way while current is flowing in the coil primary winding. They also operate in the same way after the coil primary current is stopped. *They differ in the way they stop and restart the primary current.*

The coil primary current is stopped and restarted for each spark plug firing. In an eight-cylinder engine running at 4000 rpm, there are 266 spark plug firings each second. It is impossible to follow this action with a meter because the meter cannot move fast enough. If it could, you could not read it. An engine scope (cathode ray oscilloscope) can follow the voltage change, so it is used to show the constantly changing voltage in the ignition system.

Point-Type Ignition. When the ignition switch and points are closed, the primary circuit is completed, through ground. This allows electrical current to flow in the primary winding of the ignition coil. The current flow builds a magnetic field in the coil (Figure 11–1). As the engine rotates, it turns the breaker cam within the distributor housing. The cam pushes against the point rubbing block, forcing the points apart. This stops the primary current flow. When the current flow stops, the magnetic field in the coil collapses through the secondary windings (Figure 11–2). The **condenser** (also called a capacitor) within the distributor minimizes point arcing as it helps control the rapid collapse of the magnetic field. You will remember from Section 1–9 that the collapse of the magnetic field induces a momentary high voltage in the coil secondary windings. At this instant, the rotor tip is lined up with the correct distributor cap electrode. You can see that there is a rotor gap between them in Figure 11–3. The high voltage is carried by the secondary

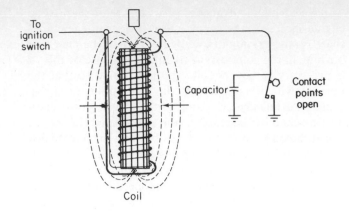

Fig. 11–2 The magnetic field around the ignition coil collapses when the current stops flowing through the primary winding.

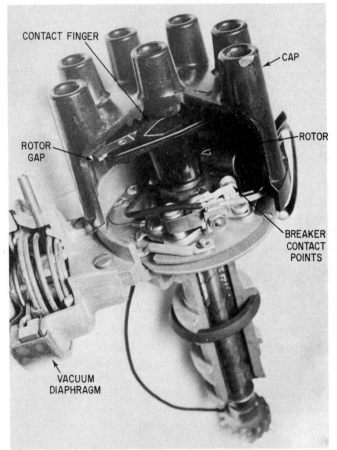

Fig. 11–3 Parts of a typical point-type distributor showing the rotor gap between the rotor tip and cap electrodes.

ignition cables to the spark plug in the cylinder to be fired. This high voltage causes an electrical arc to form across the spark plug gap. The arc ignites the compressed intake charge in the combustion chamber at the correct instant in the combustion cycle. Figure 11–4 is a schematic drawing of a typical point-type ignition system.

Fig. 11–1 A magnetic field builds up when there is current flowing through the primary winding of the ignition coil.

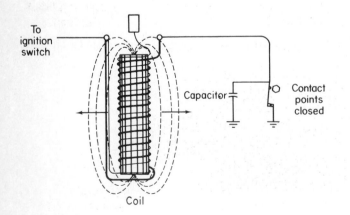

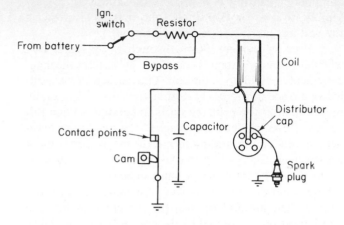

Fig. 11-4 Schematic drawing of a typical point-type ignition system.

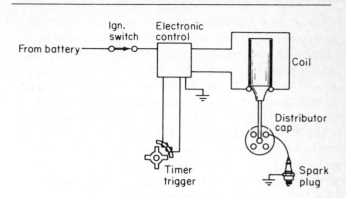

Fig. 11-5 Schematic drawing of a typical solid-state ignition system.

Solid-State Ignition. Starting in 1971, solid-state ignition systems were put on some Chrysler automobiles. By 1975, all domestic automobiles had solid-state ignition systems. These ignition systems do not require a regular tune-up. Only routine maintenance is needed. The spark plugs should be replaced at specified service intervals.

In solid-state ignition systems, a timer in the distributor takes the place of points. A signal produced by the **timer** is sent to an electronic control. The electronic control is called a module by Delco-Remy and Ford (ECM). Chrysler calls it an ignition control unit. Sometimes it is called an electronic control unit (ECU). When it controls more than basic ignition timing, Ford calls this unit an Electronic Engine Control (EEC). The ignition control unit stops and restarts the primary current flowing through the coil, just as points do. Other than stopping and starting the primary current, the solid-state ignition system works the same as a point-type system.

Figure 11-5 is a schematic drawing of a solid-state ignition system.

Coil. The typical standard automotive ignition coil, shown as a cutaway in Figure 11-6, has from 100 to 180 **primary** coil windings using AWG 20 copper wire. The primary winding has resistance and it carries a high current, so it becomes warm. It is therefore wrapped on the outside of the secondary coil winding to help keep it cool. The **secondary** coil has 18,000 winding turns of AWG 38 wire. The wires in both coils are coated with insulating varnish and the winding layers are separated with oiled paper for insulation. A soft-iron core made of a number of soft-iron strips is placed in the center of the coils. The coils are wrapped with a soft-iron shield. The laminations of the core and shield limit **magnetic eddy currents** that would reduce coil efficiency. *Eddy currents are like whirlpools in a stream that slow the flow.* The coil assembly

Fig. 11-6 Cutaway view and identification of parts of a standard automotive ignition coil. (Courtesy Delco-Remy Division, General Motors Corporation.)

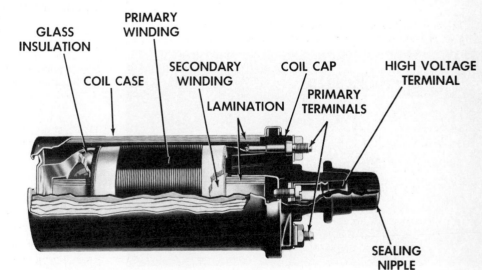

is placed in a can with a ceramic insulator, filled with insulating transformer oil, then sealed. Coils are not repairable. If tests show them to be faulty or if they leak oil, they must be replaced.

A new type of coil, illustrated in Figure 11–7, is used in solid-state Delco-Remy HEI ignition systems and in some Ford ignition systems. The coil has E-shaped laminations. The open side of the laminations are leaved together. Remember how the battery plates are leaved together. The center of the E laminations are short, so there is an air gap between them. The gap is just the right size to give the coil the correct inductance.

The primary winding is wrapped around the middle of the laminations in this type of coil. Wrapping the primary first allows the coil to have the same number of turns as a standard ignition coil while using much less wire. The shorter wire has less resistance, so it will not get as warm, even when it carries more current. The secondary winding is wrapped around the outside of the primary winding, using 100 secondary turns for each

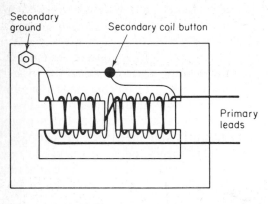

Fig. 11-7   E-type ignition coil.

primary turn. The coil assembly is potted in an epoxy compound. **Potting** is a process of saturating the assembly, so it becomes a single solid mass. This protects the coil against moisture and vibration.

Primary current flows through the primary coil when the primary circuit is complete. This causes the magnetic field to build up in the coil. You can see on the oscilloscope trace in Figure 11–8 that the current gradually builds up after the primary starts to conduct. When full current flows, the coil has reached the maximum magnetic saturation. **Saturation** means the magnetism will not get stronger. Energy is stored in the coil by induction as magnetism. The total energy that can be stored in the coil is based on the size of the coil and the maximum primary current. The amount of primary current in point-type ignition systems is limited by the current-carrying ability of the points. Normally, the primary current across the points is limited to 4.2 A. The points will last thousands of miles with this current flow. If primary current flow were increased to 5.4 A, the points would burn in a very few miles. The ability to operate with high primary currents is one of the advantages of solid-state electronic ignition systems. The power transistor in an electronic ignition system can carry twice as much primary current as the points can carry without being damaged. This allows more energy as magnetism to build up in the coil.

The primary current may not have time to build up to the full magnetic strength. The time is controlled by the number of degrees the crankshaft turns while the primary current is flowing. The longer the primary current can flow through the coil, the more energy will be stored in the coil, until the coil is saturated with magnetism. At low engine speeds, there is more time to store energy in the coil than at high engine speeds. You can see this in the oscilloscope traces in Figure 11–9. The primary circuit saturates the coil to produce available voltage in the secondary circuit. The greater the magnetic saturation of the coil, the higher the available voltage.

Capacitance, described in Section 1–10, is another

Fig. 11-8   Oscilloscope trace of the ignition primary voltage and current in one firing of a spark plug.

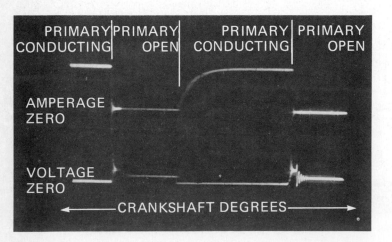

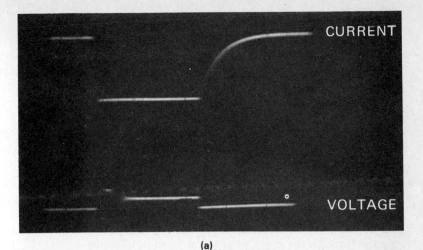

(a)

CURRENT

VOLTAGE

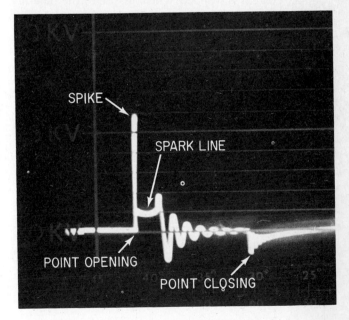

CURRENT

VOLTAGE

(b)

Fig. 11-9 Oscilloscope traces of the ignition primary voltage and current at two different distributor speeds. The upper trace (**a**) shows slow speed and the lower trace (**b**) shows high speed.

Fig. 11-10 Oscilloscope trace of the secondary voltage of a point-type ignition system. There is no primary current between the point opening and point closing.

SPIKE

SPARK LINE

POINT OPENING

POINT CLOSING

electrical property that affects the ignition system. The ignition coil has conductors close together and insulated from each other. Negative charges in one conductor attract positive charges in the conductor next to it. These charges remain as long as the conductors are insulated from each other. Some electrical energy is stored in the ignition coil in this way. The capacitance of the secondary ignition circuit is based on the design of the secondary coil windings and on the length, routing, and position of the secondary ignition cables in relation to each other and to the engine metal.

When the primary current flow stops, the magnetic field of the coil quickly collapses, cutting across both coil windings. Rapid collapse of the magnetic field produces voltage in both coil windings, charging their capacitances. The capacitive part of the electrical energy builds up in the ignition secondary until the voltage is high enough to ionize gases in the spark plug gap. This voltage produces the spike on ignition scope patterns. You can see spike in Figure 11-10. The ionized gases reduce the resistance of the spark plug gap so that the required voltage falls to about one-fourth of the maximum spike voltage as the spark plug fires. Duration of the arc is fed by inductance as the magnetic lines of force continue to collapse through the secondary windings. This part of the ignition scope pattern is called the spark line. Ignition takes place during capacitive discharge and during the first part of inductive discharge.

The energy stored in the coil must be released very rapidly for the best ignition. To do this the secondary voltage must increase very rapidly. This is called **fast rise time**. Fast rise time reduces problems with slight electrical leaks in the ignition secondary circuit. Energy is discharged through the spark plug so fast that despite any slight leaks, such as slightly fouled spark plugs, energy does not have time to leak away. Fast rise time needs good secondary insulation because the sudden high-voltage surge will try to flash through the insulation.

Condenser or Capacitor.   A condenser or capacitor is installed electrically across the points in the point-type ignition system. It connects between the negative terminal of the coil and ground. The capacitor is made from two long strips of electrical conductor foil, called **plates**, separated by **insulating paper**. The foil strips and insulation are rolled together, then placed in a can and sealed. A lead wire contacts one foil strip and the can case contacts the other. A disassembled ignition capacitor is shown in Figure 11–11. It is also shown as a line drawing in Figure 1–37. The strips of foil are close together, so there is attraction between electrons and holes across the insulation paper. The operation of a capacitor was described in Section 1–10.

The coil magnetic field starts to collapse when the primary current is stopped. The collapse of the field induces voltage in the primary winding that tries to keep the primary current flowing by inductance, as discussed in Section 1–9. This induced voltage (as high as 250 V) is high enough to force electrons across the gap between the points as they begin to open. The electrons would form an arc if they could cross the gap. An arc would absorb electrical energy that would reduce the available voltage in the coil secondary. The capacitor is a place for

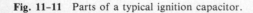
Fig. 11–11   Parts of a typical ignition capacitor.

the electrons in the primary current to go as points start to open. This keeps them from forming the arc and reducing available voltage. The attraction of the positive capacitor plate is so great that the electrons move freely into the negative plate, producing a high-voltage charge on the negative plate. As the electrons pack into the capacitor, they bring the primary current to a quick, controlled stop. This causes a rapid collapse of the magnetic field. During this time, the points have opened far enough so that the voltage will not flash over and cause an arc across the point gap.

The electrons race back and forth through the primary circuit in an attempt to balance on each side of the capacitor. This can be seen as oscillations at the left side of the primary oscilloscope trace pictured in Figure 11–12. It can also be seen as the oscillations between the spark line and point closing on the secondary pattern in Figure 11–10.

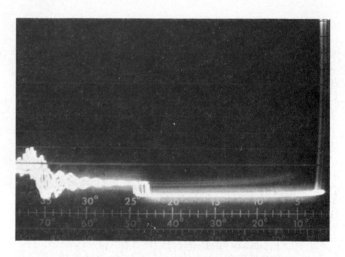

Fig. 11–12   Oscilloscope trace of superimposed primary voltages while firing all cylinders.

Solid-state ignition systems do not have points, so they do not need a capacitor to stop the point arc. Most solid-state ignition systems have a capacitor connected between the positive terminal of the coil and ground. This capacitor is used to reduce ignition noise in the radio. It does not affect the operation of the ignition system.

Leakage.   Available voltage is produced by the total energy stored in the coil. The amount of usable energy from the total energy is reduced by secondary leakage. One of the main causes of ignition leakage is spark plug fouling. Spark plugs are fouled when conducting deposits build up on the nose of the spark plug insulator. The spark plug will fire when there is a little leakage. As the leakage increases, it drains away electrical energy. The spark plug will not fire when there is too little energy left to produce the spark. You can see spark plug fouling on the oscilloscope. It has a low spike with the spark line slanting steeply downward to the right. This is shown in Figure 11-13. Compare this scope pattern with the normal secondary pattern in Figure 11-10. The effect of secondary leakage is minimized by fast rise time.

Secondary current will also leak through weak or cracked secondary insulation, especially at brackets supporting the ignition cables, across dirty coil tops, across dirty spark plug insulators, and across dirty distributor caps. Moisture and carbon tracks inside the distributor are other paths of electrical leakage.

Corona can be seen as a glow when you look at the secondary ignition cables in the dark. It is an external leakage along ignition cables. Corona increases as the conductor becomes wet and dirty. In time corona will lead to insulation failure and secondary leakage. Keeping the ignition secondary circuit parts clean will minimize corona leakage.

From this discussion, it would seem desirable to increase ignition system energy to overcome all leakage. An overcapacity ignition system, however, rapidly erodes the spark plug electrodes and insulators to give short spark plug life. It also overloads the secondary insulation so that it will fail prematurely.

Ignition Resistor. Point-type ignition systems use a primary resistor or ballast. This may be a separate resistor or it may be a resistance wire between the ignition switch and coil. The ignition resistor or ballast has about one-half of the total resistance in the primary circuit. The resistor is the only part of the ignition system that is temperature compensated.

During cranking, the ignition resistor is bypassed so that the entire electrical system voltage is placed across the coil. You can see how this is done in Figure 11-4. The voltage in the electrical system during cranking is lowered to about 10 V by the heavy starter current draw, and therefore the voltage of the coil during starting is not too high. The low cranking voltage limits the current flow across the points. When the engine starts, the electrical-system voltage increases to the regulator voltage setting, about 14 V. The resistor then becomes effective when the switch is allowed to return to the run position to limit the running voltage of the coil to approximately 7 to 8 V.

11-3 DISTRIBUTOR OPERATION

The ignition distributor is usually driven by the camshaft. On some engines it is driven from the end of the camshaft. The distributor shaft may drive the oil pump, as shown in Figure 11-14. The distributor is even driven from the crankshaft on some engines (Figure 11-15). In

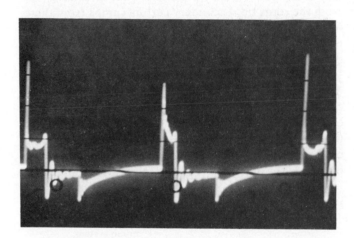

Fig. 11-13 Oscilloscope trace of a fouled spark plug. From the top of the spike the trace of the firing line slopes steeply to the right.

Fig. 11-14 Typical distributor drive from a camshaft.

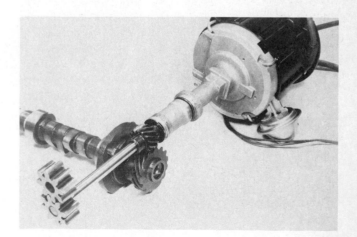

all cases it rotates at one-half the crankshaft speed. The points, inductive timer, Hall-effect timer, capacitor, rotor, cap, and timing advance mechanisms are in the distributor. This puts all the moving parts of the ignition system into a single unit. The solid-state module and coil are included with the distributor in HEI ignition systems. This can be seen in Figure 11–16, which shows the major sections of the system.

The distributor gets its name from the part that directs the electrical energy from the secondary coil winding to the spark plug cables. The electrical energy of the coil secondary goes to the center distributor cap tower. A spring clip on the distributor rotor contacts the center button in the cap. The rotor has a metal plate from the spring clip to an extended tip that comes close to the distributor cap electrodes as the rotor turns. You can see this in the cutaway distributor in Figure 11–3. As the distributor rotates, the rotor tip passes near one distributor cap electrode each time the coil discharges. This design allows as much as 20° of distributor advance. The two-to-one distributor drive ratio gives 40° of engine timing advance. Some rotors have short wires extending out from the rotor tip. Secondary current jumps from these wires to the cap electrodes. The secondary electrical energy goes from the cap electrodes to each spark plug cable, in turn, in the correct firing order.

Ford developed a bilevel rotor and cap to allow the distributor to give more ignition advance. This bilevel distributor has a center electrode plate fastened inside the cap. Secondary current jumps from the electrode plate to either of two upper high-voltage electrode pickup arms on the rotor. One pickup arm connects to an upper level blade and the other connects to a lower level blade. This

Fig. 11–15 Distributor driven from a gear on the crankshaft.

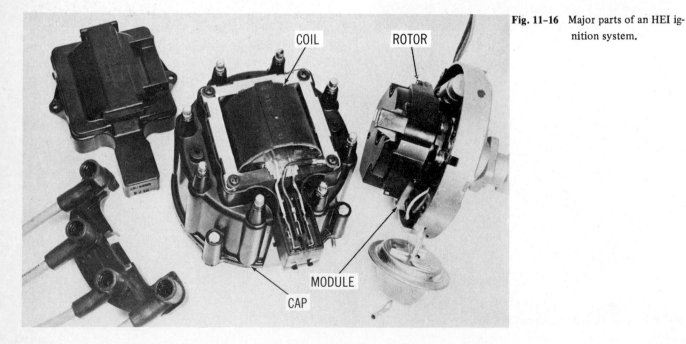

COIL

ROTOR

MODULE

CAP

Fig. 11–16 Major parts of an HEI ignition system.

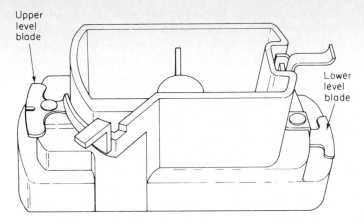

Upper level blade

Lower level blade

Fig. 11-17 A bilevel rotor allows greater ignition advance.

is shown in Figure 11–17. The upper and lower electrode blades line up, alternately, with the upper and lower electrodes in the distributor cap. This arrangement increases the space between the cap electrodes to reduce the chance of cross firing at as much as 30° distributor advance. **Cross firing** is firing the wrong spark plug. It allows the engine to have up to 60° of ignition advance.

Point-Type Timer. It is convenient to locate the point cam (Figure 11–18), timing inductor (Figure 11–19), or Hall-effect timer (Figure 11–20), on the same shaft as the rotor. They always have the same position relative to the rotor and electrode alignment. A point set or timer is mounted on a movable plate within the distributor. There are adjustments to move points closer to the cam for a larger point gap or away from the cam for a smaller point gap.

Fig. 11-18 Typical point-type timer in a distributor.

Fig. 11-19 Inductive timer in a distributor.

Fig. 11-20 Hall-effect timer in a distributor.

There is one cam lobe for each cylinder. The cam lobes for four-cylinder engines are spaced at 90°, even-firing six-cylinder engines at 60°, and eight-cylinder engines at 45°. Within each of these angles, the primary circuit must be complete long enough for the primary current to store energy in the coil. The points must open far enough to minimize point arcing. Normally, the points are closed from 65 to 70% of the total **cam angle**. This gives enough time to saturate the coil with magnetism. The number of degrees the distributor shaft rotates while the coil primary is carrying current is known as **dwell**. Any change in the point gap will change the dwell approximately 1° for each 0.001 in. (0.025 mm) change in point gap. This is illustrated in Figure 11–21.

133

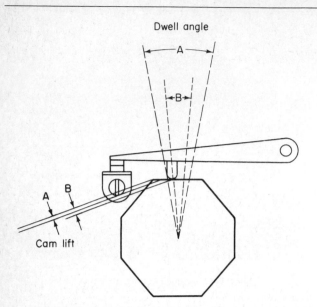

Fig. 11-21 Any change in the point gap will change the dwell.

Fig. 11-22 Chrysler and Ford type (a) and Delco-Remy type (b) inductive timers.

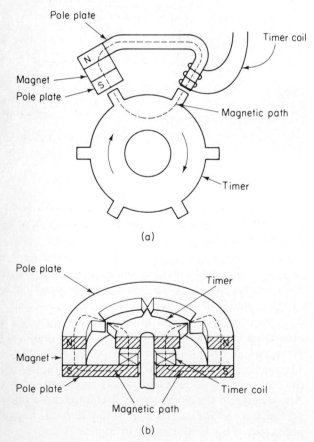

Inductive Timer. An inductive timer is used in distributors for solid-state ignition systems to trigger an ignition electronic control unit. The electronic control opens the coil primary circuit to stop the primary current.

The rotating part of the timer is called a reluctor (Chrysler), timer core (Delco-Remy), or armature (Ford). As it rotates, the teeth of the timer come very close to pole plates of a small permanent magnet. Being close reduces the reluctance to concentrate the magnetic lines of force as shown in Figure 11-22 (reluctance was discussed in Section 1-5). Continued rotation starts to open the space between the timer and plates to increase the reluctance. This will separate the magnetic lines of force. As they separate they cut across a small trigger coil made of many turns of fine wire. This induces a voltage in the trigger coil, similar to the voltage shown in Figure 11-23 (see Section 1-9 for a discussion of induced voltage). The voltage gets stronger as the speed of the rotating trigger increases.

A wire from each end of the trigger coil connects to the electronic control unit. This was shown in Figure 11-5. The change in voltage from positive to negative stops the current flow in the base circuit of the power transistor in the control unit. This stops the primary current long enough to allow the ignition coil secondary windings to discharge (see Section 11-2). The electronic circuits in the control unit turn the power transistor base circuit back on long enough for the primary current to saturate the coil before the next discharge (dwell). The coil is turned back on right after the spark plug fires in Chrysler control units. You can see this just to the right of the firing line of each cylinder on the scope pattern in Figure 11-24. The Ford electronic module turns the primary current back on after the coil and condenser have

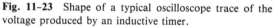

Fig. 11-23 Shape of a typical oscilloscope trace of the voltage produced by an inductive timer.

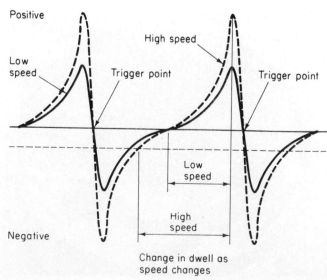

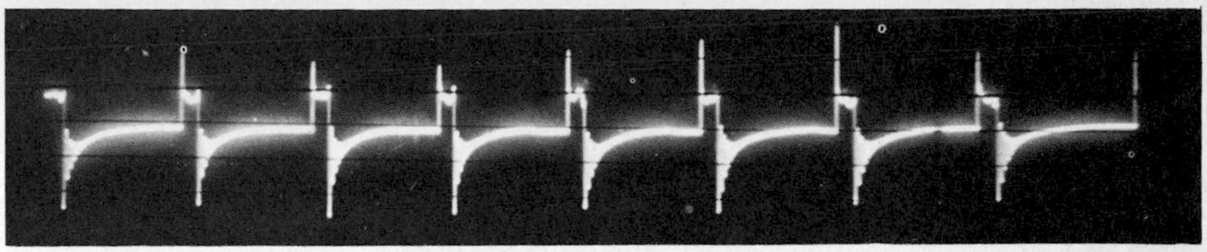

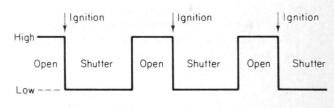

Fig. 11-24 Oscilloscope trace of the secondary voltage from a Chrysler solid-state electronic ignition system.

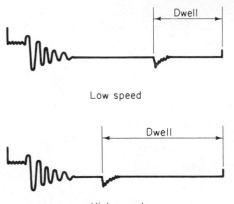

Fig. 11-25 Changes in dwell with a change in speed on Delco-Remy HEI ignition systems.

Fig. 11-26 Shutter in a Hall-effect sensor.

Fig. 11-27 Typical oscilloscope trace of a Hall-effect timer.

fully discharged. Its scope pattern looks like the pattern of the point-type ignition system shown in Figure 11-10. The ignition module used in the Delco-Remy HEI distributor adjusts the primary turn-on time in relation to engine speed. At low speeds the primary current is turned on a long time after the spark plug fires. As the engine speed increases, the primary current is turned on shortly after the coil and condenser have fully discharged (Figure 11-25). At very high speeds the secondary ignition pattern will look like the Chrysler electronic ignition pattern shown in Figure 11-24.

Hall-Effect Timer. The newest type of distributor trigger uses the Hall effect. This distributor trigger has a steel shutter connected to the distributor rotor. You saw this in Figure 11-20. As the distributor rotates, one shutter blade passes through the sensor (Figure 11-26). This is followed by a gap before the next shutter blade passes through the sensor. The sensor has a small permanent magnet. The shutter changes the shape of a magnetic field between the magnet and sensor. A semiconductor circuit in the sensor reads the change in the magnetic field. It amplifies the change and forms a square-wave signal such as that shown in Figure 11-27. The signal from the Hall-effect sensor is sent to an electronic control module. The module controls the primary current. The signal from the trigger sensor has constant signal strength, regardless of the rotation speed. As a result it gives the same signal strength even at the lowest cranking speeds. The

Hall-effect trigger is gaining in use because it is the easiest type of timing signal to use with digital computerized engine controls.

Ignition Advance. You will remember from Section 11-1 that the timing must advance when the engine runs faster and when there is less load on the engine. Timing advance is decreased for low speeds and heavy loads. A mechanical advance mechanism is used on older engines to increase the advance as the engine runs faster. A vacuum advance mechanism on these engines advances the timing when there is more manifold vacuum at light engine loads. Modern computer-controlled timing systems advance the timing even with changes in altitudes and temperatures.

Mechanical advance. The distributor shaft rotates the distributor timing trigger through a mechanical advance mechanism. The mechanism has centrifugal flyweights held with springs. An exploded view of typical mechanical advance parts is shown in Figure 11–28. The advance flyweights in this mechanical advance are below the movable plate. This location is typical of Chrysler and older Ford distributors. Delco-Remy and newer Ford distributors have the advance flyweights above the trigger (see Figures 11–19 and 11–29). As the distributor rotates faster, the flyweights swing outward against the force of the springs. Cam-shaped surfaces on the flyweights advance or move the timing trigger position forward **in the direction** of distributor shaft rotation on the distributor shaft.

The distributor shaft drive is timed to a specific crankshaft angle while the distributor advance mechanisms are in full retard. This is called **basic timing**. The distributor shaft always has this position in relation to the crankshaft. Distributor advance mechanisms always move ahead from the basic timing. The mechanical advance is sensitive only to engine speed. Flyweights and springs control the amount of timing change at any specific engine speed by rotating the timing trigger in the direction of shaft rotation. When this happens the points or the solid-state module (Figure 11–29) turns the primary current off before the crankshaft rotates to the basic timing point to advance ignition timing.

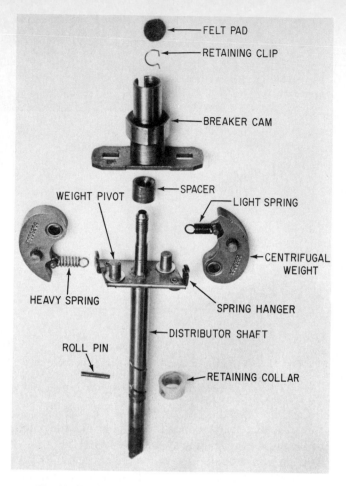

Fig. 11-28 Exploded view showing the parts of a mechanical advance mechanism.

Fig. 11-29 Mechanical advance above the timing trigger.

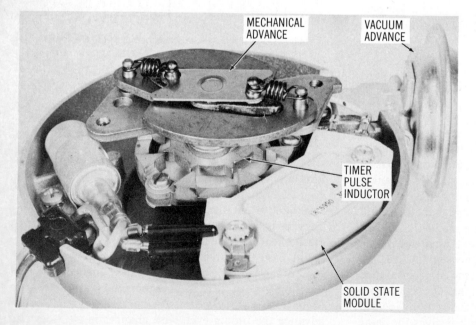

Vacuum advance. The points and inductive pickups are mounted on a movable plate within the distributor housing. A link from the diaphragm in the vacuum advance unit holds the movable plate position. You can see the vacuum advance unit in Figures 11–19 and 11–29. The outside part of the vacuum diaphragm is connected by tubing to sense vacuum at a port within the carburetor or throttle body. There is no manifold vacuum on the vacuum advance unit when the throttle plate is closed (Figure 11–30). Manifold vacuum can reach the vacuum advance unit when the throttle plate opens past the vacuum port. Vacuum pulls the movable plate in an advance direction **against the direction** of distributor shaft rotation. This opens the points or turns the control module off before the basic timing degree is reached for ignition advance. The vacuum advance mechanism is sensitive to ported vacuum. This, in turn, comes from manifold vacuum. Manifold vacuum results from the engine load and throttle position.

Mechanical and vacuum advance mechanisms work together to give the ignition advance needed for the most efficient combustion and the lowest practical emission level. Any change in the basic timing or timing advance will reduce normal engine performance. If, on the other hand, the engine is modified from the manufacturer's original design, timing and advance curves should also be modified to produce the most performance. Follow emission decal or reference manuals on emission controls

when you make vacuum hose connections and adjustments to minimize exhaust emissions.

Computer-controlled advance. The computer takes the place of the mechanical and vacuum advance mechanisms in modern ignition systems. It provides more exact ignition timing for low emissions and good fuel economy. The basic wiring of a computer-controlled ignition advance is shown in Figure 11–31. Compare this figure to Figures 11–4 and 11–5.

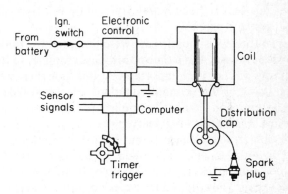

Fig. 11–31 Basic wiring of a computer-controlled ignition advance.

The computer-controlled ignition advance uses a solid-state timing trigger. In most engines the trigger is in the distributor. On some advanced designs the trigger is on the crankshaft. The basic advance trigger signal is sent to the computer. At the same time, the computer receives signals from engine coolant temperature, engine speed, vehicle speed, throttle position, manifold vacuum, atmospheric pressure, and so on. The computer compares these signals to the program built into the computer. Next, the computer delays the ignition pulse signal the correct amount of time, it triggers an electronic control unit, which, in turn, triggers the coil primary. When running at basic timing the delay is just long enough to fire the following cylinder in the firing order. Reducing the delay time fires the cylinder sooner so that timing is advanced.

11–4 IGNITION SYSTEM CHANGES

Have you ever wondered why there were so many changes in ignition systems and engine controls in the 15 years from 1970 through 1985? The changes were made because the vehicle manufacturers had to meet federal and state

Fig. 11–30 Line drawing showing where the distributor vacuum advance port opens into the carburetor or throttle body.

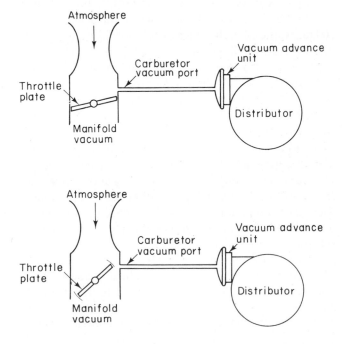

emission and fuel economy standards. Fortunately, automotive engineers learned a great deal through research of the combustion process. As a result, the engine is much finer tuned than would have been possible without this research.

During this time automotive service technicians would just learn one new system when it was changed again in new model vehicles. As a result of different ignition systems it is very important that you follow procedures in the service manual for the vehicle you are servicing. This is the only way you will be able to service these systems properly.

In the 1960s muscle cars were designed for power and speed. It was also a time of low-cost gasoline, so fuel economy was not very important. At this time there were no emission or fuel economy standards. The first federal vehicle emission standards applied to the 1968 automobiles. Each following year or two the standards became tighter, reducing emissions. First the manufacturers modified the engine and added engine controls. The engine controls became more complex through the 1974 model year. They did reduce emissions but they also reduced the engine power, speed, and fuel economy. In 1975 the engine control systems were simplified and the engine was modified to give better performance and economy. This was made possible by installing a catalytic converter to **oxidize** hydrocarbons and carbon monoxide left in the exhaust gas. Engines with catalytic converters required unleaded gasoline. In addition, a solid-state ignition system was used. This ignition system would not change basic timing in use, as point-type ignition systems had done.

By 1974 the oil-producing countries were raising the price of crude oil and Congress passed a law requiring improved fuel economy. The law became effective for the 1978 automobiles. To meet the new standards requiring lower emissions and better fuel economy, the automobile manufacturers improved the combustion efficiency of the engine and reduced the weight of the automobiles, primarily by making them smaller. The combustion efficiency was improved in a number of ways. The shape of the combustion chamber was changed. The engine intake and exhaust passages were modified. The timing and fuel metering systems operated more accurately by using computer controls. The catalytic converter reduced the emissions left in the exhaust gas.

Standards. You can see from Figure 11–32 that there were decreases in the emission standards in 1972, 1975, 1977, and 1981. Each of these decreases were accom-

Year	Federal HC/CO/NOx	California HC/CO/NOx	Cafe (mpg)	mpg change
71	4.6 / 47 / –	4.6 / 47 / 4.0	–	–
72	3.4 / 39 / 4.0	3.4 / 39 / 3.1	–	–
73	3.4 / 39 / 3.0	3.4 / 39 / 3.0	–	–
74	No change	No change	–	–
75	1.5 / 15 / 3.1	0.9 / 9 / 2.0	–	–
76	No change	No change	–	–
77	No change	No change	–	–
78	1.5 / 15 / 2.0	0.41 / 9.0 / 1.9	18	–
79	No change	No change	19	1
80	0.41 / 7.0 / 2.0	No change	20	1
81	0.41 / 3.4 / 1.0	0.39 / 7.0 / 0.7	22	2
82	No change	No change	24	2
83	No change	No change	26	2
84	No change	No change	27	1
85	No change	No change	27.5	0.5

Fig. 11–32 Changes in emission standards from 1971 through 1985.

panied by major changes in engine controls. In 1978 when fuel economy regulations became effective the corporate average fuel economy (CAFE) was 18 mpg. The CAFE increased each year until it reached 27.5 in 1985. Notice in Figure 11–32 that in 1982 and 1983 the fuel economy made big jumps of 2 mpg each year.

Let's see how the CAFE is determined by using two vehicles, one that gets 20 mpg and the other that gets 40 mpg. If you add the mpg of the two vehicles and divide by 2, you will see that their average is 30 mpg. This is not the CAFE of the two vehicles. If each were driven 100 miles, the 20 mph vehicle would use 5 gallons of fuel. The 40 mpg vehicle would use 2.5 gallons. Together they used 7.5 gallons to go a total of 200 miles. Divide the 200 miles by the 7.5 gallons to get the CAFE. In this case the CAFE is 26.67 mpg. You can see that it takes more than one high-mileage vehicle to offset one low-mileage vehicle to reduce the corporate average fuel economy.

With this background you can see why automobile manufacturers had to change the engine controls. Some of the changes in engine controls were put on a few vehicle models in the year before the standards were required. This gave the manufacturers experience in making the new systems. It also gave service technicians a chance to get some experience on the new systems before they were put on all the corporate vehicles.

Both domestic and import vehicle manufacturers have made similar changes in their ignition systems to meet the changing standards. Let's take a look at some of the major changes made by the domestic manufacturers.

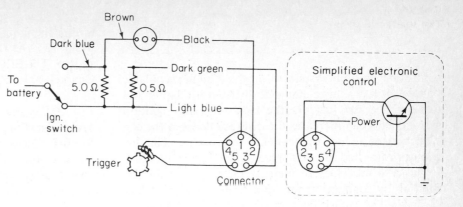

Fig. 11-33 Wiring circuit of a typical Chrysler solid-state ignition system.

Chrysler. In 1971 Chrysler put electronic ignition systems on a few automobiles. By 1973 this system was in use on all Chrysler automobiles.

The Chrysler electronic ignition system is the simplest of all solid-state ignition systems. The electrical circuit of this system is shown in Figure 11–33. A new plate with the timer pickup coil replaced the breaker plate in the distributor. A timer rotor (reluctor) replaced the distributor cam. An electronic control unit and a second resistor were added to the ignition circuit. The power transistor in the control unit turns the primary current on and off when it is signaled by the timer.

An analog computer-controlled advance, called Lean Burn, was put on some 400 CID engines in 1976. There was only a small amount of mechanical advance (5°) in the distributor. The rest of the ignition advance (about 45°) was made by the computer. All the mechanical advance was taken out of the distributor in 1977. In 1978 Chrysler introduced the Hall-effect timer on their new four-cylinder engines (see Figure 11–20). The Hall-effect timer puts a reverse bias on the base of a primary current power transistor, just like the induction timer does. The control unit and digital computer used with the Hall-effect timer are different than the one used

with the inductive timer. Feedback fuel metering with an oxygen sensor and a knock sensor-controlled timing retard were introduced in 1981. These are discussed in Chapter 13.

Ford. In 1973 Ford put solid-state Motorcraft ignition systems on the Continental Mark IV. It was put on all Ford automobiles in 1974. There are a number of different ignition modules in use on Ford engines for use on different vehicle models and years of manufacture. The wire positions and the connectors are different between modules so that they will not be used in the wrong ignition system. You can use the color of the wire **sealing block** on the module to identify which module should be used. Fortunately for automotive service technicians, Ford has kept the same wire color for the same part of the ignition circuit for each module connection, regardless of the module, the wire arrangement, or ignition system used. The wiring diagram of a typical Ford solid-state ignition system is shown in Figure 11–34. The wire color codes on this figure match the color codes on all solid-state Motorcraft ignition systems but not the location on the module.

In 1977 Ford introduced the Motorcraft Duraspark ignition. This ignition system is a modification of the

Fig. 11-34 Wiring circuit of a typical Ford solid-state ignition system.

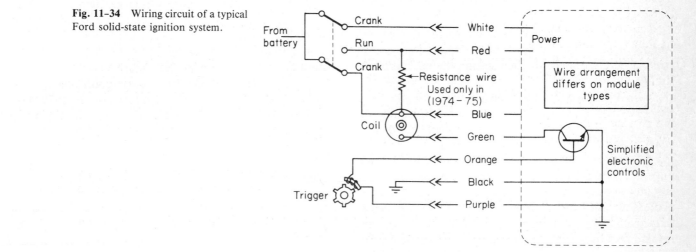

solid-state ignition system to produce higher available voltage. It has a large-diameter distributor adapter and cap but operates just like the 1974 solid-state ignition system. This cap increases the distance between the cap electrodes to reduce the tendency to crossfire. The distributor rotor had to be enlarged to match the larger cap. It was also necessary to increase the ignition cable insulation by changing from 7-mm cable to 8-mm cable.

The Duraspark ignition was put on all Ford automobile engines in 1978. The resistance wire feeding the coil used in the Duraspark ignition primary was changed from the 1.3 Ω wire used on solid-state ignition systems to 1.1 Ω. This change increased the flow of primary current. The greater primary current increased the available voltage. To prevent excess primary current, the Duraspark ignition module was designed to change the dwell with engine speed so that only enough primary current would flow to saturate the coil. The ignition system would get too hot if it had too much primary current. It has low dwell at low speeds. The dwell increases as the engine speed increases.

Duraspark ignition was modified for 1978 for use at high altitude. This system had a third connector on the ignition module that led to a BARO sensor. The high-altitude carburetor was calibrated lean for use in high altitudes. When these automobiles are driven at low altitudes, they have a tendency to spark knock. Using electronics, the BARO sensor signal is used by the module to retard the timing from 3 to 6° when the automobile is at low altitude. This retard prevents spark knock that would damage the engine.

The same three connector module is used on engines that have economy calibration. The third connector leads to a manifold vacuum sensor. When the vacuum is low (open throttle) the timing is retarded 3 to 6° to prevent spark knock.

If the third connector is disconnected the ignition will operate like all other Ford solid-state ignition systems. It must be disconnected when setting the basic ignition timing.

In 1978 Ford first used the Electronic Engine Control (EEC). This system controlled ignition timing advance with electronics instead of mechanical advance weights and a vacuum advance diaphragm. To do this the orange module lead wire connects to the EEC processing unit. The purple module wire is not used. In this system the basic timing and speed signals feed the EEC processing unit from a crankshaft position sensor, rather than from a distributor trigger. In 1981 an oxygen sensor and feed back fuel metering were added to the system. A Hall-effect trigger was used in some 1984 Ford vehicles.

You will see that the same procedure is used for testing the ignition part of the EEC system as you will use to test the Duraspark and Ford solid-state ignition system. The EEC systems are discussed in more detail in Chapter 13.

Delco-Remy. Three different types of ignition systems saw limited use on a small number of General Motors vehicles between 1962 and 1975. Each type added a new feature in the development toward the solid-state High Energy Ignition (HEI) system that became standard in 1975. The 1963 Delcotronic ignition on a few models replaced the ignition points with an inductive trigger. The trigger used a solid-state pulse amplifier to control the primary current. The Chrysler electronic ignition system introduced eight years later is quite similar to this system. A capacitive discharge (C-D) high-voltage ignition system, with an inductive pickup, was introduced in 1967. It used a large capacitor and solid-state controls to fire the coil. This system gave excellent performance in the engine of some of the GM muscle cars that used rich air/fuel mixtures. It did not work as well as an inductive ignition system on the lean mixtures used in engines with emission controls. This lead to the 1972 Unitized ignition system. The Unitized ignition system was the first ignition system to use integrated solid-state circuits and to place the coil in the distributor cap. Like the other two systems, it used an inductive trigger. The Unitized ignition system has the same secondary voltage as the Delcotronic ignition system because it used a standard-type coil, had the same diameter distributor cap, and the same size ignition cables.

In 1974 the High Energy Ignition system was introduced on a few General Motors engines. It was put on all their engines in 1975. The large diameter distributor cap and 8-mm spark plug cables allowed this system to operate at a higher secondary voltage for better ignition of lean air/fuel mixtures in engines with emission controls. Because the distributor was large, there was enough room to place the four-terminal integrated ignition module inside the distributor cap. The wiring for this ignition system is shown in Figure 11–35. You can see this module in the distributor on Figure 11–29.

The first Delco-Remy computer-controlled ignition system, called MISAR, was introduced on the 1977 Oldsmobile Toronado. It used a three-terminal ignition module in the distributor. In 1978 Buick added Electronic Controlled Spark (ECS) to the HEI ignition system on turbocharged engines. This system used a five-terminal ignition module (Figure 11–36). When a knock sensor noticed vibration caused by detonation, it retarded the ignition timing. This allowed high ignition advance for good economy at cruising speeds and high power at full throttle without detonation that could damage the pistons and valves.

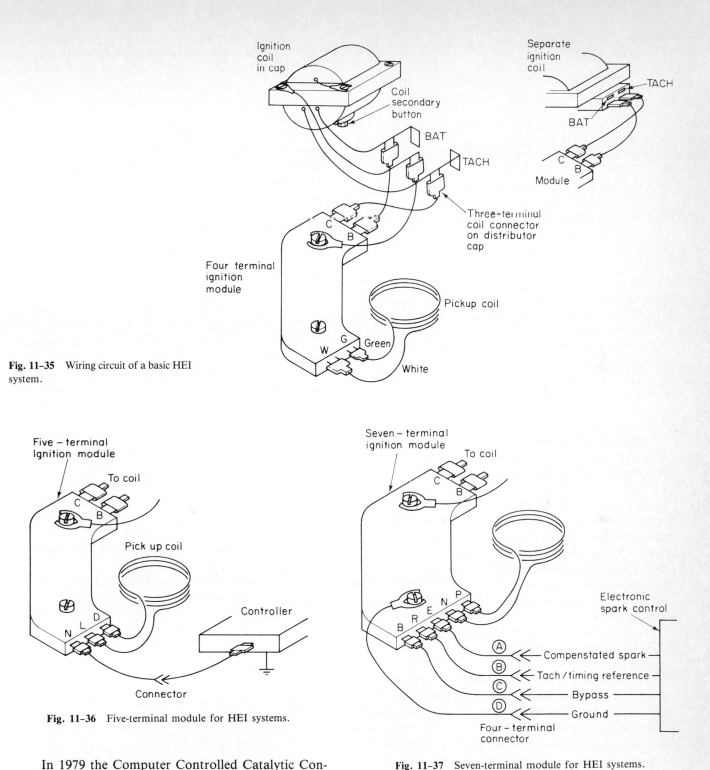

Fig. 11–35 Wiring circuit of a basic HEI system.

Fig. 11–36 Five-terminal module for HEI systems.

Fig. 11–37 Seven-terminal module for HEI systems.

In 1979 the Computer Controlled Catalytic Converter (C4) system was introduced in California. It was used on some vehicles in the rest of the 49 states in 1980. The ignition module in this system has seven terminals (Figure 11–37). The system uses an electronic spark timing (EST) computer to control ignition advance. There is no mechanical or vacuum advance in the distributor. It uses an oxygen sensor in the exhaust pipe to check the oxygen remaining in the exhaust gas. The computer uses information from the sensors to control the air/fuel mix-

ture going into the engine. The C4 system was updated in 1981 as the Computer Command Control system. The distributor was further updated in 1983 by limiting the use of the inductive pickup to starting and an engine speed signal. A Hall-effect trigger was added above the inductive trigger for use during all engine operating conditions (Figure 11–38).

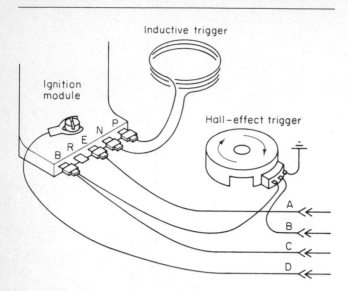

Fig. 11–38 Hall-effect trigger added to the HEI system using a seven-terminal module.

Distributorless Ignition. You will remember that the first step to reduce ignition system maintenance was to use a solid-state trigger in place of the ignition points. Ignition points would wear out in time, so they had to be replaced. The trigger did not wear, so it did not need to be replaced. As a result the basic ignition timing would never change. The ignition advance still depended on mechanical and vacuum advance units. These units would stick and wear, so the timing advance would change. The next development was computer-controlled advance, first introduced by Chrysler in 1976. This system gave a more accurate timing advance than mechanical and vacuum units throughout the life of the system. The distributor was still needed to distribute the secondary current to each cylinder at the correct time. In time the distributor gears, shaft, and bearings will wear. Each time a cylinder fires, a spark jumps from the rotor to one electrode in the cap. In time the electrodes will burn, a carbon path will cause cross firing, or the parts will wear out. As a result, the cap and rotor must be replaced. Because a computer will control the ignition advance, it was possible for Buick to introduce in 1984 the Computer Controlled Coil Ignition (C^3I) system, which did not use a distributor. It was first used on the sequential port injected, turbocharged 3.8 liter engine. The only maintenance required on this type of ignition system is to replace the spark plugs.

To understand this system we must go back to some basics. You will remember that there are four strokes in the engine combustion cycle: intake, compression, power

and exhaust. Both valves are closed during the compression and power strokes. At least one valve is open during the exhaust and intake strokes. Ignition is timed to fire the intake charge near the end of the compression stroke. Halfway through the combustion cycle (one full revolution of the crankshaft) the exhaust valve is gradually closing. A spark at this point in the engine cycle has no effect on the engine because only burned combustion gases are in the combustion chamber. The C^3I system fires the spark plug once **each** crankshaft revolution: near the end of the compression stroke to ignite the compressed charge, and a 360° crankshaft rotation later, at the end of the exhaust stroke. This is shown in Figure 11–39.

Each end of the coil secondary winding is connected to a spark plug in this ignition system. The spark plugs are in paired cylinders that fire halfway through the combustion cycle from each other. On a four-cylinder engine with a firing order of 1342, cylinders 1 and 4 are paired and 3 and 2 are paired. On a V-6 engine with a 165432 firing order the pairs are 1–4, 6–3, and 5–2. A separate coil is needed for each spark plug pair. When the secondary current flows it jumps the gap in **both** spark plugs to complete the secondary ignition circuit. Each secondary coil fires once during each revolution of the crankshaft. First it ignites the charge in one of the cylinders. On the next revolution it ignites the charge in the other cylinder of the pair. You can see how the spark plugs are paired in Figure 11–40. Remember that in an ignition system with a distributor the spark jumps a gap between the rotor tip and cap electrode as well as the gap between the spark plug electrodes. There is very little pressure in the cylinder that is on the exhaust stroke. As a result it will take about as much energy to jump the gap in this spark plug as it does to jump the gap between the rotor and distributor cap electrode. Therefore, the coil delivers about the same amount of energy in the C^3I system as it does in an ignition system using a distributor. In addition, the spark occurs in the cylinder where it is electrically shielded so that the spark does not produce radio noise

Fig. 11–39 Ignition fires at the same point on each revolution.

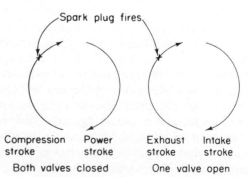

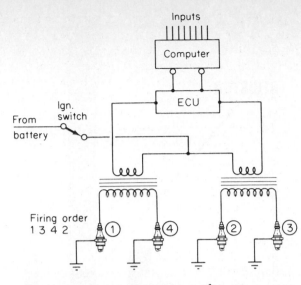

Fig. 11-40 Paired cylinders using a C³I ignition system.

as the spark does when it flashes between the rotor and cap electrode in a distributor. With no rotor-cap electrode alignment the ignition timing can be advanced or retarded as far as necessary with no cross firing between the spark plug cable electrodes.

Triggers on the crankshaft and camshaft let the computer know when each piston reaches the basic timing point. The computer also gets signals from the other engine and vehicle sensors. The computer compares the information and adjusts the ignition advance to the exact advance required for the engine operating conditions. It then stops the primary current in one of the coils to fire the pair of spark plugs connected to the coil secondary winding. It does this at the correct time for each of the spark plug pairs.

11-5 SPARK PLUGS

The ignition system is made so that it will send an electrical arc across the gap between the spark plug electrodes. If the correct spark plug is not used, there will be problems igniting the charge. This will cause a misfire or it will damage pistons. The spark plug changes the electrical energy of the ignition secondary circuit to heat energy in the electrical arc. The arc will ignite enough of the intake charge so that the charge will keep burning.

Construction. The spark plug has three major parts: the shell, the insulator, and the electrodes. These can be identified in Figure 11-41. The shell supports the insulator and it has threads that screw into the cylinder head. The thread must be long enough to allow the electrodes of the spark plug to be flush with the combustion chamber (Figure 11-42). The thread length is called the spark plug

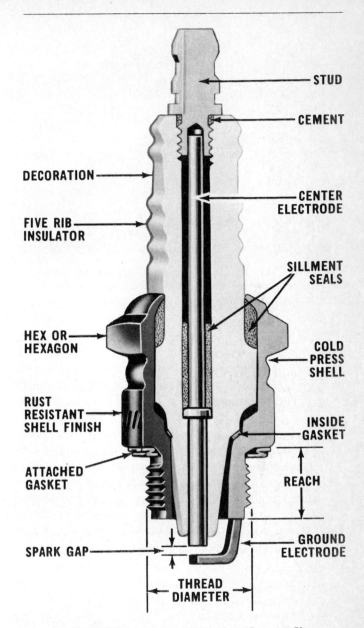

Fig. 11-41 Parts of a typical spark plug. (Courtesy Champion Spark Plug Company.)

reach. If the reach were too long, it could damage the valves or piston. The end of the spark plug could get hot enough to cause preignition. Threads on the automotive spark plug have metric 14- and 18-mm threads. The shell seals the spark plug hole in the combustion chamber. Some shells seal with a tapered spark plug seat. Others seal with a metal spark plug gasket (Figure 11-43).

The center electrode is placed in the center of the insulator. Modern electrodes are made from two pieces.

Fig. 11-42 The spark plug reach is made just long enough to reach the combustion chamber. This spark plug seats on a metal gasket seal.

The spark plug cable is connected to the top piece. The bottom piece goes into the hot combustion chamber. Using two pieces lets the spark plug manufacturer use the type of metal that will best meet the needs of the spark plug. The center electrode is sealed with a gastight electrical conducting seal material.

Some spark plug types use a resistor between the two sections of the electrode. The resistance changes the electrical radiation from the ignition system so that it does not interfere with television and radio reception or other electronic equipment in the automobile. The resistor also increases the life of the spark plug electrode by cutting down peak current that would burn the electrodes. Figure 11-44 is a section view of a resistor spark plug.

RESISTOR

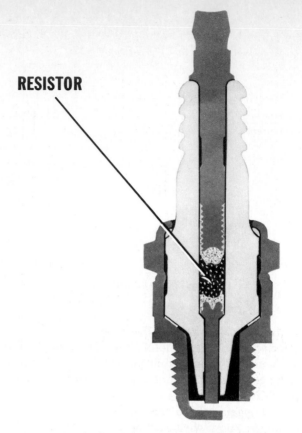

Fig. 11-44 Section view of a resistor spark plug. (Courtesy AC Spark Plug Division, General Motors Corporation.)

Heat Range. Spark plugs must operate between specified temperatures. If the spark plug operates too cold, it will foul with deposits. These deposits will leak secondary electrical energy to ground, so the spark plug will not fire. The scope pattern of a fouled spark plug was shown in Figure 11-13. If the spark plug operates too hot, the

Fig. 11-43 Typical spark plug designs used in automotive engines. The two on the right have tapered seats.

electrodes will burn rapidly and cause preignition. Preignition will lead to physical engine damage, usually burned pistons. The piston shown in Figure 11–45 was damaged by preignition. The minimum spark plug temperature for nonfouling operation is 650°F (340°C). Preignition will generally occur above 1500°F (815°C). This range is shown in Figure 11–46. The spark plug must be within these temperature limits under all normal engine operating conditions.

When an engine is running under heavy loads, such as pulling a trailer, the combustion chambers become hot.

They also become hot in high-compression engines. Cold-heat-range spark plugs are needed to keep the spark plugs from overheating. Spark plugs that have a hot heat range are used in engines that have a tendency to run with low power, such as driving in traffic and in engines with low compression. Cold-running spark plugs used in these engines would foul with oil or with carbon from light-duty operation. Hot-heat-range spark plugs are needed in these engines to keep the temperature of the spark plug nose high enough to stop fouling. The spark plug heat range does not affect the temperature of the electrical arc.

A cold-heat-range spark plug rapidly transfers heat from the spark plug nose through the shell. Some spark plugs have a copper core in the center electrode to help carry heat from the electrode tip. In a hot-heat-range spark plug the heat transfers slower. It can be seen in Figure 11–47 that the heat has to travel farther in a hot-heat-range spark plug. The spark plug heat range you use to replace spark plugs should be the one the manufacturer recommends. Modified engines may require a different-heat-range spark plug than the one specified for the original engine. Spark plugs for modified engines should be selected by working up from cold-heat-range spark plugs. If the cold-heat-range spark plug fouls, the next-hotter heat range should be used. The correct heat range is reached when the spark plug does not foul. In this way

Fig. 11–45 Piston damaged by preignition.

Fig. 11–47 Heat transfer path through a cold- and a hot-heat-range spark plug. (Courtesy Champion Spark Plug Company.)

Fig. 11–46 Temperature range of spark plugs. (Courtesy Champion Spark Plug Company.)

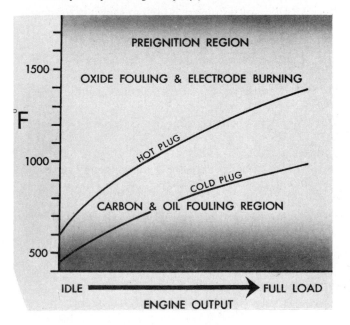

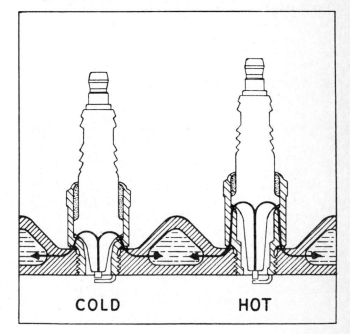

you can avoid preignition while you find the correct-heat-range spark plug.

It is interesting to note that the center electrode of automotive spark plugs has negative polarity. Hot bodies have increased electron activity. The center electrode is the hottest part of the spark plug. It therefore requires the lowest voltage to force free electrons to form an electrical arc. The hot negative voltage center electrode helps to minimize the required ignition voltage. If the polarity is reversed, a higher secondary voltage is needed to force an arc across the spark plug. Secondary polarity can be changed by reversing the primary coil leads, so care must be taken to see that the primary leads are correctly connected to the coil.

11–6 SPARK PLUG CABLES

Modern engines use nonmetallic resistance-type conductor secondary cables. As with spark plug resistors, these cables have good ignition radiation suppression (IRS cable). The television and radio noise suppression (TVRS cable) reduces the radio-frequency emissions that come from the ignition system. Aluminum distributor cap electrode inserts are used with suppression-type ignition cables. Old model engines used metal conductor secondary cables with copper distributor cap inserts. Mixing distributor caps and cable types will cause corrosion in the tower of the cap. The corrosion will add resistance to the secondary circuit.

Suppression-type ignition cable with nonmetallic conductors should not be replaced with metal conductor cable. Ignition systems are designed to operate with the resistance built into the cable. The use of metal conductor cables on these systems will lead to rapid spark plug electrode wear. Metal conductors also cause radio-frequency emission that causes interference in nearby radios and television sets. Finally, Federal Communication Commission laws prohibit the use of metal conductor secondary cables.

Emission-controlled engines run much hotter than engines without emission controls. Old-style ignition cables will not last in high underhood temperatures. You will have to make sure that you replace secondary cables with the proper high-temperature insulation on cables used on emission-controlled engines. Insulation on high-temperature cable is made from either Hypalon or silicone materials.

High-energy ignition systems need more insulation. The insulation on the spark plug cables used with these systems has been increased. The outside diameter of the cable is 8 mm instead of the typical 7 mm.

STUDY QUESTIONS

Section 11–1

1. What type of charge mixture needs the highest ignition voltage?

2. Why were point-type systems replaced with solid-state electronic controls?

3. What two changes were made in the high-voltage parts of solid-state ignition systems?

4. Why is the ignition advanced as the engine runs faster?

5. Why is the ignition advanced as the manifold vacuum increases?

6. What is the main reason for having vacuum advance on an ignition system?

7. Under what three engine operating conditions does the engine produce the most unburned hydrocarbons and carbon monoxide?

8. How does retarding the ignition timing reduce hydrocarbon and carbon monoxide emissions?

Section 11–2

9. How do point-type and solid-state ignition systems differ?

10. What type of instrument is used to show the constantly changing voltage in the ignition system?

11. What does the capacitor do in a point-type distributor?

12. Where are the two gaps in the secondary ignition system?

13. What stops and restarts the ignition primary current in a point-type ignition system?

14. What stops and restarts the ignition primary current in solid-state ignition systems?

15. Why is the primary wound outside the secondary winding in a standard ignition coil?

16. Why do coils have laminated cores and shields?

17. What is the advantage of wrapping the primary winding inside the secondary winding on E-type coils?

18. What is the advantage of potting E-type coils?

19. What is the form of energy stored in an ignition coil?

20. What determines the amount of available voltage in the secondary circuit?

21. When is the capacitance of a coil charged?

22. During what part of the coil energy release does ignition take place?

23. How does fast rise time help ignition?

24. How does the capacitor reduce point arc?

25. Ignition systems may have a capacitor on each primary terminal of the coil. What is the purpose of each capacitor?

26. What is the main cause of ignition leakage?

27. What is the advantage of a high-energy ignition system?

28. What is the disadvantage of a high-energy ignition system?

29. What part of the ignition system is temperature compensated?

30. What does the ignition bypass do?

Section 11-3

31. How fast is the camshaft driven?

32. What problem would occur in the distributor if the ignition timing were advanced too much?

33. What happens to the dwell when the point gap is reduced 0.002 in.?

34. How does changing the induction trigger gap affect the dwell in solid-state ignition systems?

35. When does the inductive trigger signal the electronic control to fire a spark plug?

36. What is the advantage of a Hall-effect sensor?

37. Which way does the mechanical advance rotate the position of the timing trigger?

38. Which way does the vacuum advance rotate the movable plate in the distributor?

39. When should the timing advance be modified to produce the most performance?

40. Where can you find out what the correct vacuum hose connections and engine control adjustments should be?

Section 11-4

41. Why were so many changes made in ignition systems between 1970 and 1985?

42. What was the advantage of using a catalytic converter?

43. How can you identify which Ford ignition module to use?

44. Why is a large-diameter distributor cap used on Ford Duraspark distributors?

45. Why was the Duraspark module designed to change the dwell with engine speed?

46. What does the Ford EEC system do that was not done by the Duraspark system?

47. How does the HEI ignition system differ from the Delco-Remy point-type system?

48. What does a Computer Command Control system do that an HEI system does not do?

49. What ignition parts wear on a Computer Controlled Coil Ignition system?

50. What spark plugs are fired by each coil in the C^3I system?

51. What are the advantages of the C^3I system?

Section 11-5

52. Name the three major parts of a spark plug.

53. What should you call the thread length of a spark plug?

54. What does the resistor do in a spark plug?

55. What would be the result of using a spark plug with a heat range that is too cold?

56. What would be the result of using a spark plug with a heat range that is too hot?

57. How does the heat range of the spark plug affect the temperature of the electrical arc?

Section 11-6

58. What is suppressed with suppression-type ignition cables?

59. What causes suppression in the ignition cables?

60. What is special about ignition cables used on emission-controlled engines?

IGNITION SYSTEM MAINTENANCE

Ignition system secondary operating voltage is the voltage required by the spark plug. The ignition has to produce this voltage if the engine runs. Any change in combustion chamber conditions, such as compression pressure, temperature, and air/fuel mixture ratios, will affect the required voltage. These must be considered when testing ignition systems.

The ignition system is serviced (1) to produce its original high available voltage at the correct instant in the cycle, and (2) to reduce the voltage required to fire the spark plug.

The performance of the ignition system is reduced as the primary wires and secondary cables develop resistance or become shorted. The condition of all wires and cables, including their terminals and junctions, are checked when servicing the ignition system. Distributor caps can crack or form an electrical path called a **carbon track**. This allows the secondary electrical energy to leak to ground or cross fire to another cylinder. A faulty rotor will allow leakage to ground or it will increase secondary resistance as the rotor tip erodes away.

All types of ignition systems use spark plugs. They operate in a combustion chamber with the hot combustion gases together with some oil that leaks past the piston rings and valve stems. Combustion deposits that form as the engine runs will coat the entire combustion chamber,

including the tip of the spark plug. Some of the combustion deposits will conduct electricity. These tend to bleed electrical energy from the ignition system so that the spark will be weak or there will be no spark. This condition is called spark plug fouling. Sometimes deposits build up on the spark plug between the electrodes. These deposits prevent the charge gases from getting between the electrodes, where they must be if they are going to ignite. In either case the voltage required to fire the spark plug is affected, so the spark plugs must be serviced.

The ignition timing advance must be checked. Mechanically operated timing advance mechanisms stick and wear. Electronic advance controls may fail so that the timing does not advance correctly. Faulty timing advance affects the ignition timing for fuel economy, engine power, and minimum exhaust emissions.

Point-type ignition systems require additional service. As the rubbing block wears, the distributor point gap will reduce. This retards the ignition timing. Burning of the contact surface of the points will widen the gap. This too will cause a change in timing. Corrosion of the point contact surface will also increase resistance in the primary circuit. This resistance reduces current flow in the ignition primary circuit. The resistance allows less coil saturation and lower available voltage. Using correct testing and servicing procedures, you can recondition the ignition system so that it will deliver the same performance as it had when it was new.

Routine service of the ignition system includes replacing spark plugs, points, and condenser. You set basic ignition timing to complete the routine service. After this work is done many technicians assume that the ignition system will operate correctly.

One way to make sure that the ignition system is operating correctly is to test each part of the ignition system, including each wire and connector. You must repair or replace faulty parts when you find them. After this is done you can be sure that the ignition system will work correctly.

12-1 SPARK PLUG SERVICE

The spark plug is the end point in the ignition system. Its tip is in the combustion chamber, where it is covered with combustion deposits, eroded, and corroded. Spark plugs require periodic service, regardless of the type of ignition system used.

Do not remove spark plugs when the engine is hot. This is especially important when working on engines with aluminum heads. The aluminum in the head expands about twice as much as the steel in the spark plug shell when both have the same increase in temperature. The greater expansion causes the aluminum to clamp tightly around the spark plug when the engine is hot. If you try to remove the spark plugs from the aluminum head, you are likely to strip the threads from the spark plug hole in the head. Be sure to let your customer know why you must let the engine cool down to room temperature before removing the spark plugs.

Spark plugs are removed by first removing the spark plug cable. The spark plug cable boot is loosened by carefully twisting the boot. The cable can then be removed by pulling on the boot without damaging the spark plug cable. Special boot-pulling tools make this job easier. Blow air around the spark plug to remove any loose material before removing the spark plug. Use a good spark plug socket, with an internal cushion, to remove the spark plug without damage. Spark plugs will come out of all engines easier if you let the engine cool before you try to remove them. Use penetrating oil around the base of the spark plug if it seems to be too tight. Do not jerk on the wrench. Just pull steadily until the spark plug loosens. A better removal practice should be followed when a compression test is to be run. Loosen the spark plugs about one-quarter turn, then connect the spark plug cables. Start the engine and speed it up two or three times. Loosening the spark plugs will break any carbon at the surface of the combustion chamber and the spark plugs. You can see in Figure 12-1 how the carbon covers across the head and spark plug. The carbon will break away

Fig. 12-1 Normal carbon deposits build up across the joint between a spark plug and the head inside the combustion chamber.

when the spark plug is loosened. The carbon chips will be blown from the engine when it is run so that they will not get under a valve and cause faulty readings during the compression test. Remove the spark plugs.

The spark plugs should be examined carefully. This examination is often called **reading the plugs**. The condition of the electrodes and the type of carbon on the spark plug nose give a good indication of how that cylinder has been operating.

The spark plug condition you can see most easily is the type of carbon on the spark plug nose. Examples are shown in Figure 12-2. Normal spark plugs will have a light tan to gray deposit, depending on the additives in the gasoline and oil that have been used in the engine. If there are almost no deposits, the deposits are white, and the electrodes are badly eroded, the spark plug has been running very hot. Heavy sooty black deposits are caused by rich air/fuel mixtures. Heavy wet deposits are caused by high oil consumption. Incomplete combustion causes dry fluffy carbon deposits. Some engines, especially ones with high mileage, tend to develop heavy white deposits that bridge the spark plug gap. This keeps the charge from getting into the gap so that the cylinder misfires. You can see in Figure 12-3 how this could happen. These deposits resulted from oil getting into the combustion chamber past the valve stem seals. Spark plug manufacturers supply full-color pictures of spark plug deposits for use to diagnose spark plug problems. You can compare the spark plug from the engine to the colored pictures.

Spark plugs can be cleaned and serviced; however, it is the general practice to install new spark plugs when

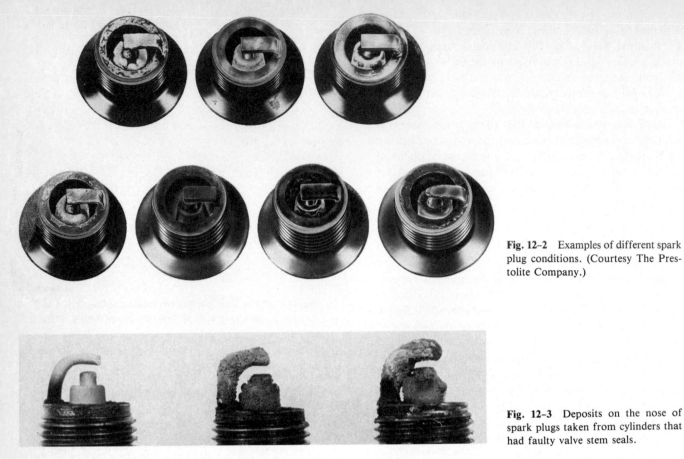

Fig. 12–2 Examples of different spark plug conditions. (Courtesy The Prestolite Company.)

Fig. 12–3 Deposits on the nose of spark plugs taken from cylinders that had faulty valve stem seals.

a tune-up is done on a customer's engine. New spark plugs should be installed at specific periodic service intervals in automobiles that have a catalytic converter. This will minimize the chance of having misfiring that causes damage to the converter.

It is good practice to run a spark plug tap into the spark plug hole to clean the threads. This should always be done where it was hard to remove the spark plug. The head must be at room temperature when cleaning the threads to avoid cutting metal. This is especially important on aluminum heads.

You must use the correct spark plugs for the engine on which you are working. You can find spark plug specifications wherever spark plugs are sold. The specifications show the correct spark plug number and the correct gap. Spark plug gaps run from 0.035 to 0.80 in. Sometimes the ground electrode is bent from shipping and handling. Be sure to check the gap of the new spark plugs before you install them.

If a gasket is needed, it is already on the new spark plug. It is a good practice to use a special high-temperature antiseize on the spark plug threads, especially when they are used in aluminum heads. You will find that spark plugs are easily installed, even in hard-to-reach places, if you start them in with a spark plug boot taken from an old ignition cable. The spark plug should be tightened against the seat by hand. Spark plugs with gaskets are tightened 1/4 turn with a spark plug wrench. Spark plugs with tapered seats are tightened only 1/16 of a turn with the wrench. Be sure that you do not overtighten them. Tightening this way gives the correct heat transfer from the spark plug to the head.

12–2 DISTRIBUTOR CAP AND ROTOR SERVICE

The distributor cap is fastened with spring clips, screwdriver lock clips, or screws. The cap is loosened and raised from the distributor. Sometimes some of the spark plug cables will keep you from moving the cap away from the distributor. You can carefully pull the cable from either the spark plug or out of the distributor tower (the cables are locked in the cap on Chrysler four-cylinder engines, as shown in Figure 12-4). Be sure that you know which cable goes to each cap tower or to each spark plug so that you can reconnect it easily. You can do this easily if you wrap tape on the cable and mark the cable position on the tape.

The rotor is pulled off from the shaft on distributors having the mechanical advance below the movable

Fig. 12-4 Locking clips that hold the spark plug cables in the cap and form the cap electrodes.

plate. Two screws will have to be taken out to remove the rotor from distributors having the mechanical advance mechanism above the movable plate. If the rotor tip or distributor cap electrodes show a lot of burning, they should be replaced with new parts, especially if the engine has been misfiring before you started to work on the distributor. A new rotor is put in place of the old rotor. Be sure to fit the rotor into the correct aligning notches, round holes, and square holes. Some Ford engines use a 1/32 in. coat of silicone grease on the top and bottom of the rotor tip. Make sure to put this grease on the new rotor. Use an ohmmeter or a self-powered test light to make sure that the shutters are grounded when installing a rotor on a distributor with a Hall-effect trigger.

If you need to replace the distributor cap the best procedure is to hold the new cap beside the old cap. Position the alignment lugs of the two caps so that they point the same way. Remove one spark plug cable at a time and put it in the new cap. In this way you will not mix the cables in the cap towers. The cables will be the correct length and they will be in the correct firing order. The cap is placed on the distributor and moved to engage the alignment lug, then the fasteners are locked in place.

If the ignition cables have been taken out of the distributor cap, they can be easily put back in the correct tower of the cap. The number 1 cable goes into the number 1 distributor tower. Following around the cap in the direction the distributor rotates, the ignition cables are installed in the engine firing order. The cylinder firing order is usually shown in raised cast numbers on the intake manifold. If it is not, the firing order will have

to be found in a specification book. Moving in the direction of distributor rotation, place the spark plug cable leading to the next cylinder in the firing order into the next distributor cap tower. Follow this by putting each following spark plug cable into the distributor cap towers following the engine firing order. The one exception to this procedure is the cables on the Ford bilevel rotor and cap (see Figure 11-17). The firing order on this cap alternates from one side of the cap to the other side.

12-3 DISTRIBUTOR SERVICE

Remember that the primary circuit between the battery and coil and the whole secondary circuit are about the same on all types of ignition systems. Ignition systems differ in the way they make-and-break the primary circuit between the coil and ground. The make-and-break is done with points (see Figure 11-4) and solid-state electronics (see Figures 11-5 and 11-31). Parts of solid-state electronic systems have no routine service. They are replaced when they fail. Distributor points are replaced at normal service intervals, usually during a tune-up. The professional automotive service technician will remove the distributor to replace the points and check the operation of the distributor advance mechanisms.

Distributor Removal. Loosen the cap and place it at the side of the distributor. Leave the ignition cables in the cap towers. Sometimes a few spark plug cables have to be removed from the cap so that it will clear the distributor. Use tape on the cables to mark their location in the tower of the cap. Note and mark the position of the vacuum advance unit and rotor. A felt-tip pen can be used for marking. This will allow you to replace the distributor in the same position to maintain timing after you have replaced the points and capacitor. Remove the primary lead from the coil and the vacuum hose from the vacuum advance unit nipple. Remove the distributor hold-down clamp, then pull the distributor straight out of its engine opening. These parts are identified on the distributor pictured in Figure 12-5. Heavy internal engine deposits will sometimes make the distributor hard to remove. Careless prying can break the distributor housing and bend the shaft. The distributor shaft will rotate a little as the distributor is removed from most engines. This is caused by the angled-drive gear teeth. You can see the angled gear in Figure 11-14. Note the amount of rotation as you remove the distributor. It will help you when you reinstall the distributor.

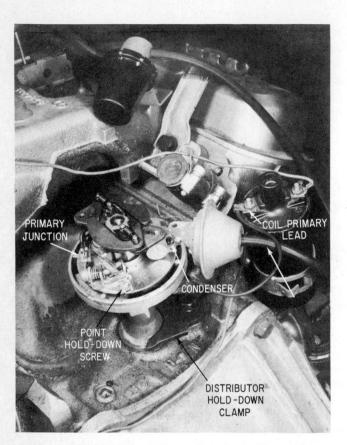

Fig. 12–5 Identification of parts used when replacing distributor points.

Point Replacement. There are still a number of vehicles in use that have point-type ignition systems. The points wear, so they need to be replaced. You can see the points when the rotor is removed from most distributors. On some distributors you will have to remove a metal shield cover before you can see the points. The metal shield is used to reduce radio noise on vehicles having the antenna in the windshield glass. Late models of these point distributors combined the points and capacitor, as shown in Figure 12-6, for the same reason.

The primary wire and capacitor are connected to the points at a single primary junction (see Figure 12-5). The junction may have a screw, a bolt and nut, or it may be held by the force of the point spring. The junction is separated and the screws holding the points to the movable plate are removed so that the points can be lifted from the distributor. If the capacitor is to be replaced, it can also be removed by taking out one hold-down screw. After wiping the old lubricant from the cam, a new capacitor and point set can be installed, reversing

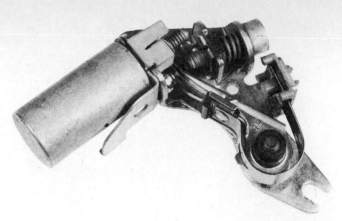

Fig. 12–6 Capacitor combined with points to help minimize radio noise.

the order you used to remove them. If you drop a screw into the distributor, you must get it out. If it jams within the distributor, it will break the distributor or distributor drive. Wipe a thin coat of fresh cam lubricant smoothly over the cam surface. Put a drop of oil on the felt plug inside the cam (Figure 12-7). This lubricates the cam movement on the distributor shaft during mechanical advance. If you use too much, some of the oil will get on the points and cause them to burn. The bearings should be oiled if the distributor has an oiler. Most modern distributor bearings have permanent lubrication or they are lubricated with engine oil from within the engine.

When a distributor is in good mechanical condition, the dwell will be correct if the point gap is correct. A point gap between 0.016 and 0.018 in. (0.04 and 0.045 mm) will allow the engine to start. Some four-cylinder engines require a point gap of 0.025 in. (0.055 mm). This much point gap will usually put the dwell within its correct

Fig. 12–7 Lubrication points when replacing distributor points.

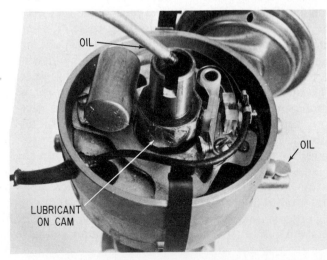

Fig. 12-8 The rubbing block is placed at the high spot of the cam to set the gap of the distributor points.

range. The point gap is adjusted while the rubbing block is on the highest part of one of the cam lobes. An example of this is shown in Figure 12-8. Most technicians adjust the points until they have the correct dwell. Putting a feeler gauge between the points may accidentally put dirt between the points. This would make a poor contact and lead to burned points. The dwell should be rechecked after making any point gap adjustment. In a professional shop, the dwell, mechanical, and vacuum advance mechanisms would be checked on a distributor machine at this time. The distributor can be reinstalled in the engine with the rotor pointing to the mark you made as you removed the distributor.

Installing the Distributor. If someone rotated the engine while the distributor was out, you will have to reset the initial timing. To do this you will start by rotating the crankshaft in its normal direction of rotation until there is compression on cylinder number 1. You can usually rotate the engine with the starter. You can find the compression stroke by covering the number 1 opening with your finger as the crankshaft is rotated. Continue to rotate the crankshaft slowly as compression is felt until the timing marks on the damper line up with the timing indicator on the timing cover. At this crankshaft position, both valves are closed. With the timing marks aligned, you have set the crankshaft at the point ignition **should** occur. Do not turn the crankshaft from this position until the distributor has been installed.

The direction the distributor rotates can be determined easily when the distributor has a vacuum advance unit. The arm on the vacuum advance unit points in the direction of distributor rotation. This can be seen in Figure 12-9. The vacuum advance unit must be set in the correct position on the engine. This is necessary so that the vacuum advance unit has clearance and the hose and wires have the correct position. When the distributor does not have a vacuum advance you will have to look at the distributor drive as the engine is being cranked to determine the direction of rotation. You will also need to know in which distributor cap tower you will be placing the number 1 spark plug cable. This is called the number 1 tower. With the distributor cap lifted straight up from the distributor, rotate the distributor in its normal direction until the rotor points toward the number 1 tower. In a point-type distributor, the points should be just ready to open. In inductive trigger distributors, a tooth must line up with the pole plate (see Figures 11-22 and 11-29). If the distributor is turned any farther in the normal direc-

Fig. 12-9 Distributor rotation shown by the location of the vacuum advance unit.

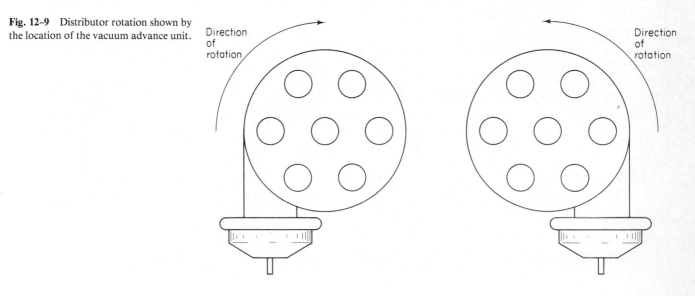

tion of rotation, the points would open or the inductor will trigger. At this point, the distributor will fire the number 1 spark plug. Remember when you removed the distributor the angle of the drive gear caused the distributor to rotate a few degrees. Before you install the distributor, rotate the shaft to allow for the gear angle. If, after installation, the rotor is in the wrong position, hold the rotor as you lift the distributor just enough to clear the gear teeth. Reset the rotor to mesh with the next drive gear tooth, then lower the distributor into the engine. With a little practice you will be able to estimate the amount of rotation you will need to engage the next gear tooth.

Sometimes, the distributor does not go all the way down into the engine because the end of the distributor shaft does not mesh with the oil pump drive. A simple method to get the distributor shaft to line up with the oil pump drive is to crank the engine with the distributor installed as far as possible in the engine. Be sure to keep track of the number of crankshaft revolutions. As the engine is cranked, the rotating distributor shaft will line up with the oil pump drive and then the distributor can be pushed down to fully seat. The engine will have to be cranked through two full revolutions to realign the timing marks correctly on the compression stroke.

The points or trigger tooth are set by eye. With the distributor hold-down clamp loose, rotate the housing of the distributor slightly to set the cam so the points are just ready to open. On inductive trigger distributors, the tooth of the timer and the inductor plate must line up. This distributor position is close enough to basic timing to start the engine. If the distributor hold-down clamp is slightly loose, the distributor housing can be adjusted to make the engine run smoothly after the engine has been started. Dwell and timing on distributor points are set after the engine is running.

Setting Dwell. Point dwell is checked only on point-type ignition systems. It can be most easily set while it is on the distributor machine. It can be set after the distributor

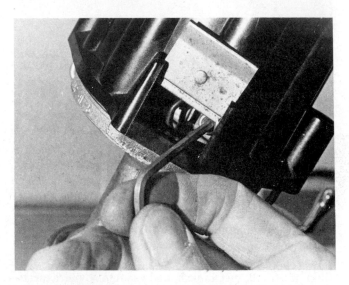

Fig. 12–10 Dwell being adjusted on a Delco-Remy external adjustment distributor.

Fig. 12–11 Screwdriver being used to adjust dwell.

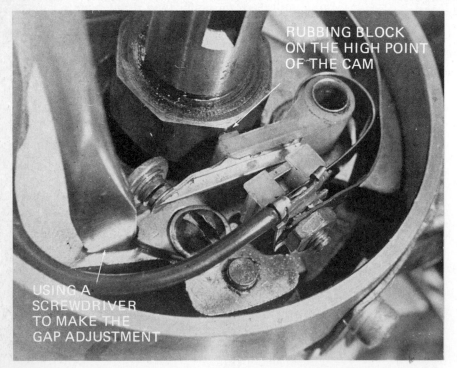

RUBBING BLOCK
ON THE HIGH POINT
OF THE CAM

USING A
SCREWDRIVER
TO MAKE THE
GAP ADJUSTMENT

is on the engine. Connect one lead of a dwell meter to the distributor side of the coil and the other lead to ground. Dwell can be easily adjusted through a window on a Delco-Remy external-adjustment distributor while the engine is idling (Figure 12-10). If dwell is incorrect on the other types of distributors, the engine will have to be stopped and the distributor cap removed. The point gap is changed only enough to correct the dwell (Figure 12-11). Some dwell meters can check dwell while the engine is being cranked. If one of these meters is used, the rotor must be removed to set dwell. The dwell can then be adjusted as the engine is cranked. The rotor and cap are reinstalled, the engine is restarted, and the dwell is rechecked. Basic ignition timing should always be reset after adjusting dwell.

12-4 IGNITION TIMING

It is not only important to have a good electrical arc at the spark plug, but it must come at the right time. Basic ignition timing is usually checked with a timing light triggered by the firing of number 1 spark plug. Some new test equipment uses a magnetic pickup at the crankshaft damper or flywheel. The timing from the crankshaft pickup is usually shown on a digital display. Timing advance can also be measured with some timing lights and magnetic pickup testers with either meter or digital readouts.

Basic Timing

Mechanical and vacuum advance. Use the following procedure to set basic timing on engines that do not use an ignition advance computer. Connect the timing-light pickup cable to the number 1 ignition cable and connect the light to its proper power source. Set the parking brake and place the transmission in neutral. Connect an exhaust hose to the tailpipe, then start the engine. Let the engine run until it is fully warm. Set the engine speed to curb idle. Remove the vacuum line to the distributor and plug it so that air does not go into the carburetor. With the timing light aimed at the timing marks and the distributor hold-down clamp slightly loose, adjust the distributor until the timing mark lines up at the specified degree (Figure 12-12). Tighten the hold-down clamp and recheck the timing. If the timing changes, readjust the timing as necessary; then reconnect the distributor vacuum line.

Basic ignition timing is more exact if you use the averaging method. First, measure the ignition timing with the timing light pickup connected to the number 1 spark plug cable. Next, connect the pickup to the paired cylinder halfway through the firing order, number 4 on a four-cylinder engine. For example, if the timing of number 1 cylinder was 4°BTC and number 4 cylinder was 8°BTC,

Fig. 12-12   The timing light is aimed at the timing marks while the engine is running.

the average timing would be 6°BTC (4° + 8° = 12°, 12° ÷ 2 = 6° average).

When basic timing is measured with a magnet-type timing pickup, slip the pickup into a round opening at the damper (Figure 12-13) or flywheel. Sometimes you will have to use a plastic sleeve adapter around the timing pickup to make it fit the opening correctly. The timing pickup is pushed against the damper. The trigger slot does not line up directly under the pickup when number 1 piston is at top center. Therefore, it is necessary to adjust the instrument to the correct **timing mark offset.** The amount of offset differs among engine makes. The offset is specified in the instruction manual that comes with the tester (Figure 12-14). You will also have to connect an inductive pickup on the number 1 spark plug cable. The difference in time between the ignition firing, the magnetic signal, and the engine speed is measured by the instrument and it is displayed as degrees of ignition advance. The display can be either an analog meter or a

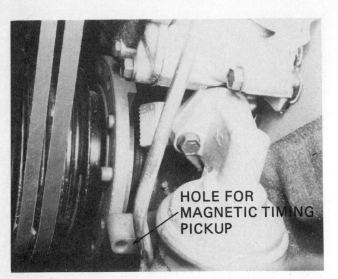

Fig. 12-13 Hole for magnetic timing pickup.

Magnetic timing offset	
Make	Offset
American Motors	−9.5
Chrysler	−10.0
Ford	−13.5
2.5 L	−52.5
General Motors	−9.5

Fig. 12-14 Typical hole offset for magnetic timing pickups.

digital readout. You will still have to set the parking brake, place the transmission in neutral, connect the exhaust hose, and plug the vacuum line before you start the engine. With the engine running, the instrument readout will show the degree of ignition advance.

It is fortunate that the basic timing does not change during engine operation when electronic and computer ignition systems are used. As a result, the timing does not have to be checked during normal engine periodic service. It is only checked when there is a problem in the distributor or when the distributor is replaced. Most ignition timing problems on computer-controlled ignition advance systems are caused by faulty electrical connections or by faulty sensors.

Computer advance. Checking the basic ignition timing requires more steps when computers are used to control the timing advance. These steps may be listed on the emission and tune-up decal. They are always specified

in the service manual for that engine. Be sure to follow them exactly.

Following are some examples of the steps that must be used before you can check the timing with a timing light on some typical computer-controlled ignition systems.

Chrysler. Ground the carburetor throttle position switch with a jumper (Figure 12-15). This keeps the computer from advancing the timing. Remove the vacuum line at the computer and plug it so that air does not go into the carburetor. You can now use the timing light to check basic timing. The timing marks are on the flywheel of front-wheel-drive automobiles (Figure 12-16).

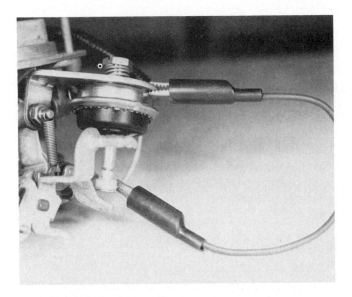

Fig. 12-15 Jumper used to ground the carburetor throttle position switch on a Chrysler engine.

Fig. 12-16 Timing marks on the transmission case used with a Chrysler engine with front-wheel drive.

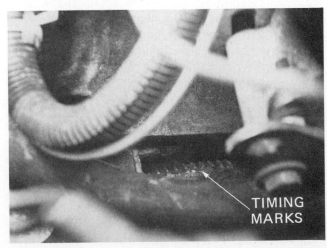

Ford. (In all Ford systems, disconnect and plug the vacuum advance hose.)

EEC I and EEC II ignition systems: The timing will not advance when the calibration assembly is removed from the processing assembly of the electronic engine control assembly. The processing assembly is located under the left side of the dash on automobiles. The calibration assembly is held on the processing assembly with two screws (Figure 12–17). Basic timing is checked while the calibration assembly is removed and the engine is running.

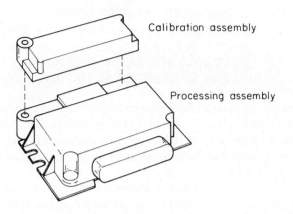

Fig. 12–17 Calibration assembly on the processor assembly of EEC-I and EEC-II ignition systems.

EEC III ignition systems: The timing is not adjustable on some EEC III systems. Remove the calibration assembly from the processing assembly or use a vacuum pump/gauge as follows:

1. Connect a timing light to the number 1 spark plug cable.
2. Tee the vacuum pump gauge between the diverter valve and diverter valve solenoid.
3. Apply more than 20 in. of vacuum for 15 seconds, then release the vacuum.
4. The vacuum gauge should pulse two or four times. The pulses show that the computer is starting to self-test.
5. The throttle kicker will automatically raise the engine speed. At this time check the timing with a timing light. The ignition should have 27 to 33° advance.
6. After a minute the vacuum should raise to a high steady reading, then drop and the throttle kicker will disengage.
7. The vacuum gauge will then pulse two or three times to show that the self-test has finished.
8. If the system is normal, the vacuum gauge will

pulse, pause, and pulse. This is code 11. If there is a problem in the system, the gauge will pulse to give the trouble code of the problem. You will have to look at trouble-code descriptions in the service manual to determine the faulty part of the system.

EEC IV ignition systems: Separate the black-and-white connector on the yellow wire with green dotting that comes from the ignition module on the distributor. This disconnects the computer so that the engine runs on basic timing. Timing is checked while an analog voltmeter is connected to the six-terminal diagnostic connector coming from the microprocessor control unit (Figure 12–18). The black voltmeter lead is connected to terminal 4. The red voltmeter lead is connected to battery positive. A jumper is connected between terminals 2 and 5. The voltmeter needle movement indicates the test in the EEC IV system just as the vacuum gauge does in the EEC III system.

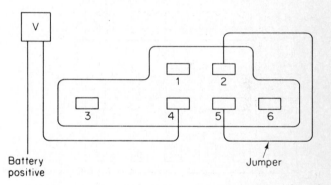

Fig. 12–18 Jumper connections to check the timing on an EEC-IV system.

General Motors. (Differences in systems depend on vehicle division, model, and year.)

C-4 and CCC systems without fuel injection:

1. Separate the four-wire connector from the distributor (Figure 12–19). This keeps the computer from advancing the timing so that the timing light will show the basic ignition timing.

CCC with fuel injection:

2. With the engine running put a jumper between test terminals of the ALCL diagnostic connector (assembly line communication link) under the dash (Figure 12–20). This activates the fault test

Fig. 12–19 Four-wire connection coming from the distributor on a Delco-Remy CCC system.

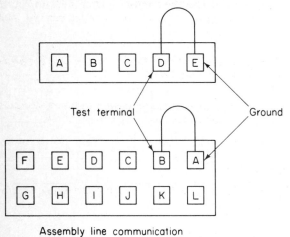

Test terminal   Ground

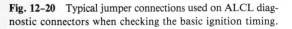

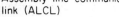
Assembly line communication
link (ALCL)

Fig. 12–20 Typical jumper connections used on ALCL diagnostic connectors when checking the basic ignition timing.

codes as well as holding basic timing. Fault test codes are discussed in Chapter 14.

3. Separate the junction on a tan wire of the four-wire connector coming from the distributor.
4. Separate the connector between a pink wire and green connector.
5. Check the timing.

Cadillac with digital display: This sytem can be checked from inside the car with the engine running. It has an interesting series of switch positions that

must be used before it will display the timing degree. The switches on one model of Cadillac must be moved in the following sequence:

1. Press the air conditioner OFF and WARM buttons at the same time. An 88 or 1.88 should show on the display.
2. Next press the air conditioner ECON button, then press the OFF and HIGH buttons at the same time.
3. When a 7 or 7.0 is shown on the display, press the reset button on the miles-per-gallon panel to show a 9.0 on the display.
4. Press the INSTANT/AVERAGE button on the miles-per-gallon panel to advance the display from 0.1, 0.2., 0.3, . . . to 0.8. The number following 0.8 will be the ignition timing. It should be 30° at hot idle on 1983 automobiles.

Making the timing checks puts a fault code into the computer memory in most General Motors vehicles. This fault code is removed from the memory by removing the ECM fuse for more than 10 seconds after the engine timing has been checked.

Be sure to remove all jumper wires and reconnect all connectors after the timing has been checked and adjusted.

These are examples of procedures that must be followed to check the timing on several computer-controlled ignition systems. You can see that it is very important to follow the procedure **exactly** if you are to get an accurate measurement of the ignition timing of an engine.

Ignition Advance. In addition to basic timing both the timing light and magnetic-type timing pickup can be used to see if the mechanical and vacuum advance mechanisms in the distributor are operating. To do this, remove and plug the distributor vacuum hose so that air does not enter the carburetor port. With the timing light aimed at the timing marks, gradually increase the engine speed. The timing marks should appear to move in the advance direction when the mechanical advance is operating. With the engine running and held at approximately 1200 rpm, observe the timing mark with the timing light as you reconnect the vacuum line. The timing mark will again move in the advance direction if the vacuum advance mechanism operates. This test will indicate that the distributor advance mechanisms are operating. It does not indicate that the advance mechanisms are operating correctly.

Some timing lights are made with a built-in-advance meter. Figure 12–12 shows this type of timing light. When doing basic timing, you must be sure to have the meter turned off so that it will operate as a simple timing light. After basic timing is set, the engine rpm is adjusted to a specified test speed. While holding this speed, the advance meter control is turned until the timing mark looks like it did when the basic timing was set. The meter reading now shows the number of degrees the distributor has advanced. This advance check can be done with the vacuum line off to measure mechanical advance. The vacuum line is reconnected to measure the total advance produced by both mechanical and vacuum advance mechanisms. The amount of vacuum advance is the total

advance less the mechanical advance. The distributor vacuum advance hose must be connected at the end of this test. If the timing advance is not correct, the distributor should be removed from the engine and tested on a distributor machine.

STUDY QUESTIONS

Introduction

1. What are two reasons that ignition systems are serviced?

2. What two things result from a carbon track in a distributor cap?

Section 12–1

3. What part of the ignition system always requires periodic service?

4. When should the spark plug cables be reconnected after loosening the spark plugs?

5. What does the service technician check to determine how a cylinder has been operating?

6. What is the general service practice followed by service technicians when the spark plug electrodes are worn?

7. List the steps, in the correct order, that you should follow to install new spark plugs.

Section 12–2

8. Describe the procedure that you should follow to install the spark plug cables in a new distributor cap.

9. In what way do ignition system types differ?

Section 12–3

10. List the steps to be followed when removing the distributor.

11. What causes a distributor shaft to rotate slightly when a distributor is removed?

12. What parts of a distributor should be lubricated?

13. Describe how you should set the gap of the distributor points.

14. Describe the procedure you should use to set the timing of an engine if it was cranked after you had removed the distributor.

15. What should be done if the distributor does not go all the way into the engine?

16. At what point should the ignition be timed when installing a set of points in a distributor?

Section 12–4

17. What should you do to the vehicle and engine before you check the basic timing?

18. What is the averaging method of checking timing?

19. What is the timing mark offset?

20. When does the basic timing need to be checked on electronic and computer ignition systems?

21. Describe the procedure used to check ignition advance with an adjustable timing light.

13

IGNITION DIAGNOSIS

The modern ignition system is not normally checked unless the operator notices some trouble. This includes poor fuel economy, hard starting, and no-start problems. Faulty spark plugs, spark plug cables, and timing advance in the ignition system can cause poor fuel mileage. Some hard starting and no-start problems are caused by the ignition system. These ignition system problems are usually the result of poor electrical connections or faulty parts.

Solid-state ignition and computer-controlled advance ignition systems sometimes fail to operate. These systems are as likely as point-type systems to have a failure in the coil, resistor, or connections. When solid-state or computer-controlled ignition systems fail, it is natural for technicians first to blame the electronic control, because they know very little about it. The electronic control should be the **last** thing to check when the ignition system fails to operate. Remember that electricity in the primary circuit must first flow through the insulated ignition system and coil before it reaches the electronic control. You saw this in Figures 11–5 and 11–31. The rotor, cap, and ignition cables are nearly the same in all types of ignition systems. Make sure that these parts are operating normally **before** you even think about replacing the electronic ignition control unit, module, or computer.

You should develop a systematic step-by-step diag-

nostic approach. Ideally, you will follow the testing procedure given in the service manual for the vehicle being serviced. You perform the tests in the order given in the manual. Make sure that you do **only** the tests specified. Reconnect the wires after each test is made. If you make other tests, the information you get from these tests will mislead your analysis. This will cause you to take more time to identify the cause of the problem.

In general terms, you will first check the vehicle to make sure that it has the problem reported by the operator. Then make sure that the battery is in normal operating condition. The battery cables must be clean and tight. Check all the wires in the circuit you think has the problem to make sure that they are in good condition. Make sure that the ignition switch is off when you remove or connect wires going to the electronic ignition control. Separate the connectors to make sure that the connections are not corroded, bent, or loose. Do not remove the dielectric compound (looks like grease) in the connectors. It is there to minimize corrosion that causes resistance. After inspection, push the connector halves together tightly so that they latch. Make sure that the spark plug cables are secure in the distributor cap and on the spark plugs. Do not remove the dielectric compound from the distributor cap towers or rotor.

It is quicker to check the overall operation of the

ignition system than it is to check each part. If the whole system is working correctly, you do not need to check each part. The parts are checked only in the section of the ignition system where the operation is faulty. This test method, together with spark plug replacement, is the fastest and best way to service the ignition system.

Testing the operation of the ignition system can show you only what the system is doing during the test. It cannot tell you that the system will continue to operate correctly. This is like a race car that runs well during the race, then suddenly fails on the last lap. If it could have been inspected, the potential problem would have been found before it failed. A good visual inspection is the best method you have to show you that the ignition system will continue to operate properly. You can often see, while they are still operating normally, parts that are about to fail. Typical examples of this are a loose wire, a wire with damaged insulation, a wire with several broken strands, a wire rubbing against another part, dirty or oil-soaked wires, or loose connectors. During a visual inspection you should try to find anything that looks unusual about the wires and the parts of the ignition system. Faults found should be carefully examined and tested, then repaired, replaced, or tightened for normal service.

13-1 NO-START PROBLEM

Remember that an engine can be started and it will run if it has (1) enough compression, (2) an intake charge with a combustible air/fuel ratio, and (3) ignition at the correct time in the cycle. One of these three things is missing when an engine will crank but not start. You should learn to hear the sound of a normal engine as it is being cranked. When you learn this you will be able to hear the change in cranking speed when compression is low or uneven. You also know that a rich fuel charge is pulled in as a cold engine cranks. The charge can be made richer on an engine with a carburetor by holding the choke closed, and it can be made leaner by holding the choke open as the engine is cranked. By moving the choke you can find a combustable air/fuel mixture for starting the engine. If the engine has compression and a combustable mixture and still won't start when it is cranked, the problem is in the ignition system.

The operation of the ignition system can best be checked by connecting a test spark plug onto one of the ignition cables (Figure 13-1). Ground the shell of the test spark plug. The ignition system should send a bright blue arc across the test spark plug while the engine is being cranked. If there is good arc at the test spark plug, the probable cause of the no-start problem is fouled spark plugs. It is common for spark plugs to foul in short-trip operation on unleaded gasoline. This is especially true

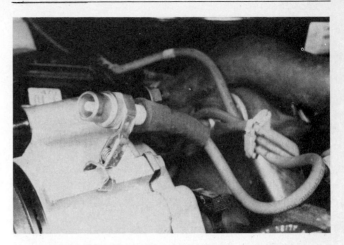

Fig. 13-1 Test spark plug connected to one ignition cable to check the operation of the ignition system.

when the vehicle is moved from place to place around the shop and the engine is never thoroughly warmed. Fouled spark plugs are corrected by cleaning or replacing the spark plugs.

If there is no arc across the test spark plug, remove the distributor cap and look for signs of burned electrodes on the rotor and cap. Also look for signs of insulation burning and carbon tracks on the cap or rotor from flashover (see Figure 13-2). While the distributor cap is off, look for broken wires, loose ground wires, or loose connections. You can connect the test spark plug to the secondary tower of the cap (ground the shell of the test spark plug with a jumper) to make sure that the coil is sending a charge to the distributor (Figure 13-3). There should be a bright blue arc across the test spark plug while the engine is being cranked. If all the distributor parts are normal and there is no arc, you should check the electrical parts of the ignition system to find the cause of the problem.

The primary circuit of the ignition system is most likely the part to cause a no-spark condition. Electricity must get to the electronic ignition control unit through the ignition switch, resistor, and coil. With the ignition switch turned on you should have voltage at the BAT terminal of the ignition coil. There must also be a voltage drop between the primary terminals of the coil. There should be no voltage drop between the metal case of the electronic ignition control unit and ground.

You can make a simple test jumper (illustrated in Figure 13-4) to check the operation of solid-state ignition systems. It takes the place of the electronic control to make and break the primary circuit. The switch on the test jumper and ignition switch are off while the jumper

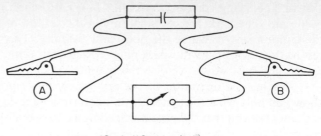

0.33 — mF ignition capacitor

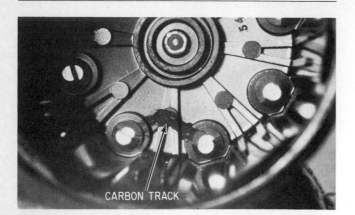

CARBON TRACK

(a)

FLASH-OVER
CRACK

(b)

Fig. 13–2 Flashover carbon track on a **(a)** distributor cap, **(b)** rotor.

Fig. 13–3 Test spark plug connected to the secondary tower of a coil with a shortened spark plug boot.

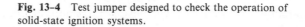

10–A, 110–V switch
(spring loaded toward off)

Fig. 13–4 Test jumper designed to check the operation of solid-state ignition systems.

is being connected. The best type of switch for this test jumper is one that is spring loaded toward off. This type of switch is only on while it is being held in the on position. The test jumper is used to check the operation of the ignition system after it is connected to the system.

Test Jumper Connections

Chrysler. Remove the connector from the electronic ignition control unit. Connect test jumper clip A on a prod placed in the connector cavity for the wire coming from the coil. This is cavity 2 connected to the black wire (see Figure 13–5). A paper clip can be used for the prod. Connect clip B to a good ground.

This test jumper can also be used on computer-controlled Chyrsler ignition systems that have inductive triggers. Remove the connectors from the computer. Connect the A clip of the test jumper to the connector cavity with the black wire connecting to the negative coil terminal. You will have to follow this wire to the connector or check the wiring diagram to find the connector cavity. The B clip of the test jumper is connected to a good ground.

Delco-Remy. Remove the three-wire connector (inner connector) from the distributor cap. Connect clip A on the tach terminal, which is the negative side of the coil primary winding (see Figure 13–6). Connect clip B to a good ground.

Fig. 13–5 Test jumper connection in cavity 2 on Chrysler solid-state ignition systems.

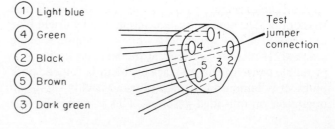

① Light blue
④ Green
② Black
⑤ Brown
③ Dark green

Test jumper connection

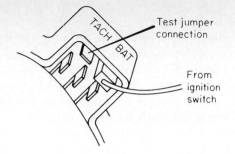

Fig. 13–6 Test jumper connection on an HEI system.

Ford.   Separate the four-wire connector from the ignition module. Connect the A clip of the test jumper on a prod placed in the connector cavity for the wire coming from the coil. It is the cavity going to the green wire on Ford ignition harnesses (Figure 13–7). Connect clip B to the connector cavity going to the black wire that grounds in the distributor.

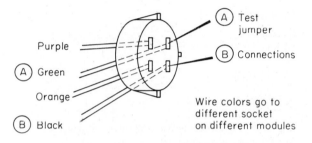
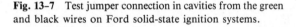

Fig. 13–7 Test jumper connection in cavities from the green and black wires on Ford solid-state ignition systems.

Test Procedure.   Remove the secondary coil cable from the secondary tower of the distributor cap of Chrysler and Ford systems. Connect the cable to a test spark plug. On Delco-Remy HEI systems with the coil in the cap, remove the cap and connect the test spark plug to the coil button (see Figure 13–3). Ground the shell of the test spark plug. Turn on the ignition switch. Turn on the test jumper switch and wait for 10 seconds. Watch for an arc at the test spark plug when you turn off the test jumper switch. Turn the switch on for 1 second, then off. Do this several times as you watch for the arc. If there is an arc, the primary circuit is normal until it gets to the electronic ignition control unit. If there is no arc at the test spark plug, start at one end of the primary circuit and check each part. When the test is finished, reconnect all wires.

Chrysler Hall-Effect.   On Chrysler ignition systems with Hall-effect triggers in the distributor the test jumper is connected slightly different. Leave the computer con-

nected. With the test jumper switch off, connect the A clip on the negative terminal of the coil primary. Connect the B clip to ground. Connect the test spark plug on the coil secondary cable and ground the spark plug shell. Turn on the ignition swich. Watch for an arc on the test spark plug as you momentarily turn on the test jumper switch, then **immediately** turn the jumper switch off. If there is no arc, remove the 10-cavity connector from the computer and try the test again. If it arcs when the computer is disconnected, there is a ground in the computer.

If there is spark when the system is being checked with the test jumper but no spark while the engine is being cranked, there is a problem in the ignition start circuit, trigger, or control unit. You can check the ignition start circuit with a voltmeter connected to the BAT terminal of the coil and ground. The voltmeter should be within 1 V of the battery voltage while the engine is cranking. If the voltage at the coil is low, the ignition bypass system will have to be checked.

13–2 IGNITION CIRCUIT

It is unusual for the primary circuit to have too much resistance. Available secondary voltage is less when the primary circuit has too much resistance. This, in turn, will cause hard starting. It will also cause misfiring on acceleration and at high engine speeds. The most common cause of high resistance in the primary circuit is loose or corroded connectors and junctions. These can be identified by testing the ignition circuit. Too much resistance in circuits going to engine control computers will cause more trouble than primary circuit resistance because these circuits operate on low voltage (usually 5 V) and they carry very little current (around 6 A).

It is important for you to know that automobile manufacturers use the **same** wire color codes between car lines year after year. For example, Chrysler uses a dark blue insulation on the wire for all circuits that have electrical power when the ignition switch is turned on. Ford uses red and General Motors uses pink for wires in this same circuit. Manufacturers also use the same pin and cavity number or letter in the connection for the same circuit in their different model vehicles. The pins and sockets may be placed at a different point in the connector. If you learn the wire color codes and the pin and cavity identification numbers and letters of vehicle makes, you can follow these circuits on the other vehicles produced by the same manufacturer.

Ignition Primary Resistance. Electrical resistance in most vehicle electrical circuits is checked by the voltage-drop method. This includes the check of ignition primary circuit resistance. Normal current must be flowing in the circuit while you are measuring the voltage drop. Except for an ignition resistor, all ignition systems use the same primary ignition circuit between the battery and coil. We will call this the insulated ignition circuit. The ignition primary current will flow with the ignition switch turned on when you follow these instructions.

On all point-type ignition systems, bump the starter until the points are closed. You know the points are closed when you connect the positive voltmeter lead on the distributor wire at the coil. The negative voltmeter lead is connected on a good ground. The voltmeter shows battery voltage when the points are open. It shows no voltage when the points are closed.

On engines with Hall-effect distributor pickups use the same connections as you would for point-type ignition systems. Bump the starter until the voltmeter shows no voltage. The shutter is now in the slot of the pickup. This will let primary current flow when the ignition switch is turned on.

The primary circuit of solid-state ignition systems with inductive coil triggers are complete to ground at all times when the engine is not running. Connect the positive voltmeter lead to the positive terminal (BAT) of the coil and the negative voltmeter lead to ground. You can read the primary circuit voltage when the ignition switch is turned on. On HEI systems the voltmeter is connected to the BAT terminal in the distributor cap (see Figure 11-35).

After making sure that the primary current is flowing, use a voltmeter as follows. First, you will need to make sure that the coil primary is operating on enough voltage. When a resistor is used in the primary circuit, connect the voltmeter positive lead on the battery terminal of the resistor. (In this discussion the term "resistor" will include a resistor wire.) When there is no resistor, connect the voltmeter positive lead on the BAT terminal of the coil. Connect the negative voltmeter lead to ground. With the ignition switch turned on and current flowing through the primary circuit, the voltage should be within half a volt of the battery voltage. There is too much resistance between the battery and resistor or coil if the voltage is not this high.

Keep the ignition switch on as you move the voltmeter leads to check the voltage drop of the primary wires. Connect the voltmeter positive lead to the positive terminal of the battery. Connect the negative voltmeter lead on the BAT terminal of the resistor or the coil when no resistor is used. The insulated side of the primary ignition system is normal if the voltage drop is less than 0.5 V. There is too much resistance in the primary ignition system if the voltage drop is greater than 0.5 V.

You can find the connection that has the high resistance by checking voltage drop along the circuit while current is flowing. Leave one voltmeter lead connected. Check the voltage at each junction along the circuit with the other lead, as shown in Figure 13-8. The high resistance in the system is in the wire or junction where you find a large change in the voltmeter reading.

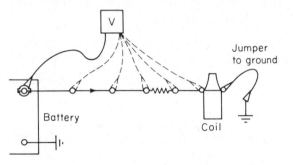

Fig. 13-8 Method of checking the voltage drop in the insulated primary ignition circuit.

When a resistor is used you will have to check the voltage drop between the resistor and coil. Connect the positive voltmeter lead on the coil side of the resistor. The negative voltmeter lead is connected to the BAT terminal of the coil. With current flowing in the ignition system there should be less than 0.1 V in this part of the circuit.

The last primary circuit check on ignition systems is the ground circuit. Connect the positive voltmeter lead on the distributor side of the coil. Connect the negative voltmeter lead to a good ground. The negative battery terminal makes the best grounding point. With the ignition switch on and the primary current flowing, the voltmeter should read less than 0.1 V. Voltage higher than this indicates distributor or electronic ignition control unit resistance. The resistance is usually in the point contacts or the ground connection of the electronic control unit.

Resistor. The resistance of an ignition resistor or resistor wire is measured with an ohmmeter to make sure it has the correct resistance for the system. The resistor must be disconnected from the circuit while you are measuring its resistance. Wire-wound resistors usually fail by breaking. A broken resistor wire opens the circuit so that no current will flow. The resistance is infinite on the ohmmeter any time a resistor is open. You should always measure the resistance of a new resistor before you install it to make sure it has the correct resistance.

Coil. Coils are measured for their resistance. Ignition coil resistance specifications are given in the service manuals for both the primary and secondary windings (Figure 13–9). Low resistance indicates a short between turns of the winding. High resistance indicates a poor or broken internal connection. If the resistance is not correct (either too high or too low) the coil must be replaced. All wires are removed from the coil when measuring the resistance. The resistance of the primary winding is measured between the coil terminal marked BAT and the terminal marked negative, DIST, DEC, or TACH, depending on the make of the coil. The resistance of the secondary winding is measured between the coil secondary tower or button to the BAT terminal. There will be infinite resistance on some Delco-Remy coils that are mounted in the distributor cap. These coils have the secondary winding separate from the primary winding. The secondary winding on these coils is checked between the center coil button in the cap and the center (ground) terminal of the three inner terminals that connect the cap to the ignition module (see Figure 11–35). The secondary is open if there is infinite resistance when you make both tests.

Make	Ignition coil resistance (Ω)	
	Primary	Secondary
Chrysler	1.4 - 1.7	8,000 - 11,000
Delco-remy	0.4 - 0.5	6,000 - 30,000
Ford		
Can-type	0.8 - 1.6	7,700 - 10,500
E-type	0.3 - 1.0	7,600 - 13,600

Fig. 13–9 Typical ignition coil resistances in ohms.

Most ignition analyzers have coil testers. They may use a meter, digital readout, or scope pattern. The coil should be tested with one of these testers when there is a question about the operation of the coil. Faulty coils must be replaced.

13–3 TRIGGERS, CONTROL UNITS, AND MODULES

Some shop equipment manufacturers make specialized testers for solid-state ignition systems. These testers are usually used when there is a no-start problem. They are normally found in new car dealerships. Chrysler has an Electronic Ignition Tester and General Motors a Module Tester. The Chrysler Lean Burn System Analyzer and Ford Self-Test Automatic Readout (STAR) testers are especially useful for checking computer engine controls when the vehicle has drivability problems. Specialized testers make the correct diagnosis of the cause of an engine problem much faster than it can be done without the testers.

All manufacturers have test procedures to be used to find the cause of ignition system problems using voltmeters and ohmmeters. When all parts you can test with these meters show normal readings and the problem has not been found, you will have to substitute a known good part for the part you think is faulty. You can see that this diagnosis procedure takes more time than it would take when using specialized testers. It usually costs the customer more money when you do not use specialized testers because the customer pays for your time. Often good parts will be replaced as you guess which part is causing the problem. Most parts departments will not accept returned electrical parts, especially electronic parts, that have been used for testing. If the cause of failure had not been corrected before installing the new part, it is likely that the new part could also fail. Unnecessary part replacement will increase the repair bill the customer must pay.

Trigger. The inductive trigger has a toothed timer that rotates close to a pole plate (see Figures 11–22 and 11–23). The pole plate is fastened to a magnet. A trigger coil is connected to the pole plate so that it senses changes in the strength of the magnetic field.

A broken wire or worn wire insulation is the most likely cause of trigger failure. You can quickly check this by connecting a test spark plug on the secondary cable coming from the coil (inside the cap in HEI distributors as shown in Figure 13–3). Turn on the ignition switch and hold a soldering gun next to the distributor. If the trigger coil is operating there should be a series of arcs at the test spark plug when the soldering gun is turned on.

The resistance of the trigger coil is checked with an ohmmeter. Disconnect the trigger coil lead from the control unit or module. Calibrate the ohmmeter on the required scale before you use it. Measure the resistance in ohms between the trigger coil leads (Figure 13–10). The coil is shorted if the resistance is too low. It is open if the resistance is infinite. Check the resistance between one of the leads and ground. The ohmmeter will show nearly infinite resistance if the trigger coil is properly insulated. Wiggle the wires and connectors while you are making

Make	Resistance (Ω)
Chrysler	150 – 900
Delco – remy	500 – 1500
Ford	400 – 1100
TFI	800 – 975

Fig. 13-10 Typical trigger pickup coil resistances in ohms.

these tests. If the distributor has a vacuum advance diaphragm, pull a vacuum in the diaphragm while the ohmmeter is connected. If wiggling the wires or pulling a vacuum changes the ohmmeter readings, you have found a cause of intermittent failure, at least a potential failure. Other tests using a body shop type of heat gun on the coil and light tapping may be recommended by some manufacturers on specific vehicle models.

In Chrysler vehicles (see Figure 13-5) the harness is disconnected from the control unit. The trigger coil resistance is measured between the control unit harness cavities 4 (green wire) and 5 (brown wire). Typically, the resistance is between 150 and 900 Ω. The resistance should be infinite between either one of these wires and ground. This is a good time to check the electrical power coming to the control unit. The voltage on the other harness cavities should be within 1 V of the battery voltage when the ignition switch is turned on. Turn the ignition switch off after making this test. You can make one last check while the harness is disconnected. There should be no resistance between pin 5 on the control unit and ground when measured with the ohmmeter.

If the trigger coil assembly is replaced in Chrysler distributors, the clearance between the toothed timer and pole plate must be adjusted with a **nonmagnetic** feeler gauge. It is usually made of brass. Clearance specifications run from 0.006 to 0.012 in., depending on the specific distributor. Reconnect the harness after the faulty parts are replaced and all tests are normal.

On Delco-Remy HEI distributors, remove the distributor cap. Slip the green and white wire terminals off from the ignition module (see Figure 11-35). Measure the resistance between terminals on these wires. Typically, there will be between 500 and 1500 Ω. Next, check to make sure that there is infinite resistance between either one of these wires and ground. This verifies that the coil is not grounded. The HEI distributor must be disassembled to replace the trigger coil. Replace the faulty parts, reassemble, and test the system. When all tests are normal, install the distributor, then retime the ignition.

In Ford vehicles the four-wire harness connector is

disconnected from the ignition module. The trigger coil resistance is measured between the harness connector cavities for the orange and purple wires (see Figures 11-34 and 13-7). Typically, the resistance of the trigger coil is between 400 and 1100 Ω. The insulation of the trigger coil is measured between one of these connector cavities and the cavity for the black wire. The black wire is grounded in the distributor. The resistance should be infinite between the orange or purple wire cavities and the black wire cavity. There should be no resistance between the blade coming from the module that connects to the black wire, and ground. Replace any faulty parts, test the repair, and reconnect the harness.

The distributor cap and ignition module must be removed from Ford distributors that have the ignition module mounted on the side of the distributor (TFI ignition systems) to measure the resistance of the trigger coil. This model distributor is shown in Figure 11-19. To do this you will have to remove the distributor from the engine. The resistance of the trigger coil should be between 800 and 975 Ω. The distributor will have to be disassembled to replace the coil. After repairs are made the distributor is reassembled, tested, and retimed to the engine.

The Hall-effect trigger switch has metal shutters that pass between a magnet and a sensor (see Figures 11-20 and 11-26). Solid-state electronics are used to signal changes that the magnetic field makes on the sensor in the switch assembly. The ignition control unit or module uses these signals to fire the ignition coil. Hall-effect trigger switch failure results from failure in the solid-state electronics or the connectors. This is often the result of a poor electrical connection between the shutter and ground when the rotor is installed in the distributor. An ohmmeter should show no resistance when its leads are connected between the shutter and ground.

The Chrysler Hall-effect switch is checked by making sure that the rest of the system is operating normally. First, connect a test spark plug on the coil secondary cable. Connect the spark plug shell to ground. Disconnect the distributor harness connector. Turn the ignition switch on. Momentarily touch a jumper between harness cavities 2 and 3 (Figure 13-11). These are the cavities next to the flat positioning surface of the connector. If this causes a spark at the test spark plug, all the electrical parts of the ignition system except the Hall-effect switch are working normally. The Hall-effect switch assembly will have to be replaced.

The Delco-Remy Hall-effect switch can be checked in the distributor. Remove the distributor cap and slip the three-terminal connector from the Hall-effect switch. Carefully note the polarity as you connect leads from a 12 V battery to the two outside terminals of the switch (Figure 13-12). Connect a voltmeter between the center terminal and the negative (ground) terminal. The voltmeter should show less than 0.5 V. If the distributor has

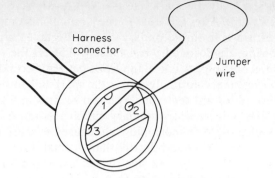

Fig. 13-11 Momentarily connecting a jumper wire to cavities 2 and 3 will cause the electronic control of a Chrysler Hall-effect ignition system to make the coil secondary discharge.

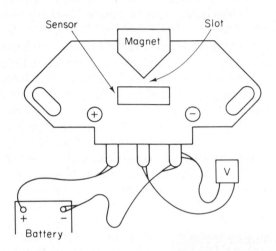

Fig. 13-12 Test connection on a Delco-Remy Hall-effect switch.

not been disassembled, rotate the distributor until one of the shutter blades is in the slot of the switch. If the Hall-effect switch is out of the distributor, place a feeler gauge straight down in the slot. Let the feeler gauge rest against the magnet. This should increase the voltage to within 0.5 V of the battery voltage. If the battery had 12.4 V, open circuit, this voltage should be at least 11.9 V. If the voltage is too low on either test, the Hall-effect switch assembly will have to be replaced. The switch assembly has slots for adjustment. Make sure that it is positioned so there is no contact with the shutters as the distributor shaft rotates.

Control Unit and Module. The ignition control unit or module is the last unit to be checked or replaced when there is a no-spark problem. First, prove that the primary circuit, coil, and triggers are normal. When this is done, the only part left in the ignition system is the control unit or module. Make sure that you have the correct replace-

ment module. Modules may look alike but have different circuits and different connector pin positions.

Control units and modules should be checked with specialized testers, when you have one to use. Some manufacturers recommend that during the test the module should be heated with a body shop type of heat gun until it is just warm enough to boil a drop of water placed on the surface of the module. Sometimes modules will run normally when they are cold but fail when they get hot.

If you do not have a specialized tester, you will have to prove that the control unit or module is faulty by replacing it with one you know will operate correctly. Retest the system to verify its operation with the replacement control unit or module installed. If the replacement part did not correct the problem, return the original control unit or module and retest the system to find where you missed finding the cause of the no-start problem.

Be careful to install the replacement control unit or module correctly. Make sure that the unit has a good ground. Delco-Remy modules use silicone grease between the module and distributor housing. The grease helps to carry the heat from the module to the housing. This keeps the module from overheating. Slide the connectors and terminals on and off several times to make sure that all dirt and corrosion has been rubbed off. This assures a good electrical connection. Where used, put silicone grease in the connector to help keep out moisture. Moisture will lead to corrosion and resistance in the connector.

13-4 IGNITION SCOPE

A cathode ray oscilloscope is the best instrument to see the overall operating conditions of the ignition system on a running engine. A special oscilloscope has been developed to show the operating voltage in the ignition system. Normal and abnormal operating conditions show up as they change the shape of the scope trace.

The ignition ocsilloscope trace displays secondary voltage on a time base. The scope sweep is usually triggered by the number 1 spark plug cable; however, any secondary cable could be used. As the voltage increases in the number 1 spark plug wire, a spike is produced at the right edge of the pattern. This is the trigger that immediately shifts the sweep to the left edge of the screen to begin a new trace.

Anything in the ignition primary circuit that has an effect on secondary voltage is reflected in the trace of the secondary scope pattern. If the scope pattern is not normal, some part of the engine, fuel, or ignition is faulty. This part should be rechecked with a specialized tester to verify its condition.

Scope Patterns. The ignition scope has a voltage pick-up that is connected to the coil-to-distributor secondary cable to measure secondary voltage. HEI distributors with the coil in the cap need a special adapter that fits on the distributor cap. A second scope lead is connected to the number 1 spark plug cable as a trigger. Each time the number 1 spark plug fires, the scope is triggered and the pattern starts on the left side of the scope screen. A typical secondary scope pattern of one cylinder firing is shown in Figure 13-13.

The ignition system must build up enough voltage to force its way across the largest gap in the secondary circuit. This gap normally is the spark plug electrode gap. It requires up to 7 kV, as indicated by the top of the pattern spike, to jump this gap when the transmission is in neutral. The ignition system has a problem when the spike goes higher. There should be little difference between the lowest and highest spike. The top of the spike is **required voltage.** As soon as the electricity arcs across the spark plug gap, the gases in the gap are ionized. This reduces the voltage needed to keep the arc going. The lower volt-

age is shown by the spark line at about one-third of the spike voltage. After the arc is formed a small milliampere current flows in the secondary circuit. Because current is flowing, any secondary resistance will affect the voltage level of the spark line in the scope pattern. Secondary circuit resistance normally causes the spark line to slope downward toward the right. You can see this in Figure 13-13. Any increased secondary circuit resistance in a spark plug cable or spark plug will cause the spark line voltage to be higher and shorter than normal. Lower resistance produces a spark line that is lower and longer than normal (Figure 13-14).

When the coil energy is nearly used up, the spark line stops. It is followed by a series of five or more oscillations as the energy leaves the ignition system. You can see them in Figure 13-13. Abnormal operation of the coil or capacitor will reduce the number of these oscillations. Compare these oscillations in Figure 13-15 to those in Figure 13-13.

Restarting the primary current causes a momentary reverse voltage signal that makes a sharp dip in the pattern trace at the right of the coil-capacitor oscillations. The trace comes up to the normal voltage as the coil saturates before the next cylinder firing. The total time the primary current flows before the next spark plug firing is called **dwell.** It is shown by the line from the primary restart (point closing) to the next spark plug firing (point opening). Most scopes are designed to allow a single pattern to be adjusted over a scale so that the scale can be

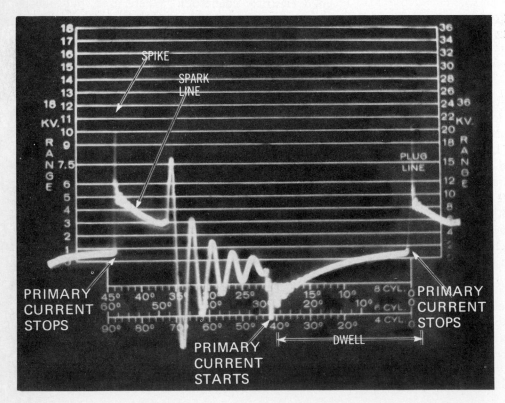

Fig. 13-13 Typical secondary scope pattern of one cylinder firing.

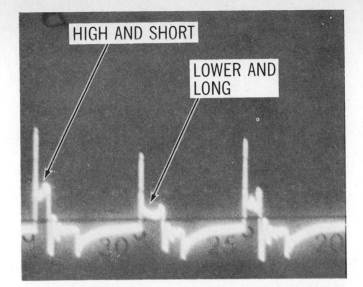

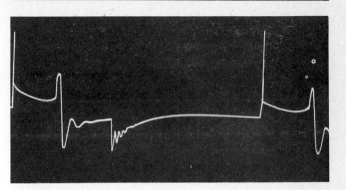

Fig. 13-15 Ignition pattern from an ignition simulator with high resistance in the capacitor lead.

Fig. 13-14 Examples of three different secondary patterns. The pattern on the left shows high resistance, the middle pattern shows low resistance, and the right pattern is normal.

used to read dwell directly without the aid of a separate dwell meter. You can see this in Figure 13-13.

It is not only important to know the required voltage, but it is also important to know the available voltage to be sure that there is enough ignition reserve. Available voltage is measured by removing one of the cables from the spark plug while the engine is running at approximately 1500 rpm. An **available voltage** spike is shown in Figure 13-16. **Ignition reserve** is available voltage less required voltage. Available voltage below 20 kV indicates problems in the primary ignition circuit. Secondary insulation can be damaged from the high voltage produced if the spark plug cable is removed for a long time. The ignition module and the catalytic converter can be damaged if more than one cable is removed at a time. One spark plug cable should, therefore, only be removed

long enough to notice how it affects changes in the pattern.

Spark plug gaps will normally increase about 0.001 in. (0.025 mm) each 1000 miles (1600 km) of operation. As a result, the required voltage will gradually increase after new spark plugs are installed. If a secondary ignition cable is damaged, its resistance can increase above the resistance of the spark plug gap. This will increase the required voltage above the available voltage and cause a misfire. Normal resistance of secondary ignition cable should be less than 20,000 Ω when measured with an ohmmeter. It is normal for long cables to have more total resistance than short cables. New secondary ignition cables have less than 750 Ω per inch (25 mm). Used cables with more than 5000 Ω per inch (25 mm) should be replaced.

Electricity will not arc across the spark plug electrode gap when the voltage required is greater than the available voltage. This type of misfire is most likely to happen when the engine is running at full throttle and at high speeds. Secondary circuit problems that cause un-

Fig. 13-16 Typical available voltage spike in an ignition scope parade pattern.

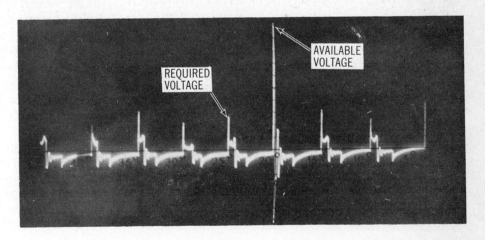

usually high required voltage are the spark plug gap and gaps in the secondary ignition circuit. Secondary resistance does **not** affect available voltage. You will remember that available voltage is developed by the primary circuit.

The secondary circuit can short or flash over the outside of the spark plug insulator so that electrical energy will go directly to ground. When this happens the spark plug will not fire. The secondary cables can crack and short to ground at their supporting brackets. Flashover can occur on a rotor or inside the distributor cap. Examples of this type of insulation failure were shown in Figure 13-2. It can even occur at the coil secondary tower. When the insulation fails, less electrical energy remains to form the arc across the spark plug gap. This is called secondary leakage. Cross firing between spark plug cables or within the distributor cap will show up as secondary leakage.

The scope pattern in the available voltage test normally has a tail half as long as the spike. A short or missing tail indicates secondary leakage. Parts that cause secondary leakage will have to be replaced.

Some ignition scopes also display a primary voltage pattern. You can use this pattern when you look at the primary stopping and starting signal and as you check dwell and dwell variation. An example of a primary ignition pattern was shown in Figure 11-12.

You will remember from Section 11-4 that the center electrode of the spark plug is normally negative. Reversed primary wires on the coil will cause the center electrode of the spark plug to be positive. This will increase the required voltage. When this happens the ignition scope pattern will be upside down, as shown in Figure 13-17. You can correct the polarity by connecting the coil primary wires in the right way on the coil.

Coil polarity can also be checked using an analog voltmeter. Connect the positive voltmeter lead to the en-

Fig. 13-17 Upside-down scope pattern caused by reverse coil polarity.

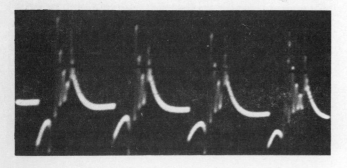

gine metal. A pointer on the negative lead is slid beside the cable into the boot of one of the spark plug cable terminals. The meter should swing upscale while the engine is running when the polarity is correct. Be careful so that you do not damage the spark plug cable or boot. You can see that there is less chance of doing damage when you use an engine scope. You can also use the voltmeter to make sure that the insulated side of the ignition primary circuit connects to the coil terminal marked positive.

You have noticed illustrations of several types of ignition scope traces in Chapters 11 and 13. Different makes and models of scopes show different displays of the voltage traces. Most scopes have switches to select several types of displays.

One popular scope display shows the voltage change during all cylinder firings lined up in parade (see Figure 13-16). This display is used to compare the height (voltage) of the patterns. You can use it to find which cylinder has a required voltage that is too high or too low, which spark plugs are fouled, available voltage, and secondary leakage.

Some scopes can be adjusted to expand any one cylinder trace so it fills the scope screen (see Figure 13-13). This display is usually used to examine the parts of an abnormal trace pattern. Other scopes can enlarge the trace of one cylinder while the other cylinder traces are shown in their normal parade or raster display (Figure 13-18). Figure 11-12 shows a complete cycle of the primary traces, one cylinder trace superimposed over the others. This display is used to compare the shape of the traces to each other. An abnormal trace that is different from the others shows up very clearly. The superimposed display cannot be used to identify *which* trace is different from the others.

Figure 13-19 shows a raster display of an eight-cylinder Chrysler solid-state ignition system. The cylinder traces are stacked, one above the other. The raster display is used to compare the events to each other along each trace. The raster display can be used to identify the cylinder with an abnormal trace. The firing order starts with the bottom trace and goes up.

Each type of display can be used to show either the primary or the secondary traces of the voltage. The most important thing you will be looking at in the scope display is the difference between the traces. With practice, as you look at the shape of the traces, you will be able to identify the part of the ignition system causing a problem.

Run the engine at different speeds while you watch the scope display. Note the speed at which the traces change their shape and how the shape is changed. If the traces on the scope display are normal, there is no ignition problem. You will need to complete the routine maintenance and thoroughly inspect the parts of the ignition

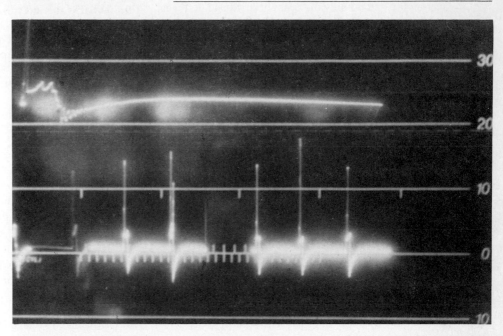

Fig. 13-18 Scope pattern of one cylinder separated and enlarged from the patterns of the other cylinders.

Fig. 13-19 Raster display of an eight-cylinder Chrysler electronic ignition system.

system to be sure that the ignition system is working normally.

If there is one abnormal trace, count along the firing order to identify the cylinder that has the faulty trace. The cylinder with the scope trigger is on the left parade trace and the bottom of the raster trace. A single faulty trace can be caused by a faulty spark plug, spark plug cable, or distributor cap electrode in the ignition system. It can also be caused by low compression, sticking valve, or an intake manifold leak in the mechanical parts of the engine. If all the cylinder traces have the same ignition fault, the problem is in the primary circuit, coil, coil secondary cable, the center electrode of the distributor cap, or the distributor rotor. Rich and lean air/fuel induction charges affect the shape of the trace. Carefully look at the shape of the abnormal trace. With practice, the shape of the trace will direct you to the part of the ignition system causing the problem. You will have to use additional test equipment to find the specific cause of the problem.

Introduction

1. Why should you do only the tests specified and do them in the order specified?

2. In what position should the ignition switch be when removing or connecting ignition circuit wires?

3. Why is dielectric grease used in some ignition connectors?

4. What can a test show you about an ignition system?

5. What is the best method you have to show you that the ignition system will continue to operate properly?

Section 13–1

6. What is missing when an engine will crank but not start?

7. How can you quickly tell that the engine has uneven compression?

8. How can you quickly check the operation of the ignition system?

9. What is the likely cause of a no-start problem if an engine cranks, has compression, fuel, and spark at the spark plug cable?

10. When should the electrical parts of an ignition system be checked?

11. What part of the ignition system is most likely to be the cause of a no-start condition?

12. What does the special test jumper do when it is used to test an electronic ignition system?

13. What do you know when there is no spark at the test spark plug while cranking but there is a spark when the special test jumper is used?

Section 13–2

14. What is the most likely cause of high resistance in the primary circuit?

15. Why does resistance cause more trouble in computer control circuits?

16. What is common in all ignition wiring produced by one manufacturer?

17. What must be done in the primary circuit before it can be tested for resistance?

18. What does low coil resistance indicate about the coil?

Section 13–3

19. What is the most likely cause of trigger failure?

20. What procedure will usually show the cause of an intermittent electrical failure?

21. What is often the cause of failure of the Hall-effect trigger?

22. What adjustment is made on the Hall-effect switch used in a Delco-Remy distributor?

23. When is it necessary to replace the ignition control unit or module?

24. What precautions should you take when installing a new ignition control or module?

Section 13–4

25. What is the best instrument that you can use to see the overall operating condition of the ignition on a running engine?

26. How much voltage is built up in the secondary circuit?

27. What is the highest voltage normally required when the engine is running with the transmission in neutral?

28. What is the maximum normal difference in required voltage between cylinders?

29. When does secondary resistance affect the voltage?

30. What makes the sharp dip in the pattern trace at the right of the coil–capacitor oscillations?

31. What is ignition reserve?

32. Why should no more than one spark plug cable be removed at a time while the engine is running?

33. What is the maximum resistance for a spark plug cable?

34. When is misfiring most likely to happen?

35. How does secondary resistance affect available voltage?

36. How will cross firing show up on the scope pattern?

37. What should be done when the scope pattern is upside down?

38. What shows up on a superimposed display?

39. What shows up on a raster display?

40. What should you do with the engine as you watch the different scope patterns?

14

ENGINE CONTROLS

The changes in emission regulations and fuel economy were discussed in Section 11-4. In addition to ignition, other engine, transmission, and vehicle controls are operated with electricity. The electrical parts of these controls are as important to the study of automotive electricity as those already discussed in Chapters 1 through 13.

Electronic parts and computers are used to control the electricity going through electrical engine and body controls. These controls can have the same types of failures as starting systems, charging systems, and ignition systems. Connectors will corrode and form a high-resistance junction. Connectors can loosen and the connecting wires can break. In time and with use sensors or operating parts can fail.

This chapter has been written to help you understand the purpose of the electrical and electronic parts in engine control systems. We are going to look at different types of electrically operated parts, how the operation of these parts affects engine operation, and how their operation can be checked.

Electrical engine controls can be divided into three types: sensors, electronic controllers, and actuators. We will study controllers only in relation to the input from sensors and output to actuators. Sensors see a change in position, temperature, or pressure. They convert this change into a changing electrical signal. The signal, volt-age, amperage, or resistance is proportional to the change in position, temperature, or pressure. For example, if the pressure doubles, the signal will also double. In engineering terms the sensors are called transducers. In automobiles signals from the controls used by the driver and the signals from the sensors are compared to the program built into the electronic controller (see Section 8-3). The controller then sends the required electrical voltage to the actuators and instrument displays. This is shown in Figure 14-1. The actuator changes the electrical force back into mechanical motion or it operates a solid-state electrical circuit switch.

Fig. 14-1 Electronic controller input and output.

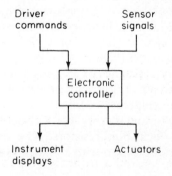

14-1 SENSORS

In automobiles, sensors will change important engine operating conditions into electrical signals. There are a number of different types of signals from sensors. They include switching, variable resistance, variable capacitance, variable inductance, voltage generation, and vibration sensing. Sensors get their electrical power from the engine control computer. The computer operates the sensors at 5 V. Make sure that you do not connect these sensors to a 12 V electrical source.

Switching. Some switching signals are operated with mechanical motion, such as the ignition switch, throttle idle stop switch, and gear selector switch. They conduct when they are closed and do not conduct when they are open. Mechanical switches can be checked with a voltmeter placed across the switch terminals. The voltmeter will show the specified voltage when the switch is open. It will show a voltge drop of less than 0.1 V when the switch is closed and carrying current. The switch can be checked with an ohmmeter when it is out of the circuit.

The transistor is the most common solid-state switch. In automotive service, it is checked as it works in an electronic switching assembly. One of these assemblies that we have discussed was the voltage regulator (see Figure 9–14). In engine controls it is part of the Hall-effect trigger in ignition systems (see Figure 11–26). A Hall-effect switch is used in some speedometers to sense vehicle speed. It is also used in some automatic-leveling shock absorbers to position the vehicle height correctly. Hall-effect switches can be tested with a voltmeter like a mechanical switch when it is operated slowly. Fast-operating Hall-effect switches are best checked using the primary side of an engine scope (see Figure 11–27).

Variable Resistance. Many of the engine control sensors use variable resistances. There are four common types: wire-wound, carbon, thermister, and semiconductor resistor.

Wire-wound variable resistors operate in two different ways. When used in temperature sensors, the resistance of the wire in the sensor coil increases as the temperature increases (Figure 14–2). When used as a position sensor, the resistance of the sensor increases as the slider moves to make electricity go through more of the resistance wire (Figure 14–3).

Some position sensors use Cermets and plastic composition thick film resistors. The ceramic-metal resistor material is mixed with a binder to form an ink.

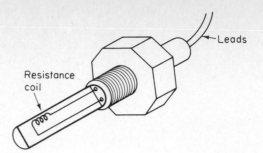

Fig. 14-2 Wire-wound variable-resistance temperature sensor.

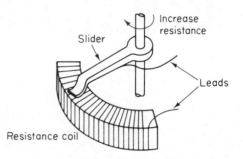

Fig. 14-3 Wire-wound variable-resistance position sensor.

The ink is silk screened on an insulator board to form the resistor. A slider moves across the resistor film to change the resistance of the circuit. Figure 14–4 shows a typical throttle position sensor that uses this type of resistor.

Carbon particles are used to form variable resistance in some sensors. You should already be familiar with this type of variable resistor. It is used as a carbon pile to control high current load while testing batteries,

Fig. 14-4 Thick-film sliding-contact variable-resistance position sensor.

starters, and charging systems. In engine sensors the carbon particles are packed together in a small cavity in the sensor. The resistance is proportional to how tightly the particles are forced together in the cavity. Resistance is increased as the cavity expands to loosen the particles. It is lowered as the particles are forced together. This type of resistance sensor is used with a plastic pellet to squeeze the carbon particles in some temperature sensors. It is used with a diaphragm to squeeze the carbon particles in some pressure sensors.

The wire-wound resistor works well for coolant temperature. It senses changes too slowly for most electronic engine controls. The thermister is the most popular type of temperature sensor for use with electronic engine controls. We first mentioned a thermister in Section 9–4 when discussing solid-state regulation. It is commonly used to sense inlet air temperature and coolant temperature in electronic engine control systems. Thermisters respond to changes in temperature much faster than do wire-wound resistors. Figure 14–5 shows a thermister used to sense the temperature of intake air in a Chrysler computer. The thermister has high resistance when it is cold (100,000 Ω at −40 °F and −40 °C) and a low resistance when hot (70 Ω at 265 °F and 130 °C).

A semiconductor resistor will respond to changes in temperature and pressure much quicker than the thermister. One example is a semiconductor bridge network fused into the diaphragm of a pressure sensor. Because semiconductor resistors are much more expensive than thermisters, they are used only where very fast response time is needed in some electronic fuel injection systems.

Strain gauges are also used in some sensors. The strain gauge is a special metal film cemented to a surface. The strain gauge will stretch or compress when the

Fig. 14–5 Thermister used to sense the temperature of intake air for a Chrysler ignition computer.

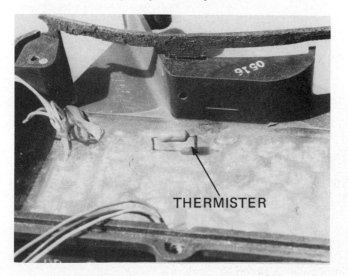

THERMISTER

surface bends or twists a very small amount. The resistance change in the strain gauge is proportional to the change of the surface on which it is cemented. The resistance change is amplified with electronics to make the signal strong enough for use in electronic engine controls.

Resistor-type sensors can usually be checked with an ohmmeter. The sensor is disconnected from the electrical circuit for test. The ohmmeter is calibrated and connected to the sensor leads. The sensor is then moved through its normal operating range by changing the position, temperature, or pressure, depending on the sensor application. The sensor assembly must be replaced if it does not have the correct resistance.

Variable Capacitance. The amount of air going into an engine depends on the throttle opening, the manifold vacuum, air temperature, and the atmospheric pressure pushing air into the manifold vacuum. You know that the piston moving down in the cylinder on the intake stroke pulls the intake charge from the intake manifold. This lowers the pressure in the manifold. In the automotive service trade we use the term "manifold vacuum" for this lower manifold pressure. A manifold air pressure (MAP) sensor is used to measure the lower pressure (vacuum) in the intake manifold. Atmospheric pressure is commonly measured with a barometer. The sensor used to measure atmospheric pressure for engine controls is called a BARO sensor.

There is a very small pressure change between high and low atmospheric pressures. Sensors used to measure these pressures must be very sensitive. Variable capacitive sensors do this very well. BARO and MAP variable-capacitance sensors have a space between a solid surface and a diaphragm. The solid surface and diaphragm are coated with a conducting material. The space between them is sealed and evacuated in the BARO sensor (Figure 14–6). The diaphragm is pushed toward the solid surface as the barometric pressure increases. This increases the capacitance of the sensor. The capacitance is converted to a voltage (between 0 and 5 V) by solid-state electronics within the BARO assembly. This design is an **absolute pressure** sensor because it compares the pressure to the vacuum in the space between the surface and diaphragm. The MAP sensor is a **differential pressure** sensor. It senses the difference between manifold vacuum and atmospheric pressure. The sensor is made similar to the BARO sensor. The solid surface in the MAP sensor has a hole so that atmospheric pressure will be in the space between the surface and diaphragm (Figure 14–7). The capacitance decreases as vacuum pulls the diaphragm away from

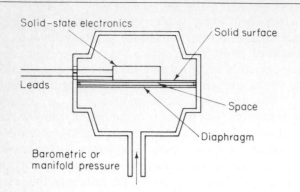

Fig. 14-6 Variable-capacitance BARO sensor.

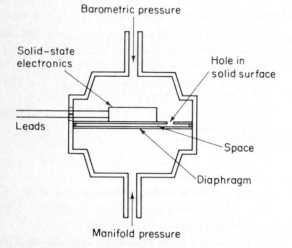

Fig. 14-7 Variable-capacitance MAP sensor.

the solid surface. Some systems combine the MAP and BARO sensors in a single sensor assembly.

Variable Inductance. You will remember from Section 4-9 that the coil causes induction as the current either increases or decreases. This means that the inductive coil sensor has to be fed by pulsing direct or an alternating current. When a core is pushed into the coil, inductance increases, so that it takes longer for the current to build up to full strength. When the core is moved out it takes less time. The inductance of the sensor is proportional to the position of the core in the coil. The engine control computer converts the analog-type inductance into a signal it needs for processing. Variable inductive sensors are built into a number of different sensor assemblies, so that you cannot see them. One you most likely have seen is the inductive sensor used with early Chrysler computers. They sense throttle position and how fast the throttle is moved. A section view of this sensor is shown in Figure 14-8. The signal from this sensor lets the computer know that the driver has moved the throttle opening so the computer can start to change the ignition timing before the MAP sensor can see a change in manifold vacuum. Chrysler also used an inductive-type sensor to sense manifold vacuum. The core of this sensor is connected to a vacuum diaphragm. The diaphragm case looks like the vacuum advance unit of a distributor, but it is part of the computer assembly.

Voltage Generation. You have studied about one of the most common voltage-generating sensors: the inductive trigger in the distributor (see Figure 11-23). An inductive trigger is also used as a position sensor on a number of modern engines with computer engine controls. A coil

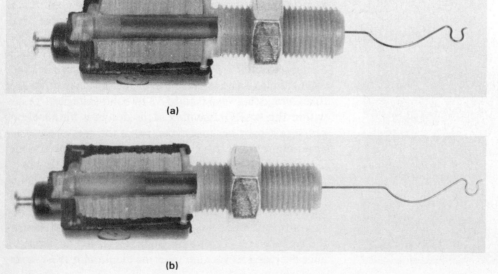

(a)

(b)

Fig. 14-8 Section view of an inductive throttle position sensor used with early Chrysler ignition timing advance computers.

and magnet are placed very close to a timing disk on the crankshaft. This can be part of the crankshaft damper assembly at the front of the engine or part of the flywheel at the rear. The timing disk has teeth or notches. As they pass the coil they move the magnetic lines of force to induce a voltage in the coil. This induced voltage signal lets the computer know the position of the crankshaft.

The crankshaft position sensor gives more exact timing than a distributor trigger. The distributor trigger is driven through camshaft gears and a shaft so that the drive has some flexibility. This changes the timing signal as the engine speed and loads change. In addition, the distributor requires some adjustment that depends on the skill of the technician. The crankshaft sensor was first used on the 1977 Oldsmobile Toronado with MISAR ignition. It was placed at the front of the engine. In 1978 the Ford EEC-I system had the crankshaft position sensor at the flywheel at the rear of the engine.

Another type of voltage-generating sensor is a vehicle speed sensor. You have seen this sensor as the cruise control sensor in the speedometer cable of Ford products (Figure 14-9). It has a magnet that rotates within a coil. The faster the rotation, the stronger the voltage produced by the sensor.

Oxygen sensors used on engines with computer-controlled fuel systems also produce a voltage. It is used to sense the oxygen remaining in the exhaust gas. The oxygen sensor is built into a shell that looks like a spark plug shell. It is screwed into the exhaust manifold near the outlet. If there is too much oxygen in the exhaust, the computer sends a signal to the fuel metering system to enrich the mixture. If there is too little oxygen, the mixture is leaned. This keeps the air/fuel mixture very close to the

ideal mixture for good fuel economy and efficient catalytic converter operation. This system is said to be in closed loop while it is controlling the mixture. It is in open loop and not controlling while the engine is cold, during idle, and at full throttle operation.

The oxygen sensor has a closed tube-shaped zirconia ceramic core. Porous platinum is put on the inside and outside surfaces. An electrical lead is connected to the inside surface, as shown in Figure 14-10. The outside is connected to ground through the sensor shell. When the sensor is hot, oxygen causes the zirconia core to become a conductor between the platinum surfaces. This is like

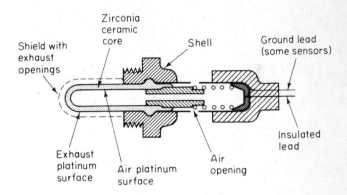

Fig. 14-10   Construction of a typical oxygen sensor.

the electrolyte between the plates of a battery.

The conducting zirconia causes negative oxygen ions to build up on both platinum surfaces. The air-reference platinum surface on the inside of the tube has more negative ions than the outside surface which is in hot exhaust gas. This makes the inside more negative than the outside, so there is a difference in electrical potential or voltage. When the zirconia oxygen sensor is heated to its normal operating temperature the voltage range is from 0.9 V with little oxygen in the exhaust to 0.1 V when there is too much oxygen. You can remember this easier if you think that the output of the sensor is nearly 1 V when the system is rich and nearly zero when lean.

The oxygen sensor does not send a signal strong enough for control until it reaches a minimum operating temperature. The operating temperature range is between 400°F (210°C) and 600°F (315°C). Notice in Figure 14-11 that the voltage changes right at the chemically correct air/fuel mixture. This ideal air/fuel mixture is called **stoichiometric.** It is the mixture that gives the best fuel economy. It is also the mixture at which three-way catalytic converters do the most efficient job of chemically oxidizing HC, CO, and chemically reducing NO_x in the exhaust.

Fig. 14-9   Voltage-generating sensor in the speedometer shaft of a Ford vehicle to sense vehicle speed.

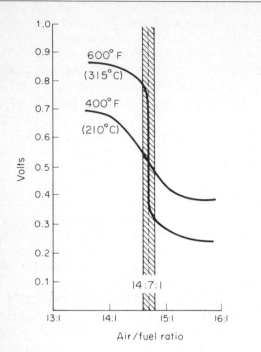

Fig. 14–11 The voltage of an oxygen sensor will change with the temperature of the sensor and the air/fuel mixture.

You should **never** try to check the oxygen sensor with an ohmmeter. Current from the ohmmeter will destroy the sensor calibration. Ford allows the use of a high-input impedance (at least 10 Ω) digital voltmeter to check the oxygen sensor. General Motors **warns against** measuring the oxygen sensor with *any* instrument. The oxygen sensor operation is checked by disconnecting the lead. This causes the computer to see a lean signal. Connecting a *digital voltmeter* between the battery positive and the insulated lead you removed from the oxygen sensor. This sends a low-voltage to the computer so it sees a rich signal. You could also use your body for this by touching the oxygen sensor lead with one hand and the battery positive with the other hand. If you remove and replace the oxygen sensor, be sure to clean the threads and coat them with a high-temperature antiseize compound.

Vibration Sensing. Knock sensors are used on some engines, especially turbocharged engines. Their use allows high advanced ignition timing for economy cruise and retarded timing at high engine power to keep the engine from spark knock. The knock sensor is tuned so that it will vibrate only at the frequency of engine knock. The most popular type of knock sensor has magnetic rods held at one end. The free end of the rods will vibrate at the engine knock frequency. The vibrating magnetic rods produce a voltage in a sensing coil which sends a signal to the computer. Another type of knock sensor uses a piezo-electric crystal transducer that is tuned to send a voltage to the computer when the engine knocks.

Knock sensors are checked with the engine running. Use a hammer to tap the engine beside the knock sensor. If the sensor is working, the engine will slow, then gradually come back to the original speed.

14–2 ACTUATORS

Signals from the sensors are sent to the engine control computer. The computer compares the signals to the program stored in its memory. It processes the signals, then controls the actuators to give the correct ignition advance, fuel metering, idle speed, EGR flow, AIR flow, canister purge, turbo boost, and so on.

Most actuators have their electrical feed from the 12 V insulated electrical circuit. This is usually the circuit that is activated when the ignition switch is turned on. The actuator circuit is completed to ground through the computer. You can see that the actuators will not operate if the computer does not have a good ground. Some of the actuator switching circuits operate on 5 V from the computer. Make sure that you do not connect 12 V to these circuits. Solid-state switches can be thought of as the simplest type of actuator. This includes the solid-state ignition switching transistors. Other actuators are solenoids and motor relays.

Solenoid. Most engine controls use solenoid actuators to move valves. Examples of the valve actuators are:

Purge valve for the carbon canister
Air injection reactor or Thermactor air switching valve
Early fuel evaporation valve
Air-conditioning clutch
Fuel injectors
Automatic transmission converter clutch valve
Exhaust gas recirculating valves
Controls on the turbocharger boost

One solenoid valve that has a lot to do with engine drivability, fuel economy, and emissions is the mixture control solenoid in a carburetor. When the solenoid is turned off, a spring lifts a needle valve to let fuel flow at the maximum rich limit. When the solenoid is turned on, the needle is pulled down to slow the fuel flow to the low limit. In operation, the solenoid is turned off and on rapidly. This causes the valve to rise and drop very rapidly. The off-on action is like voltage regulation shown in Figure 9-11. When a valve does this it is said to **dither** and it is often called a dither valve. The valve is held open for a moment, then it is closed for a moment. The longer it is held open, compared to being held closed, the richer the mixture will be. If it is held closed longer than it is held open, the mixture will be leaner.

If the mixture control solenoid does not receive power, the carburetor will go full rich. A dwell meter is used to check the action of the dither valve mixture control circuit. The dwell meter is connected between a green test lead and ground on GM vehicles. Too much dwell will indicate a lean mixture and too little dwell indicates a rich mixture. The dwell meter will be moving up and down scale between 10° (rich) and 50° (lean) while it is controlling. There is a problem in the circuit if the system should be controlling but there is no change in dwell.

Fuel injectors dither to control the fuel mixture like the carburetor mixture control solenoid does. When the injector solenoid is turned on, full fuel will flow. When it is turned off, no fuel flows. The amount of fuel delivered depends on the injector hole size, the fuel pressure, and how long the injector is turned on, compared to how long it is turned off. You can normally hear the fuel pump run for a second when the ignition switch is first turned on. You should be able to feel the injectors pulse while the engine is being cranked and while it is running.

Relay. You will remember that relays are remotely controlled switches. The computer controls the relays with 5 V in electronic engine controls. Relays turn 12 V motors like the cooling fan, idle speed, and fuel pump on and off when necessary. In some carburetors the air/fuel mixture is controlled by a stepper motor. The motor rotates exactly 180° on each electrical pulse. It rotates in one direction to enrich the mixture and in the other direction to lean the mixture.

You can check actuator circuits by measuring for 12 V coming in the feed wire from the battery or the 5 V coming from the computer. You will have to use the vehicle service manual for these tests until you become familiar with the vehicle wire color codes, sensor location, and actuator location.

14-3 SELF-DIAGNOSIS

The operator is the first to know that the vehicle has a problem. This is sensed as poor drivability or by seeing a warning lamp on the instrument panel. Be sure to question the operator so that you know exactly what problem you must look for. When you have identified the problem, check the vehicle systems exactly as you would have if the vehicle had no self-diagnosis. Any system on

vehicles with self-diagnosis are just as likely to have a problem as those on vehicles without.

Any time that a sensor signal is out of its normal range the modern automotive computer switches to a fixed value to replace the signal. This will keep the engine running, even if it does not run well. For example, it may set the timing at a fixed advance or set the fuel mixture full rich. This gives the operator a chance to drive the vehicle to a service shop for repair.

The computer is designed to remember out of range signals from the sensors. They also remember which actuator circuits will not accept normal control instructions. This information is stored in the computer as code numbers between 01 and 99. These are called two-digit numbers. Chrysler calls them fault codes, Ford calls them service codes, and General Motors calls them trouble codes. Using the correct procedures, you can read the codes stored in the memory of the computer. The code number is compared to a table of codes that applies to that vehicle. This will tell you which circuit or system is not working correctly.

General Motors. General Motors was the first domestic automobile manufacturer to use self-diagnosis in their automobiles, starting with the 1980 Computer Controlled Catalytic Converter (C-4) system. Since then, self-diagnosis has been upgraded to include more test codes. The self-diagnosis two-digit trouble code is signaled by the "check engine" lamp when a test terminal is grounded. Early models have a test terminal hanging near the computer. In later models the test terminal is in the assembly line connector link (ALCL) diagnostic connector. It is located under the dash at the left of the steering column. There are a number of ALCL connector designs (Figure 14-12), so you will have to check the service manual that applies to the vehicle being checked.

Be ready to write the code numbers down before you check them. Ground the test terminal and turn the ignition on without starting the engine to read the test codes. For example, code 32 (BARO sensor circuit on one vehicle) would flash three times, have a short pause, then flash two times. This would be followed by a longer pause, then the next trouble code would flash. The trouble codes start with the lowest-numbered code. Each code will flash three times before going to the next trouble code stored in the memory. Figure 14-13 lists typical trouble codes used on General Motors vehicles.

Trouble codes will stay in the memory of the General Motors computer for 50 engine starts unless they are erased after the faulty system has been corrected. The trouble codes are erased after correcting the cause of the

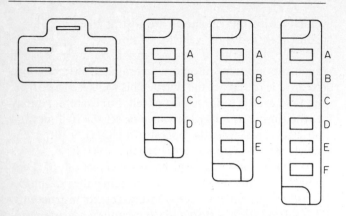

Fig. 14-12 Types of ALCL diagnostic connector designs used on General Motors automobiles.

12	No distributor reference pulse
13	Oxygen sensor circuit
14	Coolant sensor circuit shorted
15	Coolant sensor circuit open
21	Throttle position sensor high
22	Throttle position sensor low
23	M/C solenoid circuit low
24	Vehicle speed sensor circuit
24B	Park/neutral switch circuit
32	BARO sensor circuit
34	Differential pressure sensor circuit
35	Idle speed control circuit
41	No distributor reference circuit
42	Electronic spark timing
43	Electronic spark control
44	Lean exhaust indication
45	Rich exhaust indication
51	PROM
53	EGR vacuum control
54	M/C solenoid circuit high

Fig. 14-13 Typical General Motors trouble codes.

problem by interrupting power that feeds the computer. This is usually done by removing the fuse that feeds the computer. Codes can also be erased by removing and reconnecting the battery ground cable.

Special testers are manufactured by equipment companies to connect to the ACLC connector. One of these is shown in Figure 5-30. They do not use the diagnostic charts and they cannot tell exactly where the problem is in a circuit. You will have to understand what is being checked at each switch position of the tester. You will also have to know the operation of the circuit being checked so that you can identify the cause of the problem. These testers can help you to identify the cause of the problem faster than you can find them when you use test codes and diagnostic charts.

Ford. Ford vehicles introduced self-diagnosis with the 1983 EEC-IV system. This system did not use a "check engine" light. When the operator brought the vehicle into the shop to correct a problem, the technician would run all the usual tests for that kind of problem. If these tests did not find the trouble, test equipment was connected to the self-test connector. This connector is located at the right rear of the engine compartment. Ford recommends the use of the STAR (self-test automatic readout) tester. If this is not available, connect an analog voltmeter between terminal 4 of the self-test connector and the battery positive terminal. The six-cavity connector shape is shown in Figure 14-14. Do not activate the service codes until they are called for in the diagnostic procedure. At this point, the test assumes that all the circuits you have tested while following the diagnostic procedure are working correctly. When the ignition key is turned on, the service codes are shown by number on the STAR tester or by sweeps of the voltmeter needle. Three upscale voltmeter sweeps followed by a 2-second delay, then two sweeps indicate a service code 32. This shows that there is a problem with the EGR not controlling. There is a 4-second delay before the next service code is given. Typical Ford service codes are shown in Figure 14-15.

Chrysler. Chrysler introduced fault codes in 1984. Fault codes are shown by a flashing "power-loss" lamp. The fault code is activated by turning the ignition switch on–off–on–off–on within 5 seconds without starting the engine. After flashing code 88 the power-loss lamp shows the lowest-numbered fault code first. Typical Chrysler fault codes are shown in Figure 14-16. Code 55 signals

Fig. 14-14 Analog voltmeter connections to read the service codes from the memory of Ford engine control computers.

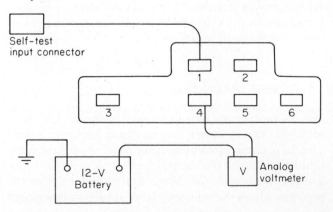

11	System "pass"	55	Electrical charging under voltage
12	Rpm out of spec (extended idle)	56	MAF (VAF) input too high
13	Rpm out of spec (normal idle)	58	Idle tracking switch input too high (engine running test)
14	PIP was erratic (continuous test)	61	ECT input too low
15	ROM test failed	63	TPS input too low
16	Rpm too low (fuel lean test)	64	ACT (VAT) input too low
17	Rpm too low (upstream/lean test)	65	Electrical charging over voltage
18	No tach	66	MAF (VAF) input too low
21	ECT out of range	67	Neutral drive switch — drive or accelerator on (engine off)
22	MAP out of range	68	ITS open or AC on (engine-off test)
23	TPS out of range	72	No MAP change in "goose test"
24	ACT out of range	73	No TPS change in "goose test"
25	Knock not sensed in test	76	No MAF (VAF) change in "goose test"
26	MAF (VAF) out of range	77	Operator did not do "goose test"
31	EVP out of limits	81	Thermactor air bypass (TAB) circuit fault
32	EGR not controlling	82	Thermactor air diverter (TAD) circuit fault
33	EVP not closing properly	83	EGR control (EGRC) circuit fault
34	No EGR flow	84	EGR vent (EGRV) circuit fault
35	Rpm too low (EGR test)	85	Canister purge (CANP) circuit fault
36	Fuel always lean (at idle)	86	WOT A/C cut-off circuit fault (all 3.8L and 5.0L Continental)
37	Fuel always rich (at idle)	87	Fuel pump circuit fault
41	System always lean	88	Throttle kicker circuit fault (5.0L)
42	System always rich	89	Exhaust heal control valve circuit fault
43	EGO cooldown occurred	91	Right EGO always lean
44	Air management system inoperative	92	Right EGO always rich
45	Air always upstream	93	Right EGO cooldown occurred
46	Air not always bypassed	94	Right secondary air inoperative
47	Up air/lean test always rich	95	Right air always upstream
48	Injectors imbalanced	96	Right air always not bypassed
51	ECT input too high	97	Rpm drop (with fuel lean) but right EGO rich
53	TPS input too high	98	Rpm drop (with fuel rich) but right EGO lean
54	ACT (VAT) input too high		

Fig. 14-15 Typical Ford service codes.

Fig. 14-16 Typical Chrysler fault codes.

11	Distributor reference signal circuit	34	EGR solenoid circuit
12	Battery feed to logic module	35	Fan relay circuit
13	MAP sensor circuit — vacuum	41	Charging system
14	MAP sensor circuit — electrical	42	Automatic shut down relay circuit
15	Vehicle speed sensor circuit	43	Ignition and fuel control interface
21	Oxygen sensor circuit	44	Logic module
22	Coolant temperature sensor circuit	45	Turbocharger overboost
23	Charge temperature sensor circuit	51	Oxygen feedback sensor
24	Throttle position sensor	52	Logic module
25	Automatic idle speed control circuit	53	Logic module
31	Purge solenoid circuit	54	Distributor synchronizer signal circuit
32	Power loss lamp circuit	55	End of test sequence
33	A/C wide open throttle cutout relay circuit	88	Start of test sequence

the end of faults stored in the memory. Fault code read-out stops any time the engine is started. Corrected fault codes in Chrysler vehicles will be automatically remove from memory after 30 engine starts. They can be removed from memory by interrupting the power going to the computer in the same way General Motors trouble codes are erased.

A special Diagnostic Readout Box has been designed to help diagnose Chrysler vehicle problems. It will quickly check the whole engine control system with no chance of doing damage to any part of the system. Other electrical test equipment may be used, but this equipment is limited to checking wiring and connectors after they have been disconnected from the rest of the system. The Diagnostic Readout Box is connected to a mating diagnostic connector in the wiring harness near the right-front shock tower.

Summary. Self-diagnosis will show the result of most, but not all, of the problems in an engine. It does not necessarily show the cause of the problem. The easiest problem cause to find is a fault that keeps the engine from running. Problems that the driver notices, such as poor drivability, are more difficult to find. It is still more difficult to find problems caused by sensors going out of range. The most difficult problems to solve are those that have no effect on normal operation. An example of this could be an air pump switching valve. The driver would not notice this until some other part also failed.

The sensor circuits and some actuator circuits operate on a maximum of 5 V. As a result, small resistances in these circuits have a great effect on the operation of the circuit. Many engine control circuits use Weather Pack connectors to minimize the chance of resistance. Figure 14–17 shows an example of this type of connector. When you mate these connectors, make sure that the connector halves are properly nested together. Make sure the sealing rings properly seat to seal the connector. These connectors are so tight that fluid from a faulty sensor will travel inside the wire insulation all the way to the electronic engine control. This results in corrosion in the wire and at both terminals. Never probe into a Weather Pack connector. The probe will form a passage into the connector that will allow moisture to enter the connector to cause corrosion. When testing circuits always use jumpers between the Weather Pack connector and your test equipment.

The connectors in the electronic engine controls may be open, misaligned, or oxidized. These conditions are difficult to find when you are diagnosing the system. About the only way you can find them is to wiggle the

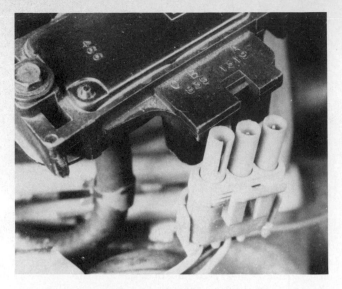

Fig. 14–17 Typical Weather Pack connection that keeps moisture and corrosion from the connector.

connection on the circuit that is causing the problem while your test equipment is connected to the circuit.

14–4 INFORMATION SYSTEMS

Electronic displays were first introduced in automobiles as warning lights, digital clocks, and digital radio dials. Vehicle downsizing reduced the space behind the instrument panel. This left less space for mechanical and electrical instruments. Electronic instrument displays can be made to fit this smaller space. In addition, information for electronic displays can be taken from sensors already being used for electronic engine and vehicle controls. As a result, the use of electronic instrument displays has increased. Together with electronic displays, electronic synthetic voice reminders are used to inform the operator about the condition of the vehicle and its systems.

Electronic Displays. There have been many different types of electronic displays developed in the laboratories. Some produce their own light. They are called **active** displays. Other types, called **passive** displays, must have light added to them for you to see them.

Each display has an electrical connection for each part, called a segment, of the display. There would be one positive and one negative connection for each dot or line segment. Numbers take seven segments. They use one power source feed and a single ground lead for *each* segment. This is illustrated in Figure 14–18. You have seen how seven segments make numbers on digital clocks and calculators. It takes a 16-segment display to show both numbers or letters on the same display. Each of the segments must have an electrical connection.

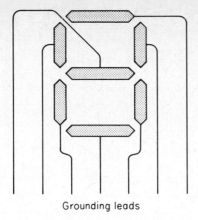

Fig. 14–18 Ground leads are needed for each segment of a number display.

Look closely at the pictures in this book with a magnifying glass. Notice that each picture is made up of dots, some darker and some lighter. Instrument displays made up of hundreds of dots (dot matrix) can be used for numbers, letters, and pictures. You have seen this type of display as animated score boards. Remember that each dot needs a ground wire connection. You can see that a dot matrix would be a complex and expensive display, but it could be made.

Light-emitting diode. The active light-emitting diode (LED) was the first type of electronic display used on automobiles. It was used with gauges as warning lights for low fuel level, high engine temperature, and battery discharge. You have commonly seen LEDs used as sound-level meters on some tape recorders.

The LED is about 0.020 in. (1 mm) square. It is usually built with a reflector to direct the light in one direction. A lens is used to shape the light into a spot or line. It can be green, yellow, or amber, but it usually is red. LEDs are most often used for small displays. Numerical displays commonly use seven LEDs, each with a lens to expand the light to form a line segment. A number of LEDs can be combined to form a large display, but these are quite expensive. Toyota used 44 LEDs to form a vehicle speed display in one of their automobiles. Each of these LEDs had a separate ground through the control.

LEDs operate on about 2 V. They are rugged and have a long operating life. Their use in automobiles is limited because rapid changes in temperature and high humidity may damage them.

Vacuum fluorescent display. A second type of active electronic display is the vacuum fluorescent display (VFD). It has become one of the popular types of electronic instrument displays. The VFD operates similar to a triode vacuum tube. A wire filament (cathode) just behind the front glass is heated with electricity so that it gives off electrons. A wire grid attracts the electrons, like a transistor base circuit. Most of the electrons go through the grid to strike a positive polarity (anode) fluorescent segment that has been silk screened onto an insulated film base. The cathode, grid, and anode assembly forms a flat box-shaped vacuum chamber (Figure 14–19). The fluorescent segment surface gives off light like a television picture tube. You have seen many VFDs as blue/green digital displays in calculators and clocks. Large luminous vacuum flourescent instrument displays are made. They have a good viewing angle, up to six colors, good brightness, wide operating temperature range, and low power consumption. VFDs use from 8 to 150 V and they respond quickly.

The VFD instrument panel is an assembly. The driver sees the display through the front frame and color filters. Electronics that drive the display are mounted on the display board. The display board is backed by a microprocessor board. The voltage converter module and mechanical odometer are fastened to the rear frame housing behind the microprocessor board.

Liquid crystal display. A liquid crystal display (LCD) was used for the instrument panel in the 1984 Corvette. It is a passive display so it needs light to be seen. You have seen this type of display on some wristwatches and on solar-powered calculators. The LCD usually has black numbers on a light background.

The LCD assembly is made up of two flat glasses with a thin liquid crystal sealed between them. Tin oxide transparent conductor segments are etched on the inside surface of the front glass. The inside surface of the rear glass is also coated with a tin oxide transparent electrode. The liquid crystal (0.0001 in. thick) layer is sealed between the front and rear glasses. The LCD assembly looks cloudy when it is not connected to electricity.

Fig. 14–19 Typical vacuum fluorescent display parts.

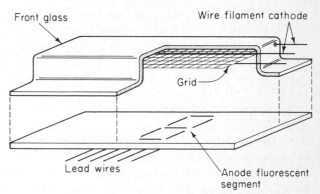

Have you ever played with Polaroid sun glasses? If you place one glass over the other and rotate them, you will find a position where the most light will pass through. Rotate them 90° from this point and they will turn black because very little light will pass through. A polarizing screen, like Polaroid sun glasses, is placed in front and another behind the LCD assembly. The polarizing screens are placed at 90° to each other so no light will come through.

A small current will flow through the liquid crystal when electricity is connected to electrodes on the front and back glasses. It uses from 5 to 10 V. The voltage causes the molecules in the liquid crystal to line up so they control the light by rotating or twisting it 90°. Polarized light coming through one polarizing screen is turned 90° in the liquid crystal so that it can go out through the other polarizing screen. This changes that part of the screen from a black to a clear transparent area.

In watches and solar-powered calculators there is a reflecting surface behind the rear polarizing screen. Light goes through the transparent part of the LCD, hitting the reflecting surface, and comes back out. This makes the clear surface look light and the nonactive surface looks black. The brighter the light that hits the LCD, the more contrast there is between the light and dark surfaces. The contrast makes the light surface lighter compared to the black surface. This would work allright in daylight, but it would be of no use at night because there is no light to reflect from the reflector.

In automotive instrument displays the back reflector is made somewhat like a one-way glass window. It is called a **transflector** because light behind it will shine through and it still will reflect light from the front. The brightness of the instrument display is controlled by the brightness of a lamp that lights the back of the LCD. Figure 14-20 shows an exploded view of a LCD assembly. The color is determined by the way the polarizers are made. Yellow, green, and red are the easiest colors to display.

LCDs will work between temperatures as low as −25°F (−30°C) and as high as 185°F (85°C). This covers the range of temperatures in which the vehicle will operate, except in unusual arctic or tropical conditions. Development work will increase the temperature range of LEDs. When the liquid crystal temperature gets too cold it becomes a solid. When it gets too warm it becomes clear. In either case it will not control the light.

The 1984 Corvette has three LCD units in the instrument cluster: speedometer, tachometer, and mulifunction driver information. They are designed with a black background and colored active areas. The colors in these units

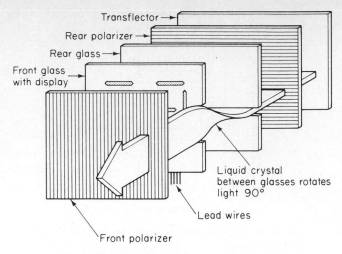

Fig. 14-20 Principle of a liquid crystal display shown in an exploded view.

are made with translucent fluorescent inks. The background is covered with a black mask. This part of the panel always looks black to aid in defining the graphics. Light for the display is carried from four 3.8 candlepower halogen lamps through plastic blocks called **light pipes.** This method of light transfer spreads the light evenly across the graphics for good visibility. A photocell sensor in the instrument panel senses the amount of light hitting the front of the cluster and sends a signal to a controller. The controller automatically adjusts the LCD lamps to hold the light for normal contrast. The system also has the usual instrument panel rheostat to set the level of lighting.

There are 256 individual electrical connections between the LCDs and the driver board in this Corvette instrument panel. The driver board has 8 integrated circuits, each driving 32 LCD segments. There is a 12-pin connection between the driver board and the processor board. The cluster assembly is connected to the vehicle through two connectors, one with 24 and one with 36 junctions.

Odometer.   The odometer is mechanical on most electronic instrument panels. It is operated with a stepper motor. Each pulse moves the stepper motor one step to keep track of the miles traveled. This type of odometer will hold its reading when the battery is disconnected. Work is being done to develop an odometer with an electronic reading.

Electronic Speech.   Sound is actually vibrating air. We speak into a microphone and the microphone changes the sound into an electrical signal. The electrical signal is carried through an amplifier and fed into a speaker to remake the sound. Electronic engineers have been able to analyze the parts of speech in the electrical signal produced by a microphone. These parts of speech are called **phoneme.** The separate parts of speech have been put into the memory of a computer as phonemes. The computer is programmed to assemble the phonemes and feed them into the speaker of a radio to make new words. The words we hear are called **synthetic speech.**

Voice information systems were introduced on automobiles about the time that electronic instruments were introduced. Vehicle computers receive and check signals from all the vehicle systems. Faults are stored in the memory as a fault code. These codes are available to the voice synthesizer to inform the driver of both nor-

mal and abnormal vehicle conditions.

Computers can check all systems much faster than the driver can. The voice synthesizer uses artificial speech to tell the driver that all systems are normal or it lists the systems that are not normal. A voice information system informs the driver about the condition of the vehicle while the driver keeps attention on driving.

STUDY QUESTIONS

Section 14–1

1. What voltage is used by automotive computers to operate sensors?

2. List six different types of signals from sensors.

3. Name three instruments that can be used to check the operation of a switch.

4. Name four common types of variable resistance sensors.

5. Why are thermisters usually used with electronic engine controls rather than wire-wound resistors?

6. What type of sensors use variable capacitance?

7. How does a variable capacitance MAP sensor differ from a BARO sensor?

8. Where did Chrysler use inductive-type sensors on their early ignition timing advance computers?

9. Name four types of voltage generating sensors.

10. What is the voltage range of an oxygen sensor when it is operating at its normal temperature?

11. What results would you expect if you checked an oxygen sensor with an ohmmeter?

12. How is the oxygen sensor checked?

13. What precaution should you take when replacing an oxygen sensor?

14. What tool is used to check the knock sensor?

Section 14–2

15. What does an engine control computer do to control the actuator circuit?

16. Name three types of actuators.

17. What does a solenoid do when it dithers?

18. What happens to the mixture if the mixture control dither valve fails?

19. What controls the relay-type actuators?

Section 14–3

20. What must be done to the ALCL diagnostic connector to read the trouble codes stored in the memory of computers in General Motors vehicles?

21. How are trouble codes erased after correcting the cause of the problem?

22. What common type of tester can be used to read Ford service codes?

23. What is done to make the power-loss lamp flash fault codes in Chrysler vehicles?

24. What precautions should you take when assembling Weather Pack connectors?

Section 14–4

25. What is needed to activate each segment of a display?

26. What is done to an LED to make a line?

27. Which displays described in this section are active displays?

28. Which displays described in this section are passive displays?

29. What problem is encountered when using a liquid crystal display in an instrument panel?

30. What is a light pipe?

31. What is synthetic speech?

32. What does the voice synthesizer tell the driver?

ELECTRICAL
ACCESSORIES

Automotive accessories are installed on vehicles either for safety or convenience. Lights, instruments, and windshield wipers and washers are needed for safety. In fact, they are required by state and federal regulations. The radio, speed control, electric window openers, and electric door locks are examples of convenience accessories. They are not required on automobiles but they make driving more pleasant. When convenience accessories help to keep the driver from becoming tired, they also add to vehicle safety. We will be looking at a number of typical automotive accessories that operate on electricity.

In Chapter 2 we covered lights, flashers, and electrical safety devices. Chapter 5 discussed the testing and repair of electrical parts and electrical circuits. What you learned in those two chapters will also apply to other electrical accessories that we will be studying in this chapter.

15-1 INSTRUMENTS

Instruments are used to indicate automobile operating conditions. All automobiles must have a speedometer to show speed and an odometer to show the distance traveled. There is some way to indicate low engine oil pressure, high coolant temperature, and battery discharge. All vehicles have a fuel gauge to show the amount of fuel

remaining in the tank. Each automobile has an indicator to show the operation of high-beam headlamps and turn signals. They are usually mechanical-electrical instruments. Some new designs use electronic instruments as covered in Section 14-4.

In addition to these basic instruments, many automobiles have instruments to give the driver more information about the operation of the automobile. These would include instruments such as a tachometer, clock, and compass. Computers are becoming popular to keep track of things like fuel economy and the miles or kilometers the vehicle can go on the fuel remaining.

Indicator Lamps.   Many operating conditions are shown by indicator lamps. These are frequently referred to as "idiot lights" by those who do not recognize their real value. A driver immediately sees a light signal that indicates a problem, even when concentrating on driving. It is interesting to note that the aerospace industry uses lights to indicate abnormal operating conditions to alert the highly skilled pilot to the problem. A gauge may also be used to check the actual operating value. Many gauges now in use have a red LED to serve as a warning when the system is out of normal range.

Indicator lamp circuits connect between the sensor, usually called the **engine sending unit,** the indicator light bulb, the ignition switch, and junction block to complete the circuit. This circuit is shown in Figure 15-1. It should be noted that these indicator bulbs are some of the few lamps in the vehicle that are not grounded at the bulb socket. The sensors are electrical switches that connect the circuit to ground to turn on the indicator light.

A diaphragm in the oil pressure engine sending unit opens the ground connection when there is oil pressure. When the pressure drops, a spring pushes the metal center of the diaphragm against the metal sensor body to complete the circuit and turn on the indicator lamp. A section view of the pressure engine sender is shown in Figure 15-2. Points on a bimetal arm are used in a temperature engine sender unit, as shown in Figure 15-3. When engine temperature is too high, the heat bends the bimetal arm in the sender so that the points close to complete the circuit and turn on the red HOT warning lamp. In some cases, the temperature engine sender unit has a second set of points to light a green low-temperature indicator lamp. These are normally closed points to light the green COLD lamp. As the engine warms, the bimetal arm bends enough to separate the points, which turn out the cold signal lamp. Further heating bends the arm enough to close the normally open points to light the red HOT lamp.

Discharge lights in the charging system operate in a different manner. Solid-state regulators use electronic circuits to operate the charge indicator lamp. This system was discussed in Section 9-4.

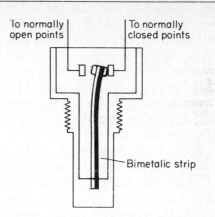

Fig. 15-3 Section view of a typical temperature engine sender.

A number of other warning lamps may be used, such as brake signal, low fuel level, seat belt fastening, and door ajar. Each helps to improve safety and convenience while adding to both the original and maintenance costs.

A relatively new indicating method makes use of fiber-optic conductors. They are made of a bundle of plastic filaments that transmit light. These light conductors are used to show the driver if lights are on or off. One end of the light conductor is at the light source and the other end can be seen by the driver.

Gauges. Electromechanical instrument gauges are used where it is important to know values such as vehicle speed and the amount of fuel in the tank. Oil pressure, engine temperature, and the charging rate gauges are used to indicate that a failure may occur. Gauges are generally more expensive than indicating lamps, and most drivers would not notice or even recognize an incorrect reading. So indicator lamps are usually used. Gauges are standard equipment on most sport and performance-model cars and optional equipment on many other cars.

The mechanical speedometer uses induction between a rotating magnet and a cup. The cup, with the indicator needle, is held against the zero stop by a hair spring. As the magnet rotates, induction pulls the cup against the hair spring. The needle movement is proportional to the magnet's rotating speed. The rotating magnet is driven by a flexible shaft, which, in turn, is driven by a gear in the transmission output shaft or by a gear in one of the wheels. An odometer is part of the mechanical speedometer assembly.

Most of the other gauges are electrically operated.

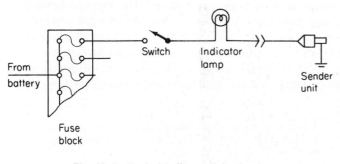

Fig. 15-1 Typical indicator light circuit.

Fig. 15-2 Section view of a typical pressure engine sender.

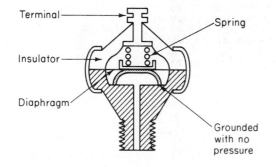

In one type of gauge, a coil of resistance wire is wound around a bimetal arm. One metal of the arm expands more with heat than the other part. This bends the arm. The more current that flows through the coil, the more it heats the arm. The heat causes the bimetal arm to bend more. The movable end of the arm is connected by a linkage to an indicator needle. Scale panels are placed behind the needle to show the correct value. This type of thermal electric gauge is illustrated in Figure 15–4.

A balanced-coil principle is another method used to operate instruments. A series coil on the left side of Figure 15–5 goes to ground, so it carries constant current. Current in the shunt coil on the right goes to a variable resistance in the engine sending unit. Current flow changes as the resistance of the sending unit changes. Low resistance in the sending unit increases the magnetic

strength of the shunt coil. High resistance weakens the magnetic strength of the shunt coil. The indicator needle is moved by the difference in the magnetic strength between the series and shunt coils. Low sending unit resistance gives a low reading and a high resistance gives a high reading.

Many instrument gauge mechanisms are sensitive to current flow. It is important for these gauges to have a constant-voltage source for accuracy. The voltage is supplied from a vibrating point voltage regulator that keeps the voltage at a constant value, usually 5 V. The instrument voltage regulator is usually a separate unit. Sometimes it is part of the fuel-level gauge.

Electronic instrument panels are being put in many new vehicles. You will be seeing many more of them. They were discussed in Section 14–4.

Senders. The gauge sender, which is the sensor at the tank or engine, connects the instrument electrical system to ground to complete the electrical circuit. In the fuel gauge sender, a variable-resistance rheostat is connected to the hinged tank float. This is illustrated in Figure 15–6. When the fuel level is high, the gauge circuit connects directly to ground, allowing full current to flow through the instrument coil. This moves the instrument needle to the top of the scale. As fuel is used, the float drops. This causes the instrument circuit current to flow through part of the variable resistor. The added resistance of the variable resistor reduces current flow through the shunt coil circuit of the balance-coil gauge. On thermal bimetal gauges less current reduces the instrument coil temperature, so the gauge reading lowers. The gauge reading is, therefore, proportional to the tank fuel level.

Oil pressure gauge senders have a spring-loaded diaphragm. Diaphragm movement from oil pushing the

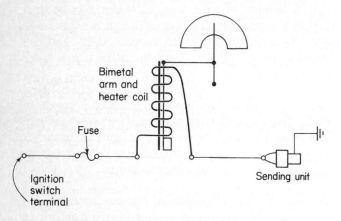

Fig. 15–4 Typical thermal-electric gauge circuit.

Fig. 15–5 Balanced coil gauge.

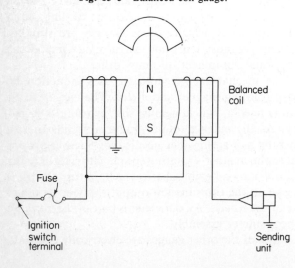

Fig. 15–6 Operating principle of a sender for a thermal electric fuel gauge. The instrument connection is at the opposite end of the variable resistance when used with a balanced coil gauge.

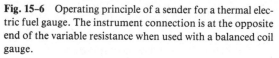

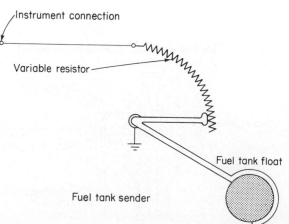

diaphragm toward the spring moves the slider on the wire-wound resistor. This will change the instrument circuit resistance proportional to the diaphragm movement (Figure 15-7). Resistance is low when oil pressure is high, giving a high instrument reading.

The temperature gauge sender has a bimetal spring. The free end of the bimetal spring is connected to the slider on a variable resistance. As the slider moves, the instrument circuit resistance is changed proportionately to the engine temperature. This can be seen in Figure 15-8. When the engine is hot, the sender resistance is low, which will give a high instrument reading.

Some temperature senders used with gauges have a plastic pellet and carbon beads enclosed in the sender bulb, as shown in Figure 15-9. The plastic pellet expands as it gets warm. This expansion forces the beads together to reduce the resistance. The change in resistance is proportional to the change in temperature.

If the sender end of the wire is grounded, the normal reading of a thermal-electric gauge will be high. If no current flows, the reading will be zero. Balanced coil gauges have opposite readings. Some service manuals give resistance values that you can temporarily connect into the circuit to check gauge accuracy. Several equipment manufacturers have made testers with resistors that can be set to the specified resistance. These resistances are also helpful in troubleshooting a gauge problem. If the gauge works when the resistor is connected in place of

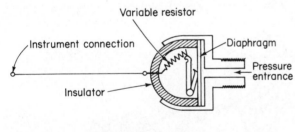

Fig. 15-7 Operating principle of a sender for a pressure gauge.

Fig. 15-8 Operating principle of a wire-wound variable-resistance sender for a temperature gauge.

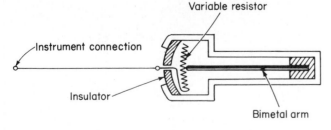

Chapter 15
Electrical Accessories

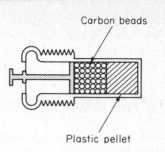

Fig. 15-9 Section view of a variable-resistance pellet-type sender for a temperature gauge.

the sender, the sender is faulty. If the gauge does not work, the tester should be connected at the next junction closer to the gauge. Continue this until you find the cause of the problem.

The ammeter is connected in the part of the charging circuit that leads to the battery. Its **only** purpose is to indicate the amount of current being put into or taken from the battery. It does not indicate generator output. The ammeter wiring circuit has a large wire size. The ammeter itself must also have heavy construction to carry high current. Several ammeter movement types are used. All use some application of electromagnetic induction. As current flows, it forms a magnetic field that deflects a permanent magnet in the instrument. High current causes more deflection than low current. The moving part of the gauge is connected to an indicator needle. The needle's normal position is upright. The needle moves to the right when the current is flowing into the battery and to the left when current flows from the battery.

Troubleshooting becomes routine when you understand the basic operating principles of these electro-mechanical instruments and when you follow the service manual instructions. The biggest problem you will have in instrument troubleshooting is to find and reach the instrument leads and junctions behind the dash panel to check them, especially in a car equipped with air conditioning and a center console.

Digital Instruments. Digital instrument displays have been increasing in automobiles. A digital display, discussed in Section 14-4, uses numbers and words rather than an instrument pointer to give information to the driver. Working with microcomputers, digital instruments display information such as miles per gallon, trip speed, trip time, miles until the fuel tank is empty, remaining miles to go, arrival time, engine rpm, engine temperature, and electrical-system voltage. Sensors are located in the vehicle to collect the information needed. The sensor signal is sent to the microcomputer, where the signals are processed. The results of the processing are sent to the instrument panel, where the information is displayed to the driver.

15-2 WIPERS AND WASHERS

Windshield wiper systems are safety-related automobile units. Fortunately, they require little service. Most of the time the only service needed is the installation of new wiper-blade inserts. Sometimes new wiper arms are required. These are held on to the wiper mechanism with cap screws or with a spring-loaded clamp built into the wiper arm.

Windshield wipers use an electric motor driving the wiper through a gear train that is connected to the wiper linkage. An exploded view of a wiper motor assembly is shown in Figure 15-10. If the wiper motor fails it can be checked using the same procedure used on other automotive-type electric motors. The motor must receive electricity through wires and switches. If it does, the fault is in the wiper assembly. If it does not get electricity, the wiper electrical circuit will have to be checked. The mechanical linkages of the wiper should be carefully inspected for binding before the assembly is removed for service. The complete wiper motor assembly is usually replaced. Parts are available to recondition the wiper assembly, but they are rarely kept in stock, so they will have to be special-ordered. In emergencies you can use parts from several used wiper assemblies to make one operational unit.

Windshield washers are another safety-related item used on automobiles. The washer system has a fluid reservoir, an electric pump, hoses, and washer nozzles. The electric pump may be a diaphragm-type pump that puts pulses of washer fluid on the windshield or it can be a turbine pump that sprays a steady stream of washer fluid.

Fig. 15-10 Exploded view of a typical windshield wiper motor. (Courtesy American Motors Corporation.)

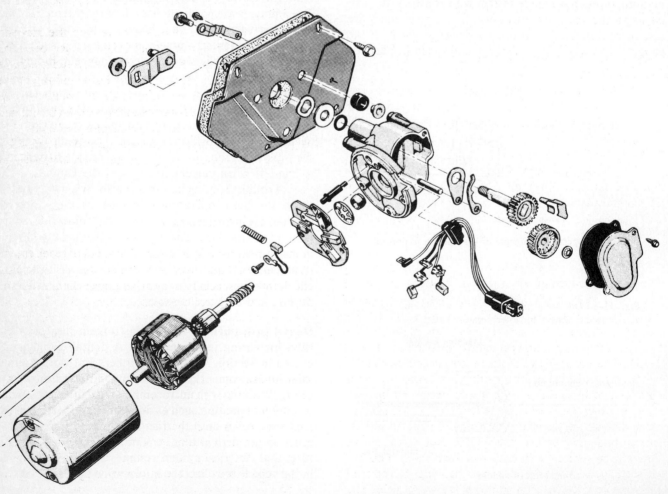

The most common washer failure is an empty washer-fluid reservoir. A second common cause of failure is plugged or poorly adjusted nozzles. Plugging can be checked by removing the washer pump pressure hose and operating the pump. If the pump supplies fluid, the nozzles are plugged. Plugged nozzles can usually be opened with air pressure. Sometimes, a small soft wire, such as those used on shipping tags, will have to be used to open the nozzle holes. If this fails, the nozzle will have to be replaced. If the washer pump does not deliver fluid, the pump is not functioning properly. Here again the electrical circuit should be checked to make sure that electricity is being delivered to the pump. The pump will have to be replaced when it has electricity but the motor does not run. Washer motors and pumps are not normally repaired. They are replaced as an assembly.

15-3 RADIO

A radio is one of the most common convenience accessories. It may be a simple AM radio or a complex AM/FM search-tune stereo with a tape deck and CB. As an automotive service technician, your only responsibility is to install or remove it properly, see that it is supplied with electrical power, trim the antenna, and adjust the pushbuttons. If you cannot correct a problem with the radio in the vehicle, you will have to remove it for repair by a specialist.

The radio is connected to the ignition accessory terminal. It may be fused in the connecting wire. In some cases, the fuse is built into the radio chassis. The light in the radio is a separate circuit. It is connected to the dash-light circuit.

Trimming the antenna is a way to balance the radio and antenna. It is done with a trimmer screw on the back or bottom of the radio chassis next to the antenna lead. The radio is tuned to a weak AM station around 1600 kilocycles and the trimmer screw adjusted to get the strongest signal.

Pushbuttons are pulled outward to release them. The station is tuned in with the dial. When the pushbutton is pushed in, it will lock the station to the pushbutton. In most cases, the driver will adjust the pushbuttons.

As an automotive service technician you should be able to remove and install the radio, speaker, and antenna. Most automobile radios are located in the instrument panel. They are held in place with panel braces and with nuts located behind the radio knobs. You will have to remove some defroster and air-conditioning ducting to reach the back of the radio. You should remove the battery ground cable before you start to remove the radio. This will prevent an accidental electrical short. You can reach the back of some radios by removing the top trim cover between the instrument panel and windshield. The

radio electrical lead, antenna lead, and speaker leads are separated. If a brace is used on the back of the radio, it should be loosened. The knobs are pulled from the front of the radio; then you can see the nuts holding the radio chassis to the dash. The nuts are loosened while you support the chassis. When free, you can remove the radio chassis. If the front speaker needs to be replaced, it can usually be easily removed after the radio chassis is out. The speaker can be removed from its mounting after taking off the retaining nuts. The radio chassis is sent to a radio repair shop for internal repair when this type of repair is needed. Faulty speakers are replaced.

The radio is reinstalled by reversing the procedure you used to remove it. The speaker is remounted, the radio chassis installed, and the retaining nuts and brace are tightened. This is followed by connecting the speaker wires, antenna, power lead, and knobs. After the radio is installed the battery ground is connected and the radio is checked. Trim the antenna. Heater and air-conditioner ducting can be reassembled after the radio is operating correctly.

Sometimes you will have to replace the antenna. Most original-equipment whip antennas are one-piece units going from the fender antenna to the radio chassis. Remove the antenna lead from the radio and the antenna trim nut. Slide the lead wire through grommets to remove the antenna and lead assembly. Push the antenna into the fender and thread it out behind the fender. The new antenna is installed in the reverse order. Windshield antennas are replaced only when a new windshield is installed.

15-4 SPEED CONTROL

A speed control is an accessory that is gaining popularity. It will hold the automobile at the set speed. This keeps the driver from accidentally driving over the speed limit. It is most useful on limited-access highways. Here it becomes a safety accessory because it reduces driver fatigue. It also improves fuel economy above the economy the driver can get by controlling the accelerator pedal.

Driver Control. There are several ways for the driver to command the speed control. An engagement switch is used to turn the system on and off. In some models the engagement switch sets the speed. Others have a separate speed set switch. Brake and clutch pedal switches disengage the system when either pedal is used. If the speed control was not disengaged while braking, it would try to increase the speed as the driver tried to slow the

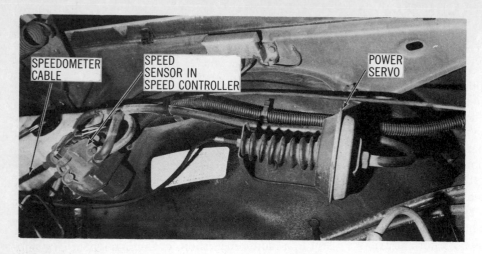

SPEEDOMETER CABLE

SPEED SENSOR IN SPEED CONTROLLER

POWER SERVO

Fig. 15-11 Typical speedometer cable speed sensor on a speed control.

automobile. If the clutch was released while the speed control was engaged, the speed control would sense the automobile slowing and it would try to accelerate. This would cause the engine to overspeed. On some speed control models the driver can close a resume switch to bring the automobile back to the set speed after slowing with the clutch or brake. The driver can accelerate above the set speed anytime without affecting the speed setting. The automobile will return to the set speed when the throttle is released after acceleration. The speed must be reset on all speed controls after the engagement switch or ignition switch is turned off and then turned back on.

Speed Sensing. There is some way to sense the automobile speed and speed changes. One of the popular locations for speed sensing is the speedometer cable. The driveshaft is another popular location, especially with add-on units.

The speedometer cable is divided and the speed sensor is placed between the sections. An example is shown in Figure 15-11. A lower section of the cable connects from the transmission to the speed sensor. An upper cable goes from the speed sensor to the speedometer. Two types of sensors are used for this type of speed sensor. One is a mechanical **flyweight** governor. The flyweights on one type are shown in Figure 15-12. The other is a **rotating magnet** that generates an electrical signal. The faster the automobile goes, the stronger is the electrical signal from the rotating magnet. This signal is the same vehicle speed signal used for electronic engine controls and electronic instruments (see Figure 14-9).

A magnetic drive shaft sensor also generates an electrical signal that gets stronger and **pulses** more often as the automobile speed increases. One drive shaft sensor uses a magnetic pickup head placed close to a tooth wheel on the drive shaft. The other is an add-on unit that cements magnets to the drive shaft. The magnets are wrapped with tape. A pickup coil that senses the mag-

FLYWEIGHT GOVERNOR

Fig. 15-12 Section view of one type of speed sensor that uses flyweights.

Fig. 15-13 Add-on speed control sensor. Two magnets are cemented to the drive shaft and wrapped with tape. A coil is mounted so that it will sense the magnetic pulses as the drive shaft rotates.

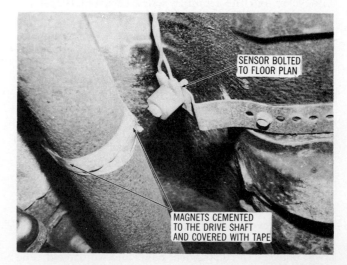

SENSOR BOLTED TO FLOOR PLAN

MAGNETS CEMENTED TO THE DRIVE SHAFT AND COVERED WITH TAPE

netic pulse is placed close to the magnets as they rotate with the drive shaft (Figure 15–13).

A distributor pulse pickup has been used as a speed sensor in a limited number of speed control systems. It works best with manual transmissions and with automatic transmissions that have lockup torque converter clutches. These are used with add-on units.

Speed Controller. The speed controller is the brain of the speed control system. It receives a speed signal from the speed sensor. The vehicle speed is compared to the speed set by the driver. The speed controller then commands a power servo to change the throttle position enough to match the automobile speed to the set speed.

In a typical original-equipment speed control, centrifugal flyweights mechanically move a shaft against a spring. You can follow the discussion of its operation by referring to Figure 15–14 as you read. When the speed control is engaged a solenoid will clamp an armature to this shaft. The armature is connected to the control plate so that the control plate moves with the shaft. The control plate is in the neutral position when the automobile

is running at the set speed. When the speed is slowed about 1/4 mph below the set speed, the plate closes the air port. This increases the vacuum in the controller housing. The housing is connected to the power servo so that the vacuum is also increased in the power servo. You can see a typical power servo in Figure 15–11. Increased vacuum in the power servo begins to open the throttle. When the speed increases about 1/4 mph above the set speed, the plate will move to close the vacuum port. Air comes into the housing through the air port to lower the vacuum. This gradually reduces the throttle opening to slow the automobile. The speed controller moves the control plate back and forth to adjust the vacuum so that it will hold the set speed within ±2 mph (±3 km/h).

Electronic speed controllers move the control plate by changing the strength of an electrical signal. Increasing the electrical signal moves the plate to close the vacuum port. Decreasing the signal closes the air port.

Power Servo. One of the first power actuators used in a speed control was a reversible electric motor that moved the throttle. Modern power servos use vacuum bellows or diaphrams. Only enough vacuum is supplied by the speed controller to position the throttle correctly. Air and vacuum are balanced while the automobile is running at the set speed.

Many power servos are connected to the speed controllers with vacuum hoses. The servo pulls the throttle open through a bead chain or cable in a housing (see Figure 15–11). In other designs the servo is made in the same housing with the speed controller (see Figure 15–12). In these units the throttle is pulled open by a cable that runs in a housing.

Speed control is a very good example of a **closed-loop** feedback system. It is operating as a closed loop while it is controlling the vehicle speed. Changes in the speed are fed back through the speed controller to change the throttle position. This corrects the vehicle speed. You can see that this action closes the loop from the original vehicle speed back to the corrected speed. The system is always comparing the actual speed to the set speed. The system goes to open loop when the speed control is disengaged or the accelerator is depressed.

15–5 ACCESSORY CONTROLS

Controls for electrical accessories make and break electrical circuits. These controls include switches and relays. Motion is produced with solenoids (Figure 15–15) and

Fig. 15–14 Drawing showing the operating principle of a typical mechanical flyweight governor speed controller unit.

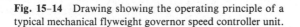

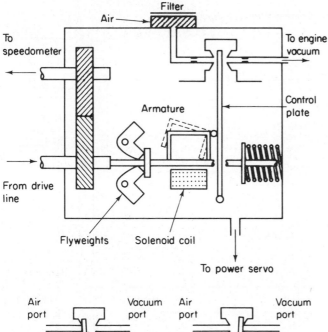

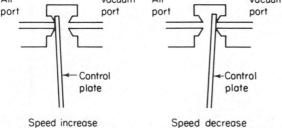

Fig. 15–16 Door lock motor that produces motion.

Fig. 15–15 Door lock solenoid that produces motion.

motors (Figure 15–16). One side (positive) is carried through an insulated circuit. This side of the circuit has the fuses, switches, and electrical junctions. The other side (negative) grounds on the metal body or frame.

Switches. A switch is manually operated. It has electrical contacts made of special metal alloys. These metals resist burning and corrosion caused by small electrical arcs that always form as a switch is closed and opened. Switches are designed to move with a **snap action** that will minimize arcing time.

A switch will fail if the contacts eventually become so pitted and burned that they can no longer carry an electrical current; or if the contacts stick together so that they carry electrical current all the time. A second type of failure is mechanical. The snap-action mechanism may fail, so the contacts will not move, staying either open or closed. Finally, the switch leads may fail. Failed switches are not repaired. They must be replaced.

Relay. A relay is a switch that is remotely controlled by a manually operated switch. It is usually used where heavy current is required. The voltage losses would be too great if the circuit ran to the driver's control switch. A horn relay is an example of this requirement (Figure 15–17). The normally open relay points on the relay arma-

Fig. 15–17 Typical electrical circuits. (Courtesy Chrysler Corporation.)

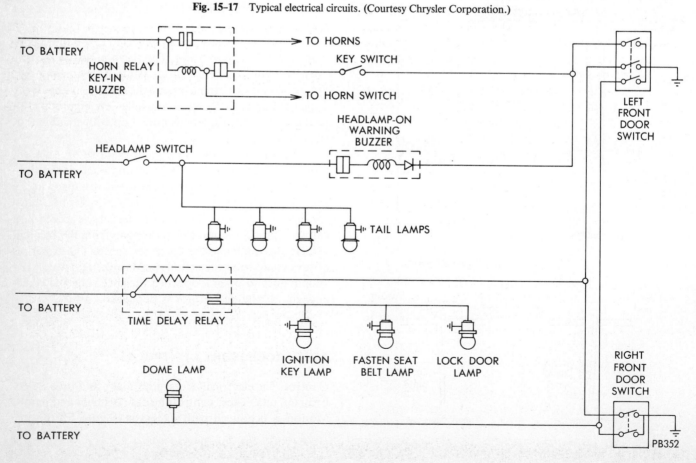

ture are heavy enough to carry current to operate the accessory. One lead of a fine wire coil is connected to the relay power input and the other end lead is connected to a switch. The parts of a typical relay can be identified in Figure 1–27. When the driver closes the switch, current flows through the relay coil. This forms magnetism to close the relay points. The closed points supply current to the electrical accessory. Upon release of the switch, the relay spring opens the points to break the circuit and the current flow stops.

Solenoid.   A solenoid provides a pull force. Solenoid details described in Section 6–3 explain its use to engage the starter drive. It is also used as a remote control to operate items such as door locking (see Figure 15–15), trunk opening, and applying the air-conditioning compressor clutch. A movable core is connected to the mechanism. When current flows through a coil in the solenoid the core is pulled toward the coil center to operate the mechanism. A solenoid electrical circuit is controlled by a switch or relay.

Motors.   Many accessories operate with small electric motors. Examples of some of these small motors are shown in Figure 15–18. In some cases, they are reversible motors. Electric motors used for accessories make use of the same motor principles as cranking motors, described in Section 6–1. The motor has a rotating armature within a field. Current is transferred to the armature through commutator brushes. The armature is supported within the housing by bearings.

   Reversible motors have two fields. One field is used when the motor runs clockwise and the other field is used when the motor runs counter-clockwise.

   Motors are used to rotate the fan in the heater, air conditioner, and defogger. They are used for power to operate power windows, power seats, power antennas, power door locks (see Figure 15–16), hydraulic pumps for power tops, windshield wipers, windshield washers, electric fuel pumps, and many other electrical units.

Buzzer.   Buzzers are used to call the driver's attention to an unusual condition, such as the key left in the ignition when the door is opened. The buzzer principle is also used for vehicle horns. In horns, the vibrating armature is connected to a metal diaphragm that is vibrated to produce the sound. Buzzers are often mounted on the fuse block, as shown in Figure 15–19.

   In the buzzer, current flows through a coil, then on to spring-loaded, normally closed points. Coil magnetism pulls the armature to open the points. This breaks the coil's electrical circuit, so the coil loses its magnetism. The spring will then close the points and the cy-

Fig. 15–18   Typical small motors used in vehicles.

cle repeats. Cycling speed or frequency is based on the balance between the spring force, coil strength, air gap, and armature weight. Different cycling frequencies produce different pitch sound. A flasher unit is essentially a slow vibrating buzzer. Some horns have an adjusting screw to change spring tension for tuning the pitch (sound) of the horn.

Fig. 15–19   Buzzers and flashers mounted on a fuse block-bulkhead connector.

FLASHER   BUZZERS

INTERIOR
AND INSTRUMENT
PANEL WIRES

THE UNDERHOOD
BULKHEAD CONNECTOR
FITS HERE

15–6 SUMMARY

It is much more difficult and it takes more time to find the cause of an electrical problem than it does to repair it. You will have to develop good diagnostic procedures and use test equipment correctly to quickly find the cause of electrical problems.

First, analyze the problem. Find out when the problem occurs. See if it affects any other circuit or if it is affected by another circuit. Next, check the wiring diagrams to find the location of the circuit connectors and the color of the wire insulation. The wiring diagram will also show where two circuits are interconnected. Follow the troubleshooting diagnosis procedures in the service manuals or service bulletins while you check the faulty circuit. Do not skip steps in the diagnosis procedure. If you do, you may miss the cause of the problem. Some electronic circuits may be damaged if diagnosis steps are missed.

When the cause of the problem is found, it is usually easy to repair or replace the part. Be sure to check the operation of the repaired circuit before trim parts are replaced. This will let you make further repairs if they are necessary.

STUDY QUESTIONS

Section 15–1

1. List eight basic electrical accessories required on vehicles.

2. What is the advantage of an indicator light?

3. What does the sensor do to turn on the indicator lamp?

4. How do indicator lamp sockets differ from the sockets of most other vehicle lights?

5. When are instrument gauges used?

6. What makes a bimetal arm bend when it is heated?

7. What force moves the indicator needle in a balanced coil instrument?

8. What does a sender do to the electrical circuit to control instrument readings?

9. What instrument reading would you expect if you grounded the instrument circuit wire at the sender unit?

10. What does an ammeter tell the driver?

11. What is the biggest problem in troubleshooting faulty instrument readings?

Section 15–2

12. What is the normal way windshield wiper systems are repaired when their motor fails?

13. What is the most common cause of windshield washer failure?

Section 15–3

14. What does an automotive service technician do to service a radio?

15. What should you do before you start to remove the radio?

Section 15–4

16. What driver controls are there on a speed control system?

17. Name three types of speed sensors used on speed controls.

18. What is done in the speed controller to hold the vehicle speed?

19. What type of actuator is used as a power servo in modern speed controls?

Section 15–5

20. How are switches operated?

21. Why do switches use snap action?

22. Where is a relay usually used?

23. What controls a solenoid?

24. What causes the pitch of a buzzer?

GLOSSARY

A

Accessory. A part or system that is not needed for vehicle operation.

Active Display. Produce their own light to be seen.

Actuator. A part that moves another part.

Adjuster Frame. Metal frame with adjusting screws that holds the glass headlamp bulb.

Air Gap. A small space between two parts.

Alloy. A small amount of metal added to a base metal to change the characteristics of the mixture.

Alternating Current. Rapidly reversing the direction of current flow, first one way and then the other.

Amperage. The amount of current flowing measured in amperes.

Ampere. A measure of the rate of electrical current flowing in a circuit.

Ampere-Hour. The number of hours a battery can supply a set amount of current before the voltage is too low.

Ampere-Turns. A term used to describe the strength of a magnetic coil.

Arc. A spark caused by an electrical current flowing across an air gap.

Armature. A moving conductor within a magnetic field. The rotating assembly of an electric motor.

Atom. Smallest part of element matter.

Available Voltage. The maximum voltage an ignition system can produce.

B

Basic Timing. Ignition timing when there is no advance.

Battery Capacity. The amount of electrical power the battery has.

Beam. Light shining in one direction.

Bench Checking. Testing an automotive part on a workbench.

Bimetallic Spring. A coil or leaf spring made of a double strip of two different metals. It will bend when the temperature changes.

Binary Logic. Has two positions, on and off.

Breaker. A switch that is automatically opened by heat, high current, or mechanical action.

Bridge. A connection across a gap. A group of diodes between a stator and the electrical system.

Brush. A carbon compound that slides against a moving surface to form a good electrical connection.

Bulb Socket. Holder with electrical contacts that fits and holds the base of a lamp bulb.

Bypass. To connect around some restriction.

C

Cable. Secondary ignition wire. Large-diameter wire that connects to the battery.

Calibrating. Adjusting a meter to a set position.

Candela. Metric unit of light brightness.

Candlepower. Standard unit of light brightness.

Capacitance. The ability to store electrons.

Capacity. Ability of a battery to change chemical energy to electrical energy.

Carbon Monoxide. Incomplete combination of carbon and oxygen to form a molecule that has one carbon and one oxygen atom.

Carbon Pile. Carbon plates made to be pressed together to reduce the electrical resistance through them so that they will carry more electrical current.

Carbon Track. A mark across an insulator produced by an electrical arc.

Check. Look at a part or measure it to find anything abnormal about it.

Chip. A small solid-state semiconductor, usually an integrated circuit.

Circuit (complete). You can follow all the way around the circuit without running into an opening.

Commutator. The part of an armature with section bars on which the brushes contact to send electricity through the armature windings.

Conductor. Metal atoms with three or less electrons in their outer orbit. A part that will carry electricity.

Contacts. The part of a switch that makes and brakes an electrical circuit.

Continuity. The result of a closed circuit through which an electric current can flow.

Counter Electromotive Force. A voltage that opposes the voltage in a circuit.

Cross Firing. Ignition secondary arcing across or through an insulator to fire the wrong spark plug.

Current. Electrical flow in a conductor.

D

Decay. To gradually lose its energy.

Diagnose. Find the cause of faulty operation by using knowledge of a system, troubleshooting charts, and testing equipment.

Diode. A semiconductor with two leads that allows current to flow in only one direction.

Dither. To move rapidly back and forth.

Doped. A small amount of material added to the base crystal of a semiconductor.

Dwell. The number of degrees the distributor rotates while the coil primary windings carry current.

E

Effective Resistance. Combined resistance of electrical parts connected in parallel.

Electrical Load. A part that uses electricity.

Electricity. The movement of electrons through a conductor in one direction.

Electrochemical. Electron movement caused by a chemical reaction.

Electrolyte. Sulfuric acid solution that forms ions in a battery cell.

Electromagnet. Magnetism formed by current flowing through a coil that is wrapped around an iron core.

Electromagnetic Induction. An electromotive force made by relative motion between a conductor and a magnetic field.

Electromagnetism. A magnetic field around an electromagnet.

Electromotive Force. The force that causes electrons to move in one direction. It is measured as voltage.

Electron. Small negative charged particle spinning around the nucleus of an atom.

Element (Battery). A group of positive plates and a group of negative plates interleaved with separators.

Energize. To fill with energy using the flow of electrical current.

F

Field. A magnetic force around a magnet.

Filament. The wire in a lamp bulb that gets hot and gives off light as electricity passes through it.

Forward Bias. Currents flow through a semiconductor in a circuit when the N-type material is connected to negative and the P-type material is connected to positive.

Free Speed. The speed a motor will rotate when it is not rotating a load.

G

Gap. Space between two parts.

Gate. Specialized circuit in a transistor that turns on or off when it receives the correct signal.

Grid. A lead frame that supports the active material and conducts electricity from the active material to the terminal.

Ground. The part of the electrical circuit connected to the negative terminal of the battery.

Group (Battery). Assembly of all the battery plates of one polarity.

Growler. A coil of wire wrapped around a U-shaped core that produces a continually changing magnetic field when the coil is connected to an ac power supply.

H

Heat Sink. A metal block that absorbs heat from an electrical device and radiates the heat to the surrounding air.

Henry. The inductance that results when the current changes 1 ampere per second to induce 1 volt.

Hole. An electron is missing from an atom that would be needed for the atomic structure to be neutral. It attracts an electron.

Hydrocarbon. Molecules made of a combination of hydrogen and carbon atoms.

Hydrometer. A float that measures specific gravity of a fluid by the depth the float sinks into the fluid.